Chicken Soup for the Soul

for the Soul®

True Love

Chicken Soup for the Soul: True Love
101 Heartwarming and Humorous Stories about Dating, Romance, Love, and Marriage
by Jack Canfield, Mark Victor Hansen, Amy Newmark

Published by Chicken Soup for the Soul Publishing, LLC   www.chickensoup.com

*Cover photo courtesy of Getty Images/ Swell Media/UpperCut Images. Back cover photo
courtesy of Getty Images/Todd Williamson/Contributor/Collection: WireImage.
Interior illustration courtesy of iStockPhoto.com/Simfo*

Cover and Interior Design & Layout by Pneuma Books, LLC
For more info on Pneuma Books, visit www.pneumabooks.com

Distributed to the booktrade by Simon & Schuster. SAN: 200-2442

Publisher's Cataloging-in-Publication Data
(Prepared by The Donohue Group)

Chicken soup for the soul : true love : 101 heartwarming and humorous stories
  about dating, romance, love, and marriage / [compiled by] Jack Canfield, Mark
  Victor Hansen [and] Amy Newmark ; foreword by Kristi Yamaguchi and Bret
  Hedican.

   p. ; cm.

   ISBN: 978-1-935096-43-6

1. Love--Literary collections. 2. Love--Anecdotes. 3. Dating (Social
customs)--Literary collections. 4. Dating (Social customs)--Anecdotes.
5. Marriage--Literary collections. 6. Marriage--Anecdotes. I. Canfield,
Jack, 1944- II. Hansen, Mark Victor. III. Newmark, Amy. IV. Yamaguchi,
Kristi. V. Hedican, Bret. VI. Title: True love

PN6071.L7 C45 2009
810.8/02/03543   2009939186

PRINTED IN THE UNITED STATES OF AMERICA
on acid∞free paper
16 15 14 13 12 11 10 09   01 02 03 04 05 06 07 08

Chicken Soup for the Soul®

True Love

101 Heartwarming and Humorous
Stories about Dating, Romance,
Love, and Marriage

Jack Canfield
Mark Victor Hansen
Amy Newmark

Foreword by Kristi Yamaguchi and Bret Hedican

CSS

Chicken Soup for the Soul Publishing, LLC
Cos Cob, CT

Chicken Soup for the Soul

www.chickensoup.com

Contents

❶

~How We Met~

❷

~Adventures in Dating~

❸
~Meant to Be~

❹
~The Proposal~

❺
~The Wedding~

❻

~Keeping the Love Alive~

❼

~Lessons in True Love~

❽

~Happily Ever Laughter~

❾

~Gifts from the Heart~

⑩
~Love Everlasting~

Foreword

*K*risti: Everyone enjoys a great love story, so we were excited about being part of the Chicken Soup for the Soul family for this wonderful book of true love stories. This is not my first time in a Chicken Soup for the Soul book. I had a story about my early years as an athlete in *Chicken Soup for the Preteen Soul 2* and my mom had a story about my skating career in *Chicken Soup for the Sports Fan's Soul*.

Skating is great, but true love is even better! After all, it's something we all strive for and most of us achieve it at some point in our lives. Bret and I are fortunate to have it all—great careers, a strong marriage, and a wonderful family. But it almost didn't happen….

Bret: We met at the 1992 Olympics when I was playing for the U.S. hockey team and Kristi was figure skating for the U.S. She won a gold medal that year. Nancy Kerrigan and Kristi were walking around meeting some of the other American team members. Kristi made an impression on all of us—she was just excited to be there and happy to be watching the hockey team and the players and be a part of it.

Kristi: There were about twenty-five hockey players and I remembered a few of them, but not Bret. When we met again a few years later in Vancouver, he told me that we had met at the Olympics. I had to go back to look at the photos to see if he was really there.

A hockey player was the last type of athlete I thought I would ever date. Hockey players are just a different breed from figure skaters. We always competed with the hockey players for rink time when I was a kid.

Bret: We had no class.

Kristi: It was pretty funny, because when we were reintroduced, one of my choreographers was with me, and he said there was this cute guy who kept looking over at me. I was so embarrassed, as if I was transported back to grade school.

We dated for about three years before Bret proposed. Bret was playing for the Vancouver Canucks and I was based in the Bay Area so we were only going to see each other over Christmas for a day and half, actually only forty hours! Bret called me and said he had missed his flight. I was not happy. There had been a snowstorm in Vancouver, and Bret's car wasn't working, and there were no cabs available since they are not accustomed to heavy snow in Vancouver.

Bret: We were spending Christmas Day with Kristi's family so I wanted us to have a nice quiet Christmas Eve dinner, just the two of us, so I could propose. But when I arrived, I discovered that Kristi had said that her sister and brother-in-law could join us. I pulled her sister aside and told her I had the ring in my pocket, and that she needed to leave right after dinner.

Kristi: He was still in trouble with me for being late, so it took me a while to figure out what was going on, and then I thought, "Don't do it because I've been so nasty all night." But we ended up at the top of the Marriott in downtown San Francisco, with a 360 degree view of the city, and he proposed. Of course I said yes.

Our parents were thrilled and excited and we decided to have a nice intimate family wedding in Hawaii. My extended family had a tradition of vacationing on the Big Island of Hawaii—25 or 30 of us at the Orchid Mauna Lani. We loved it and thought a small wedding would be nice.

You can guess what happened. We gave everyone more than a year to plan, so they could plan their family vacations around the wedding, and almost 100% of our invites said yes. Over 300 people came. We took over the whole hotel. It was awesome. It turned into a five-day wedding because everyone came early and by the time we had the ceremony on Saturday, everyone knew each other.

Bret: At the reception I scored points by serenading my bride with the Bob Dylan song "Make You Feel My Love." I saw Scott Hamilton quoted in People Magazine saying that every single woman in the room was crying.

Kristi: That was in 2000, and three years later we had our first child, Keara, and two years after that we had Emma. Our daughters are our proudest accomplishments. The minute you become a parent, you become so much closer and it reinforces the bond you have with each other. You become more conscious of the values you want to instill in your family. You also have a better understanding of your own parents—it's a lot of work!

While our marriage is still young compared to many out there, we feel a real affinity to the stories in this latest Chicken Soup for the Soul volume about true love. It's a lot of fun to read about dating, proposals, and weddings and remember our own years of long distance dating and our own wedding. And we love the stories written by long-time couples about how they keep their marriages fresh and their relationships healthy. Some of the stories are so funny, and a few will make you tear up. There is something in here for everyone, even you guys out there. We wives know that you secretly enjoy a good love story too, right Bret?

Bret: Yes, dear.

~Kristi Yamaguchi and Bret Hedican

Introduction

My very thoughtful son, who is a college senior with a long-time fabulous girlfriend, has a wonderful metaphor for relationships. He views a relationship as a machine—a box full of intermeshed gears working together. When the machine is new, the gears are shiny and sharp. They work together, but there is some roughness around the edges and a little resistance as they mesh. Over time, the gears lose some of their shininess, and their edges become a little rounded, but they work together more and more smoothly. A little dirt gets in the machine from time to time, and it must be cleaned out diligently in order to keep the gears working well and avoid permanent build-up.

Once in a while, a major problem may occur, and a piece of metal may fall into the works. But a well-maintained machine with well-matched gears will survive this. The gears will keep moving and the stray piece of metal may get thrown against the side wall of the machine, leaving a permanent dent that mars the machine but doesn't impair its performance. Or the piece of metal may actually damage a gear, bending it or breaking it, but the machine soldiers on, and the gears still mesh better and better over time, albeit with one missing tooth.

Our relationships are like that metaphorical machine. Over time, our gears may darken with age and wear down, and even show some breakage, but if we tend to them they should mesh more and more smoothly. If the machine really suffers irreparable damage, and we break up or divorce, we look to start over with new machines.

Chicken Soup for the Soul: True Love is an inspiring collection of stories about dating, romance, love, and marriage. You will find stories about everything from first dates and falling in love, to proposals and weddings, to second chances and love later in life, to making relationships work over the years. Whether you are looking for new love, basking in the glow of a successful relationship, or working on a relationship that needs a little polishing, you will find fundamental wisdom in these pages, from real people sharing their personal stories with you.

Our Assistant Publisher, D'ette Corona, and I had so much fun reading the thousands of stories submitted for this book. After all, who doesn't enjoy a great love story? We laughed and cried, nodded our heads in recognition, shook our heads in disbelief, and were disappointed when it was all over and the book was finished!

So now it is your turn. "Gear up" for a great read. We hope these stories will help your relationship "machine" work as well as ours, or give you faith that your next box of gears will be the one that operates smoothly for the rest of your life!

~Amy Newmark
Publisher, Chicken Soup for the Soul

Chapter
1

True Love

How We Met

You know you're in love when you can't fall asleep because reality is finally better than your dreams.

~Dr. Seuss

Challenged

You don't love someone for their looks,
or their clothes, or for their fancy cars,
but because they sing a song only you can hear.
~Source Unknown

I was twenty-six, single, and I had just bought my first home. It was my very first "grown-up" purchase. After signing the final paperwork, I decided to stop and visit some friends before heading home to pack.

My friend has never been one for formality, so when I arrived at her house I let myself in. As I came around the corner into her living room, I was a little startled to see a man I had never met sitting on the couch.

As I was introduced to Martin, I could not help but notice that his attire was horribly coordinated. I am no fashion diva by any means, but I had to wonder what this man was thinking when he left his house that morning.

As we sat in the living room engaged in lively conversation, I noticed that Martin was saying very little. My mother had always taught me that talking over people was not only impolite but very rude. So I tried to incorporate him into our conversation. No matter what I said to him, all I got was stammering and stuttering.

Upon hearing him speak, I mistakenly assumed he was mildly developmentally-challenged in some fashion. This would explain his speech difficulty and his clothing. For some reason, when people find themselves in a situation like this, they tend to talk louder and slower. I was no exception and I must have looked like a complete idiot, given what I learned later.

After a few hours I headed home. I had a lot of packing to do, and moving day was coming up fast.

A few days later, I went shopping for some window blinds for my new home. Once I got there, I realized that my standard screwdriver was not going to do the job. So, I headed over to my friend's house to see if I could borrow a cordless screwdriver or drill from her husband.

When I got there, she explained to me it was no problem to borrow the drill, but her husband had not made it home from work yet and she did not know where he kept it. After pausing for a moment, she said that Martin was in the other room and she would see if he had one.

Within a matter of moments he appeared. This time it seemed that his speech problem was far worse then the last time we had met. Also, I could not help but notice that he had made another not so great fashion choice. Slowly, he told me that not only did he have a cordless drill, but he would come and help me to hang my blinds… and he would drive.

My stomach twisted, not knowing what to say. Although I firmly believed that a challenged individual should be given the same chances as anyone else, I was not sure of the degree of his disability. Could he handle this task? Could he drive? Should I trust him? After all, he was a complete stranger.

I took a deep breath and agreed. I knew that if my friend was okay with this, he must be up to the challenge. Otherwise, she would have pulled me aside and told me. Hoping for the best, I got into his truck and we headed the short distance to my new home.

When we arrived, Martin pulled a tool box from his truck and went inside. I must say I was instantly impressed. Before hanging each blind, he measured and marked, taking extreme care not to damage or mar my beautiful new windows.

As he traveled from room to room hanging the blinds, I followed him. By this time I was more then comfortable with his ability. I just felt I should try to engage him in conversation. During this time I began to notice something. Martin spoke clearly whenever his back was to me. It was only during face-to-face conversations that his speech became difficult to understand.

Then it hit me. Martin was not the least bit mentally challenged. Why then, I wondered, did he have difficulty speaking at times?

At the last window, with his back turned, he told me that he and our mutual friends were going out on Friday. He wanted to know if I would like to come along. Without a moment's hesitation I blurted out yes. I surprised even myself, as that was something I never did.

I would never have guessed in a million years that Martin would be my husband when I first met him, but four months later we were married. By the time we said "I do" the stammering and stuttering came far less often. A few months later, I confessed to Martin my first impression of him. He laughed and said he stammered and stuttered only when he looked at me because he thought I was the most beautiful woman he had ever seen and it made him nervous to be around me. My heart melted… again.

You may be wondering… what about the poor fashion choices? Martin is colorblind.

I guess it goes to show you that you cannot always go by first impressions. If I had, I would have missed out on being married to the most wonderful man on the planet for the past eight years.

~Toni-Michelle Nell

Long Distance Love

In true love the smallest distance is too great,
and the greatest distance can be bridged.
~Hans Nouwens

"So how did you and your fiancé meet?" My college classmate sat down beside me in the cafeteria, leaning close to look at my emerald engagement ring.

It was a common question when people found out I was just nineteen and engaged, but I always had to fight the urge to wince. I knew that no matter how delicately I tried to answer, they would be wagering on our relationship's demise.

"We knew of each other online...."

"Oh, so this was one of those new Internet relationships?" she asked. This was 1999, and most any news about the Internet boasted that it was great for finding a date and/or a sexual predator.

"No. We knew of each other online, but not well. I was in California, he was in Ohio. We were on the same e-mail list for video game fans, and we knew that we both liked the group Journey. Well, Jason was going on a road trip to meet people from the e-mail list, and it so happened that Journey was appearing on tour not far from me at the same time. I asked if he wanted to go, and when we met, we just clicked."

"And he was in the Navy then?"

I shook my head. "No. He enlisted about six months later. We were engaged right before he went to boot camp."

When she walked away, her face was composed but I could see she was tabulating the facts in her head: two very young people in a relationship based on the Internet and video games and music; he joined the Navy; they reside on opposite coasts. It sounded like a divorce waiting to happen, if we even made it as far as the altar.

At the same time, I knew how bad it all sounded. So did Jason. He endured the same skeptical reaction from acquaintances and family. There was no way we could defend ourselves and our love with words without sounding silly and immature.

"No," Jason said. "We'll have to show them by making it."

Fairy tales and popular culture make a big deal out of love-at-first-sight, as though the heavens open in celestial chorus. The reality is much more subtle. We met in person, and we were instant friends. This was someone I could trust, someone thoughtful and respectable. To make things even more astounding, Jason made the same impression on my overly-cautious parents. I wasn't allowed to make the ten-minute bicycle ride to my grandma's house unless I called home to let my parents know that I arrived safely, yet this stoic young man instantly earned their trust and respect.

Since we lived thousands of miles apart, most of our initial courtship was done by phone and Internet. Our infrequent reunions were a delightful blur of board games and slow strolls around the local mall while walking hand-in-hand. When Jason came out to visit one final time before joining the Navy, he sold his battered car to buy my engagement ring. There was no formal wedding proposal; we were simply in consensus that we would be married, and the ring made that public. While he was in boot camp, I did the math: we had only been in each other's physical presence for a rough total of three weeks spread over a six-month span. Our engagement probably seemed hasty and foolhardy—and looking at those numbers, I could see why—but I still believed in us. Jason felt the same way, clinging to whatever correspondence I sent his way even as his fellow sailor-recruits received more and more "Dear John" letters as the weeks went by.

Our reunion took place exactly six months after he left for the

Navy. It was Christmas, and having Jason in my arms again was the best gift of all. We had both endured other people's doubts about our relationship, but our love was strong. He was still utterly ruthless at Scrabble, too, and as he strategized with his tiles, it gave me ample time to renew my memory of his handsome face. And when it was my turn to play, I would catch him looking at me the same dreamy way.

While we were out shopping for Christmas presents, Jason accidentally knocked a pillow off a high shelf and onto my head.

"Spousal abuse!" cried a fellow shopper on our aisle, a teasing grin on his face. "I was a witness!"

Jason looked at me, beaming. "Spouse!" he said. "He thinks you're my wife."

"I will be," I said, squeezing his hand.

After that visit, it was almost another six months until we were together again. This time, it was for our wedding. I walked down the aisle to an orchestral version of the theme from the Final Fantasy video game series, and Jason was waiting for me, attired in Navy dinner dress whites. The next day, we packed up a Penske truck with all of my worldly belongings and made the long drive from California to my new home in South Carolina.

I didn't expect things to be easy, which was good—they weren't. I hadn't been away from my parents for longer than a week, and quite abruptly, I was 3,000 miles away and living in near-poverty. But I had Jason, and he had me, and Top Ramen noodles are mighty tasty when you're in love. Not only did we stay together, but we were content. Years passed, and we moved from South Carolina to Washington. He began preparations for deployment, and that's when I discovered I was pregnant.

Those six-month droughts without Jason back in our courting days proved to be good practice for deployment. Those same skills—constant letter and e-mail writing, care packages laden with sweets, sleeping with the phone beside my bed just in case—kept us strong while we were apart. Under the turbulent influence of hormones and loneliness, I would cry on cue when certain songs came on the radio, especially our song—Journey's "Faithfully." Jason returned home in time for the birth of our son, Nicholas, and less than a year later he was deployed again. A year after that, Jason left the Navy, and we again hauled ourselves across the country to a new home.

Next year is our ten-year anniversary. We've endured multiple deployments, zigzagged the country in hectic moves, and yet we somehow still like each other. I still get tingles in my belly when Jason comes in the door after a long day at work, and we engage in vicious Scrabble matches on our designated weekly game night. We've worked together to cope with Nicholas's autism diagnosis and special needs. We're still together, against all odds, and still love Journey, video games, and each other. True love doesn't mean that things are easy—it just means the struggle is worthwhile.

And after all this time, I'm no longer afraid of people asking how we met.

~Beth Cato

The Girl for Me

Gravitation is not responsible for people falling in love.
~Albert Einstein

People often ask when it was that I knew that my wife of twenty-five years was the girl for me. I always tell them that I knew it before I even knew her name.

It happened on a bright, crisp, autumn afternoon on my first day at college. In fact, it happened in my first class. I was a theater major and was taking Theater Crafts 101. My college advisor had assured me that the class was a great way to meet all the kids who would be in the program with me over the next four years.

So there we were—forty boisterous, nervous, excited teenagers in their first college class. None of us knew what to expect. We didn't know each other. All of us were determined to show off how talented we were. I managed to get to the lecture hall a little early to check out my classmates. There was a pretty blonde over here, a gorgeous redhead over there, and a cute brunette sitting with her best friend towards the back. I slowly strutted my way to the far side of the room and picked a chair by the windows. I was convinced the girls couldn't help but notice my natural "leading man" good looks.

Of course, Theater Crafts 101 wasn't an acting class. It was an "Introductory" class. So, after an hour and a half of being lectured on the history of Western Theater, our professor announced it was now time for some practical experience. We all hoped that meant we'd get on stage. Well, we did get on stage. Then off it again. In fact, our professor marched us downstairs to the main auditorium, up on stage, out the back, and into the workshop. The groans of disappointment could be heard in the lobby.

"All right," our professor said, barely suppressing his laughter, "I know all you future Academy Award-winning actors would prefer to be in front of the curtain right now (ironically, one of my classmates would go on to win an Academy Award), "but here," he declared, "is where the magic starts. This is where you get your hands dirty. Theater isn't just about glamour and applause. Theater is hard work. It's pitching in when things need to get done. And speaking of pitching in, your first assignment is to clean out the storage area and pitch all the trash in the Dumpster out back." People started groaning again.

Now, the assignment didn't really bother me, but some of the girls weren't very happy about it. They'd come dressed to impress. Their make-up was flawless, their hair was carefully sculpted, and their hands were freshly manicured. They hadn't planned on getting dirty in pursuit of their craft. So the guys got to show off by hauling the larger items while the girls stuck to the smaller more manageable pieces.

Since the Dumpster was in the parking lot, and that meant going down a series of hallways and out a fire door, it became apparent that we should form a bucket brigade. One person would grab a piece of scenery, haul it down a hallway, and pass it on to the next person, who would go down another hallway and hand it off to someone else. On and on it would go until the piece reached the guy perched up on the Dumpster who would drop it in. That was me.

I'd been up there about twenty minutes and was getting pretty good at it. The blonde I'd seen in class brought down a two-foot piece of wood that I gallantly tossed one-handed into the Dumpster. The redhead had found a small piece of canvas that I flipped over my shoulder with flair. Then Catherine appeared. Only, I didn't know her name just then.

Catherine was the friend of the cute brunette who'd been sitting in the back of class. She'd actually paid attention during the lecture and had asked several intelligent questions. She was also dressed in a plain flannel shirt and blue jeans. Her make-up was understated and she hadn't groaned when we were told to haul garbage.

Catherine was carrying a two-foot by six-foot flat. Flats are wooden frames covered in canvas. Once painted, a flat could be used to represent anything from a garden wall to a sunny sky. Though not really heavy, they can be cumbersome to maneuver. I was just taken by the fact that she'd opted to pick up something that weighed more than three pounds.

"Thanks, babe," I said as I leaned down and reached for the flat. I think it was the "babe" that impressed her.

"That's all right," she said. "I've got it."

"Hey," I replied with my best Brad Pitt smile. "I'm here; let me help."

Catherine gave me a small shake of her head and then said: "Duck."

"Excuse me?"

Catherine repeated her instruction, slowly. "D-u-c-k."

I was perched on the side of a commercial Dumpster and the lip to the steel container was a good six or seven feet off the ground. I wasn't sure what she intended to do. "Look," I began, "why don't you just let me...?"

Without another word Catherine reached back, grabbed hold of the flat with both hands, and proceeded to swing it around. I dropped down in time to watch the two-foot by six-foot frame sail neatly up over my head and into the Dumpster. The steel container clanged when the wood hit the bottom. I turned in time to spot a hint of a smile on Catherine's face as she gave me a nod, dusted off her hands, and walked away. I remembered crouching there, having nearly been conked in the head by flying scenery, and thinking: "Strong girl."

In that instant I learned all I ever needed to know about my future wife. I learned about her strength (both physical and of character); I learned about her stubborn streak of independence; and I learned about her wicked sense of humor. It would be two more years before we started dating and five till we got married. But on that day, by that Dumpster, I met the girl of my dreams. I just had to wait for my knees to stop shaking in order to realize it.

~Arthur Sanchez

"I'm majoring in English, Math and True Love this term... how about you?"

One Enchanted Evening

Happiness often sneaks in through a door you didn't know you left open.
~John Barrymore

After my divorce, I dated a very charming man for several years who, despite all that he had to offer, could never really make a commitment to me or to a future together. We separated and reunited many times, and finally, we found the courage to end the relationship once and for all. It was agonizing, but the healthiest thing we could have done for one another.

After the end of our relationship, I really swore off men. I was the single mother of two small children, trying to balance a full-time career with motherhood, and managing well, most of the time. I didn't have a strong desire to have anyone else in my life, though occasionally I did long for a playmate and lover. Given the situation, it was really just easier not to get involved.

By the spring of 2001, I had been on the Board of Directors of the American Heart Association in my county for six years. As part of my duties, I volunteered annually with the AHA Annual Gala. Somehow, getting sponsors and auction items for "the Ball" just seemed more glamorous than the other service options, and Lord knows, being a single mother, I didn't have much glamour in my life.

Given that it was my last term, I worked my tail off to make the event as special as it could possibly be. It was set at the new Grand Californian Hotel at Disneyland in California. We had arranged for David Benoit to play for us that evening, and there were terrific silent and live auctions to tantalize all of our guests. My swan song looked complete, but by the night before the event, I couldn't stomach the idea of attending one more gala, especially alone.

I finished the last of my To-Do list and hugged my director, then wished the committee well. My director, realizing that I did not mean to attend the event, looked aghast. I was even more surprised when the refined sixty-something belle told me in no uncertain terms that I would get my tail to the event, OR ELSE. I had never seen her like this, and wasn't quite sure what would happen if I argued with her. I squinched up my face at her, and left the building. I began speed-dialing the sitter I had used, hoping that I could even get someone to take care of the kids at such late notice. After getting a confirmation from the sitter, I headed to the mall. I pawed through the dresses on the rack, doubtful that I would find something in time, and completed the purchase of a deep-blue gown as Security began locking the doors for the night.

By 4:00 P.M. Saturday, I was a wreck. I tried to hold myself together, glaring at the clock with every minute that the sitter was late. A half-hour later, the sitter arrived and I dashed off to the ball. I deposited my car with the valet, strode into the hotel, and tried to scan the crowd for my director. Inside the VIP lounge, I spied her across the room with a few of my close colleagues.

After a brief hug, I told her that I wouldn't be staying for dinner, and she seemed to take no notice. She handed me a glass of champagne and asked my opinion about the auction tables. We talked shop for a few minutes before she asked if I'd met Thom Breslin. "Old, fat, balding cardiologist" is what I thought to myself, knowing that the event was often attended by these types. I told her that I hadn't, and she mentioned that he'd lost his wife to cancer. The image in my mind aged a few more years, and I wondered why she'd asked. She must have caught the expression on my face, because she took that opportunity to suggest that we go join her husband, Roger. As I'd spent Christmas the year before with them, I was pleased that he was attending the event.

As she turned to join Roger's group, I turned away from them to hand the waiter my glass. When I turned back around, in front of me was one of the most handsome men I'd ever seen. I quickly averted my eyes and hugged Roger, clasping his hands. And, with a gentle steer back to the others, Roger asked me, "Have you met Thom Breslin?" That whole "old, fat, balding cardiologist" thing just fell away with his words.

I thought for a moment that I might actually faint. I don't know if it was the form-fitting dress, the champagne gone to my head, or an actual swoon, but I had to remind myself to breathe as he reached out to shake my hand.

We spoke then, about our careers, our lives, and our loves. I shared about my divorce, and he spoke about losing the love of his life to cancer after twenty-one years together. I tried to be empathic and compassionately offered, "I'm so glad that you had so many wonderful years of such deep love." And, to my surprise, he responded, "Yes—but I want to have that again!"

And, with that, we both realized that, while rapt in conversation, the room had emptied and left us in the bubble we'd created with our stories. The dinner bell rang, alerting us to find our tables. We quickly scanned the auction tables, playfully flirting and then headed toward the ballroom. There, this handsome man deposited me at my table at the back of the room and went off to join the head table, as he was a guest of the Director.

As I bit into my salad and pondered what had just happened, something caught my eye and I looked up. There, coming across the room towards me, was Dr. Thom Breslin. "How's your seat?" I asked, knowing that the head table was directly in front of the stage. "Funny," he replied, "there doesn't seem to be a seat left for me." Glancing to my right and left, I was met with open chairs. I lifted my eyes towards his, amazed by their sparkle. I pulled out a chair, and with a smile, he sat beside me. The rest of the evening, for both of us, is now a blur.

It's eight years and three children later, and we still feel blessed to have met in that crowded room. While my director finally confessed to setting us up, so much of our encounter was truly magical. Thom shared with me later that his first date with his late wife, Jennifer, had been at Disney World in Florida. And, so, it seemed simply divine that, in a ballroom, he'd find love again with me, in the "happiest place on Earth."

~Sage de Beixedon Breslin

"Is the room crowded?
I thought it was just
you and me in here!"

Hope Deferred

Hope is patience with the lamp lit.
~Tertullian

"Congratulations, girlfriend. I'd love to fly out for your wedding." I dropped the phone, the tears flowing. Not only were three close friends planning weddings, but my brother and sister had each just tied the knot as well. My thoughts turned to Jonathan and our recently cancelled nuptials. It wasn't easy going through heartbreak while those closest to me realized their heart's desires.

Four years earlier a very intuitive friend had shared a profound moment with me. She strongly sensed I would one day have a life partner who would meet my every desire. She warned me, "Be careful and wait for him."

Thrilled that her words confirmed the dreams within my heart, I believed the wait surely wouldn't be longer than a couple of years.

As my twenties evolved into my thirties, that promise turned bittersweet. The word "spinster," not yet in my vocabulary, began to nag at me. I didn't want to meet just any guy. I wanted *the* guy, the one who was destined for me—was I too picky? Tall and thin with long, curly blond hair—was I pretty enough? A Bachelor's in Sociology and a Master's in Theology—should I appear less successful, not quite as smart, more relaxed? Why was it easy for others to find someone to love, but so hard for me?

"Martha, I'm hosting a beach party tonight at my place. Would you like to join us?" asked Mark.

"Count me in," I replied. I never turned down an opportunity to meet Mr. Right.

That evening a tall stranger with black hair and green eyes approached me. "Hi, I'm Peter. Didn't I meet you at Mark's ranch last summer?"

"You might be confusing me with my twin sister, Mary," I commented.

"That's right, I remember now. So Mary's your twin?" he said.

I wondered, was this slight confusion really destiny bringing us together?

Peter, a successful entrepreneur, invited me to explore with him. We flew kites on a hillside, discovered the back streets of the city, and enjoyed fine dining with international flair. After six months of dating, I was crazy about him. I thought the time had come to take the temperature of our relationship. At the end of a long phone conversation I asked, "Peter, where do you see our relationship going?"

"Martha, I don't see myself getting married for at least five years. And you know I have this ideal picture in my mind of the type of girl I want to spend the rest of my life with. I've really fallen for you, but I don't see marriage in our future."

My heart shattered in a thousand tiny fragments. How could I make sense of this? He wanted to be with me now… but not for a lifetime. Should I continue to date him… and hope his feelings changed? How could I stop the pain without isolating myself from living?

It turned out there were many others in my same circumstance… successful, smart, thirty-something women wanting to start families before it was too late. My roommate came up with the idea of a support group. "Let's meet with other women to navigate through these singles' issues together."

"That sounds like a fantastic idea," I replied.

For two years, fifteen women met twice a month to discuss books like *Men Are from Mars, Women Are from Venus*, and *Love Must Be Tough*. We learned, laughed and cried together as we developed lifelong friendships. One by one the women found their husbands—all except me. I still waited, as doubt encroached on the hope left in my heart.

At forty, directed by a strange sense of destiny, I moved to Colorado. Everything seemed novel and exciting: the mountains, my career in real estate, interesting friends. Within a year I became engaged to a lawyer with three children from two previous marriages.

Friends warned me. "Martha, are you certain you're making the right decision?" Sure enough, within two months his controlling personality chased me away without a backward glance.

I poured myself into the home I had purchased. When the interior design resembled a model home, I studied landscape design and turned my bare slope into a beautiful, shady garden. My Cocker Spaniel, Annie, and my affectionate tabby, Oliver, took the place of children. I entertained groups of friends, traveled abroad, immersed myself in work, and began to write poetry—yet something eluded me. Joy and laughter were not a daily experience. In fact, I found it hard to find humor in anything. Almost fifty, I experienced the Proverb, "Hope deferred makes the heart sick."

One evening, engrossed in the speaker's words at a church dinner, I glanced casually at a guy with an athletic build across the table from me. What a nice-looking man. I wondered what his story was.

As we stood up and walked toward the buffet line, he slid in beside me and introduced himself. "Hello, I'm Paul, a guest of Bob and Huntley. It's nice to be out meeting new people. Tell me about yourself. Are you from Colorado?" We talked, laughed and sparked an interest in one another.

The next evening I received an e-mail from Huntley. "Paul asked for your phone number. May we pass it on?" Not only thrilled, I felt peaceful about him, his character and trustworthiness.

Paul had married his high school sweetheart after graduating from college, so he had never been part of the crazy dating world I knew. He didn't understand about playing games, being afraid to commit, or never calling after saying he would. His last seven years had been focused on taking care of a wife dying slowly of emphysema. His world of oxygen tanks, emergency wards and surgeries had finally ended when she succumbed to the disease. During her last days, she made him promise to carry on with life.

As Paul and I spent time together, my laughter returned. He instinctively knew how to make me feel secure, never comparing me to his spouse, and assuring me, "Martha, you're not the next chapter in my life… you're a new volume." He hugged me until I couldn't catch my breath and I felt our bond tighten.

For my part, I brought Paul back into the land of the living. Together we hiked, camped, occasionally hunted, water skied… and attended my nephew's wedding. As they took their vows, I realized I had fallen deeply in love.

Six months from the day we met, he led me to his hillside prayer spot. "I've never experienced what I have with you. We love the same activities, want the same things in life, and think the same way." He laughed. "You speak the words that are going through my head before I can say them. I can't imagine living life without you."

My heart stopped as I looked down at the emerald-cut diamond he placed on my finger. I flashed back to my friend's admonition to wait for the one who would be my every desire. Paul seemed more of a soulmate than I could possibly have hoped for, more like me than my twin sister. The waiting had paid off, my joy found completion as I envisioned our future together.

~Martha Eitzen as told to Margaret Lang

Love at First Flight

Nothing compares with the finding of true love;
because once you do your heart is complete.
~Anonymous

I wanted an exciting job. Sure, I needed to pay my bills along the way. But money was not the first thought on my mind when I accepted a job as a ticket agent for Midway Airlines. I was sold at the mention of free flights and buddy passes for my friends. I didn't even ask about my hourly wage. I didn't care.

Two days prior to my first day on the job, I called the company to find out a few things—things I couldn't ask the lady who interviewed me.

"Is this job fun?"

"Uh, I guess," replied a baffled male voice.

"Good," I said. "I'm starting Wednesday. What are the other employees like?"

"Well, they are mostly male. A lot of us are in our twenties—except for the boss and a couple of baggage handlers. It's pretty laid back though."

"Perfect. I'll see you then. By the way, what's your name?"

"Craig," he said. "Craig Face."

I showed up that Wednesday wearing khaki pants and a Midway polo. I had my ID badge made, filled out paperwork, and then my boss, Rizz, introduced me to my co-workers.

"I'm going to have you start training with Craig," Rizz said. "Shadow him for a while as he checks passengers in."

I recognized the name right away. He was the one I had spoken with on the phone. And in case there was a chance he had forgotten, I reintroduced myself.

"I remember you," he said shyly. "You wanted to know if this job was fun."

"Guilty!" I laughed.

"This isn't the fun part. But wait until we go out to meet the planes."

For the next couple of hours, I watched Craig book flights, hand out tickets, and assist with lost luggage. I learned about three-letter airport codes, the list of prohibited items, and how to check baggage. It was interesting—but not exactly "fun."

Since Midway was a small airline, we were also responsible for meeting the arriving planes, guiding them in with glow sticks, and unloading the luggage. That was the next part I needed to learn.

"Let's go," Craig said. "We need to head out to the tarmac before the CRJ gets here."

"What's a CRJ?" I asked.

"It's a type of plane. It stands for Canadair Regional Jet."

Craig handed me a pair of ear protectors as we walked through the terminal. I wondered why I would need them but I put them around my neck just in case.

Once we were outside in the sun, Craig and I sat on a luggage cart and waited for our plane. I was starting to have fun. I felt an adrenaline rush just watching the plane's landing gear meet the runway.

Then, I watched Craig guide the aircraft towards the gate. His tan arms were outstretched and the sun was glistening off his dirty-blond hair. He looked extremely handsome and I realized I was staring at him.

I also realized that I needed my ear protection after all. The jet engines were deafening as the plane approached.

Craig and I (and the other employees) worked together at the airport for about a week. Then our supervisor said she was sending me to Raleigh for training.

"I'm going to send you and Craig," she said. "You guys started around the same time, so it should work out."

It definitely worked out. For two weeks, Craig and I went to class during the day and went out to dinner at night. We tried every restaurant within walking distance of RDU (Raleigh Durham International Airport) and stayed up talking and laughing until the early morning hours.

I was sad when the training was over. Craig and I had gotten to know each other very well and I had fallen for his witty comments and easy-going personality. It was an amazing experience.

But once we returned home, the job wasn't as exciting as it first seemed. It was hot out on the tarmac, the customers were rude, and I was hardly ever scheduled to work with Craig. I quit the job a couple of weeks later.

Some things just aren't meant to be. That job happened to be one of them. It was fun for a while, but I needed to get serious about my life. I needed to go back to school and finish my degree.

That's exactly what I did. I enrolled in a summer class and focused on my schoolwork. But I didn't completely abandon fun. I still went out on the weekends and enjoyed the local bands with my friends and classmates. And I dated Craig.

I don't know that I believe that everything in life happens for a reason. But I do believe some things do. I believe that I was meant to work for Midway Airlines. How else would I have met my future husband?

Craig and I have been together for nine years and married for five. We've shared a lot of special memories over the years, but few are as fond as our two-week training in Raleigh.

And he still loves to pick on me about our very first conversation.

"I can't believe you actually called a job to ask if it was fun," he says.

"I know. That was pretty silly of me. But at least I knew what I was looking for."

"I did too," he argues.

"Yeah?"

"Yeah. And I found her."

~Melissa Face

"The job may not have been fun... but the benefits were wonderful!"

Loathing at First Sight

There's nothing in this world so sweet as love.
And next to love the sweetest thing is hate.
~Henry Wadsworth Longfellow

Looking at our wedding pictures always makes me giggle. I recall the young man that my brother brought home to dinner one night well over forty-seven years ago. It was not what one could call love at first sight. It was more like loathing at first sight.

The first time I had met him was a few weeks earlier. It all began with a phone call to my high school principal's office. I was a senior in high school at the time. I worked after school at a local restaurant as part of our school work-credit program.

This particular day, I was not scheduled to work, but Mrs. K (the owner) had called and left a message with the office that I would have to take another waitress's place. Mrs. K was not the nicest person in the world to work for to say the least. She never asked if I was available—she just said in her message to "be there at 4:00 P.M." Since not showing up would affect my grades for graduation, there was no way I could wiggle out of the unplanned shift.

My mother was quite the taskmaster herself, and I found myself caught in a bit of a pickle. My mother expected me to be home immediately after school to start dinner for our family. I tried to call my mom at her workplace to tell her of the change in plans but was unable to reach her. Unfortunately there was no voice-mail in those days. There was no way my mom would just let it slide if she did not know of the change in my work schedule. I could count on being grounded, no matter how good the excuse was, if I did not get my message through to her.

Mrs. K never allowed employees to use the phone while on duty and I knew she would not budge on her rules, even though she was the one who had created the situation. I had to stop for gas so I decided to call my mother again from the gas station. My dad had an account at the local Shell station, where I could sign for gas, and Ed (the owner) would bill my dad later.

I was surprised to see a total stranger running the gas station instead of Ed. The young man was quite a flirt, and took his time putting the gas in the tank, washing the windshield, checking the oil, etc. I tried my best to get him to just put the gas in the tank and forget the other routine services, but he kept on trying to impress me. I tried to be polite, but flirting with a strange guy was the last thing on my mind. He was seriously threatening my job and my big date for the Sweetheart dance the following day if I got grounded.

I finally told him, "Look sir, I am in a big hurry. I have to get to work. Now please put the gas on my dad's credit line in Ed's book." Naturally this lead to more delays as he insisted he had no idea where such a book would be or how to do it, so I had to go inside and find it behind the counter for him. I was beginning to think he wasn't very bright. It was a red ledger, exactly where I told him he would find it, right beside the cash register.

My next big mistake was in asking him to give me a dime for the payphone, and put that on the ledger charge too. Good grief! He began to lecture me about taking money from a stranger and other nonsense. By that time I was furious and stomped out hurrying to get to work, and decided to try and talk Mrs. K into letting me use the phone at work.

Naturally, with all the time wasted at the filling station, I was late to work and Mrs. K refused my request to use the phone. Not only that, she also said I had to stay late and do clean-up duty to boot. By the time I got home at midnight my mom was fit to be tied and as

I had feared, I was grounded. A rude stranger had ruined my life. I hoped I never would lay eyes on him again.

As luck would have it, a few weeks later, my mom called me at school and asked me to pick up an extra pound of hamburger as we were having a guest for dinner. Sounded normal to me, so I was totally unprepared that evening when my brother walked in the door with his new friend named Gene that he had met at the gas station. I wanted to hide in the kitchen as I was still so angry at him, but manners precluded my doing so.

By the time the meal was over, the young man apologized for all the trouble he had caused me and he became a regular visitor in our home. When time for the prom came, my boyfriend and I had broken up, so Gene offered to be my date. From there a loathing at first sight became a love story which resulted in forty-one very happy years of marriage and three beautiful children. Obviously, I decided he wasn't so bad after all.

~Christine Trollinger

My Hot Italian

The art of love… is largely the art of persistence.
~Albert Ellis

Rich man, poor man, beggar man, thief. Doctor, lawyer, Indian chief. I never dated an Indian chief, but that was probably because they're hard to come by in suburban New Jersey.

I dated a lot. I just never found anyone I liked.

My mother once said, "If a knight in shining armor came riding down the street on a white stallion, you'd say, 'But he has a red plume in his helmet. I wanted one with a purple plume!'" She couldn't understand what there was to think about. To my mother, love came after finding someone appropriate to marry. She'd say things like, "He's in med school. What do you mean you don't like him?"

Truthfully? I feared boredom. I just couldn't imagine spending the rest of my life with anyone I ever went out with. Wasn't there supposed to be a spark or something? All of these guys seemed interchangeable—same guy, different name.

Maybe I needed to broaden my search.

Teaching did afford me summers off and I was able to spend some of my vacation time in Europe. Men were so romantic there. They looked at women in a way that I had never been looked at before in my life. Was it the wine or exotic locales that made them so attractive? What ever it was, they should bottle it and sell it as souvenirs at the airport. They'd make a fortune.

Of course, September brought me back to reality.

On the first day of school there was an Italian boy in my class. This wasn't unusual. I taught in a large, inner-city school where most of the kids were from either Europe, South America, or the Caribbean. This boy's first words to me were, "You know, you'd be perfect for my big brother."

Honestly? It wasn't the first time I heard that from a student, but there was no way I would ever take anyone up on that offer. Too weird.

But Rocco never let up. Not a week went by that I didn't hear how much his brother and I had in common. This kid was relentless. Even the other kids in class were getting in on it. "You gotta meet him, Miss Maddalena. You'd like him."

And let me tell you, the big brother wasn't bad-looking. Rocco brought a picture in. You could tell it was taken without him knowing it, but the guy was a hot Italian just about my age. This was 1977, and Prospero was the spitting image of John Travolta as Vinnie Barbarino.

"How old is he?"

"Nineteen."

"Nineteen? He's way too young." I was twenty-three heading towards twenty-four. Dating younger men wasn't fashionable. Yet.

"He acts older." This coming from a fourteen-year-old.

Still, it was really too weird. I'd stick with hitting the clubs with my girlfriends, but it was getting old.

Kissing too many frogs and hearing, "What's your sign?" too many times made me decide to go on a self-imposed dating strike. I had a better time staying home and reading than standing around talking to the desperado disco-babies in three-piece suits.

Then boredom hit. Spring was in the air, hibernation time was over, and I needed to get out. Nothing serious, just a little fun. The school year was almost over. Could I? Should I? We had nothing in common. He was way too young. But we were just going out, not getting married.

"Rocco," I said, "do you think your brother is still interested in meeting me?" To tell you the truth, I wasn't even sure if he knew anything about it. I just figured that since Rocco was so persistent with me, he was doing the same thing at home. I guessed right. It turns out that Prospero had been sending his own friends past the school at dismissal to check me out. I slipped the kid a piece of paper. "Tell him to call me."

Our first date was April 30, 1977. What can I say? When I looked in his eyes it felt as if I had known him forever. Before we knew it, we were spending all of our time together. Everything was more fun when Prospero was around. Although we came from very different backgrounds, we shared the same sense of adventure and common values. We took the time to grow together.

Like the song says, we fooled around and fell in love.

Rocco was best man at our wedding in 1980 and made a lovely toast taking credit for the fix up. I still run into some of those kids from my class. They're married now, with kids of their own, and they never fail to remind me that if it wasn't for them, I wouldn't have met my husband.

If anyone ever told me that I would marry Rocco Menna's big brother, I would have laughed like crazy. But what can I say? It was the best thing I ever did. Since the day I met him, Prospero has been my knight in shining armor. And his plume is absolutely perfect.

~Lynn Maddalena Menna

Miracle by Chance

Love isn't something you find. Love is something that finds you.
~Loretta Young

ifteen years ago I hung out at a country bar called the Club Palomino. I loved listening to good bands there, and dancing to their country rock music. I used to drag my friend out to see my favourite band, Cheyenne, who were amazing and always packed the place. My friend and I used to get up and dance to their songs.

I was interested in the rhythm guitar player in the band. To me, he was the best looking one, and I loved his voice along with his rhythm guitar sound. Yes, I had the "hots" for him and would gaze at him playing his guitar and singing while I was on the dance floor or at the bar. Cheynne played at Club Palomino for a long time. I went there as much as I could to see them, and of course, to watch my favourite player. The sad part about it was I used to see him with a short blond girl, his girlfriend or wife I assumed.

When the Club Palomino was closed down, to be replaced by a real estate development project, I wanted to ask the band where they would be playing in the future. But I didn't have enough courage to do that.

Time went on. I met someone and got married. That was a mistake. Eventually we got a divorce. I starting going out to bars again but I didn't meet anyone decent enough. I wasn't crazy about the bands playing at other bars either.

Later, a friend told me to join a particular dating site on the Internet, which I thought I would never do. I checked it out for fun. I had a few dates but didn't find the right person. I gave up on it until one night, after getting home from a bar that I hated, I logged in to that site again. I got an interesting e-mail from a guy and liked his picture. We started e-mailing each other and seemed to have so much in common. We chatted every night as often as we could.

And then, a miracle happened. We started chatting about music. I told him I liked country music and used to frequent Club Palomino. He was really surprised and told me he used to play there. I wasn't sure whether to believe him or not! He said he would send me a picture of his band that played there. I thought "yeah right" to myself as I waited patiently in front of my computer for the picture. Lo and behold, a huge picture came up on my screen. He was the rhythm guitar player in Cheyenne! And he had married, and then divorced, that short blond girl I used to see with him at the club.

We finally met three weeks later, and on our first date, he got up on stage and started playing his guitar and singing in front of an audience. That did it for me. I was hooked. The guy I admired fifteen years ago was performing in front of my eyes and was my date! I was in heaven.

We have been together more than five years now, and the final surprise occurred after we bought a condo and moved in. We looked out the window, and there was the office building of the dating site where we met!

~Jeannette Gardner

Chapter 2

True Love

Adventures in Dating

Take a chance! All life is a chance.
The man who goes the furthest is generally the one who is
willing to do and dare.

~Dale Carnegie

Dating at the Speed of Light

*Two things are aesthetically perfect in the world—
the clock and the cat.*
~Emile Auguste Chartier

Speed dating sounds interesting, at least in theory. You sign up for an evening of dating and fork over some money, though less than you'd spend on dinner for two in a restaurant that doesn't feature a drive-through window. Then you show up at a pre-determined location—a coffee shop or bar—to play musical chairs.

Only in this case, every time the music stops, you meet a new person. And there begins your date.

After reading a couple of articles on it, I decide to check it out. Not that I am actually going to do it, mind you, but I am curious. Okay, more than curious, I am tempted.

A trip to a website for one company sponsoring these events makes for enlightening reading. The main reason for this fast-growing industry appears to be "too many frogs, too little lip balm." Of course, the company states it more diplomatically.

According to the website, people are interested because it's fast, cheaper than joining a dating service, and safer because you decide whom you want to meet. You meet Mr. or Ms. Possible at a supervised location and there are no matches unless both parties say they're interested. At that point, the agency contacts you with phone numbers. After that, you're on your own.

It costs $49 which covers up to nine dates in one evening as well as coffee and a dessert. Not cheap but if it's a really good dessert, with lots of chocolate, it might be worth it.

I continue to read. The "events" offered by this particular establishment are organized into four different age groups. The most popular is the twenty-five- to thirty-five-year-olds, with their next two events already sold out. That is followed by the thirty- to forty-year-olds, the thirty-five- to forty-five-year-olds, and then the forty-two plus category.

That brings up an interesting point. Do I sign up based on my own age or on the age of men I want to meet? After hearing so much about hot, steamy older women/younger men relationships, I'm tempted to shave off a year or two and run, not walk, to the thirty-five- to forty-five-year-old group. Maybe even the thirty- to forty-year-old group if I remember to take my Geritol before I go and if the bar is dark.

Or do I thumb my nose at our youth-worshiping culture and proudly sign up for the forty-two plus category, hoping to meet a suave, debonair mature man with a touch of gray at the temples and the butt of a thirty-year-old. Hey, I'm only human.

Though with my luck, I'll sign up for the forty-two plus category only to find every male under the age of ninety has signed up for younger categories.

The process is simple. You show up at the location and get a name tag with your first name, last initial and a number as well as a confidential response card on which you indicate if you'd like to go out with that person again. Oh, if you're stuck for words, there's a list of conversation starters to get the ball rolling.

As a woman, you also get your own little table for two, where every nine minutes or so another Mr. Possible is supposed to plunk himself down and start chatting. The organizers ring a bell to let you know when it's time to move on. Nine minutes? That's eight minutes too long with some men and a lifetime too short with others. But in speed-dating, all dates come in one size — short.

I'm not so sure about this table thing. Why do men circulate while women sit and wait to be chosen? Having long hair, pouty red lips and a D cup makes it pretty certain that you will get chosen. But what about the rest of us? What if no one comes to your table? Can you get up and drag someone over? Or, do you pull out a book and pretend you've wandered into this meet-and-greet exercise by mistake?

Even if Mr. Right doesn't make it to your table, all is not lost. According to the organizers, you're allowed to corner him, that is, to mingle during the break or after the event. Remember, though, stalking is a crime.

Since the last time I had a date was when the Titanic sank, the real one, I'm becoming more interested. I don't like to use the word desperate — it's such an ugly word. I have my credit card out and I'm just about to hit enter to e-mail the form when I notice something. There, in the small print, it says for every man you register they'll reduce the fee by $10. If I bring five men, I don't have to pay a thing. Hey, I might even get a dollar back.

Alarm bells start going off in my head. First of all, if I knew five single men whom I wouldn't be embarrassed to bring to an evening like this, I wouldn't need to pay for a date-a-thon to begin with. And second, that tells me right away that the ratio of men to women is not in my favor.

Still, you never know. Mr. Almost Right, or at least Mr. Not Entirely Wrong in Dim Light, could be just one cup of coffee away. On the other hand, $49 is one and a half large bags of specialty cat food, enough to feed Thomas for a whole month. And as long as I'm the only one in this house with an opposable thumb who can open the cat food container, I know he'll never leave me.

So it's coming down to feeding one big, fat, not too bright orange tabby cat or a chance to meet Mr. Right. A cat or a man? A man or a cat? Well, that's easy.

Thomas, come here. It's time to rub your tummy. You're such a good boy.

~Harriet Cooper

First Date, First Dent

One forgives to the degree that one loves.
~La Rochefoucauld

Crunch! I knew the sickening sound of metal on metal, and it wasn't the sound I wanted to hear as I was pulling away from one of the most unusual and yet promising first dates I'd ever had.

I jumped out of my car and tried to assess the damage in the inky blackness. All I could tell was that I had officially backed into my date's 1988 Mustang. Ugh! I couldn't believe what I'd just done! I trudged back to his door, dreading the confession I was about to make. As I stood waiting for him to answer my knock, I reviewed the events that had led up to this moment.

The night had started just fine. My darkroom partner from photography class had finally asked me out. I really liked this guy. He seemed genuine and caring, but he could both give and take a joke with the best of them. Definitely my kind of guy.

Since I lived off campus, I parked at his dorm, and he drove us to the movies in his Mustang, a car he was extremely proud of. The conversation flowed freely, as we had plenty to talk about, from our classes to our similar upbringing. I was truly enjoying myself.

We finally pulled up to the movie theater, but it looked abandoned. I worried that we were out of luck, but he thought there was a chance it was open. Sure enough, his positive spirit prevailed: it was open! We purchased tickets and went inside, only to find that I was also right: the place was deserted! Literally, we were the only people there, aside from the ticket-taker and the projectionist (and, truth be told, I wouldn't be surprised if they were the same person). Anyway, we settled in and watched our private screening. Then the fun really started.

About halfway into the movie, the screen started to flicker, and we heard the flapping of the film as the projector broke. We stared at the blank screen. My date took charge. He went to see what the problem was and ended up making friends with the projectionist. Soon we were receiving a tour of the projection room and enjoying an insider's view on how movies are shown.

I have to admit it was kind of fun. And even more interesting was to see how this man acted under pressure. In fact, I was starting to really admire him. As we watched the rest of the movie, my mind began to wander. Maybe we might have a chance—maybe we would end up married with lots of little children who are fascinated by how things work and who could see the possibilities and not the problems in life. I could just see Junior taking apart my blender and making a time machine….

But truly I was getting ahead of myself. Plus I had no idea at that point what a tragic (for the Mustang!) ending our date was fated to have. So the movie ended and we drove back to the dorms, happily chatting, oblivious to the impending disaster.

We said good night and bang! There I was knocking at his door again to tell him I'd ruined his muscle car. I was sure then that I'd ruined my chances as well. But he answered the door, slightly surprised to see me standing there only moments after we had said goodnight. I sheepishly confessed my crime, hung my head and waited for the worst.

But it never came. Instead, that patient man went out to see the car, barely glanced at it in the pitch black and pronounced it fine. I was shocked. And also interested. I know my reaction would have been much different had our roles been reversed. In fact, I am certain it would have involved shaking heads, wringing hands and loud voices, yet there he stood, smiling and telling me not to worry. It was at that moment that I knew I'd found a good man.

And guess what? Somehow, despite all my mistakes, he saw something in me, too. Two years later we drove away in that Mustang with a sign that said "Just Married" covering up a slightly scratched and dented bumper. It's been nearly eighteen years now, and while we no longer own the Mustang, we do have a rich history together, complete with fun stories of our adventures, beautiful twin boys and a future that's brighter than any shiny chrome bumper you could imagine.

~Lisa Tiffin

The Doberman Dates

You can discover more about a person in an hour of play
than in a year of conversation.
~Plato

Ah, Randi. Randi of the smoldering eyes and skin that's marble smooth. Randi, in whose black hair a man could lose his way. A cyclone of a woman, that Randi. And one magical night in 1972 Randi chose me.

She picked me out of at least two hundred desperate L.A. singles who had paid good money to jam into a bad restaurant and yell their hopes and dreams at each other. It started with a nod, followed by a compliment about my smile, delivered in a voice whose every syllable aroused. Randi's praise migrated to my eyes and, after we swapped a few sentences, my brain. "Ivy League," she purred when I answered the "what college" question, and her exquisite fingers touched my hand. Wesleyan is not an Ivy League school, but before I could correct her, Randi said that she too had been expensively educated.

She invited me to dinner at her home the following Friday night. She wanted to try out her gourmet cooking. Now I knew this exquisite creature and I could harmonize our lives, and I spent the week dreaming of the white hot passion that awaited me.

Friday. The night was drizzly, perfect for a quiet dinner in Randi's apartment. But she had not put out any hors d'oeuvres. Worse yet, her kitchen looked spotless, with no indication of a meal in progress. Randi steered me into a bedroom whose purple walls matched her bedspread. "There," she said, and pointed to at least a dozen diplomas hanging over a stainless steel headboard. She was expensively educated, all right, at one-week academic wonders like Perpetual Savings and Loan's Seminar on Financial Institutions, the Bellefontaine Academy for Wealth Accumulation, The Culinary Institute of the Arts, and the Summertime School for the Humanities. I said I was impressed, while my eyes traveled from her stiletto heels to the mirrors on her ceiling.

Randi squeezed my hand. "I'd like to see a movie first," she said, and added that a theater was close by. On its one screen was *The Doberman Gang*, the immortal, unforgettable yawn (I mean yarn) about a dog trainer who taught Doberman Pinschers to rob banks. Each canine got the name of a famous outlaw. Bonnie. Clyde. Baby Face Nelson. Pretty Boy Floyd. Dillinger. Someone booed when it was over. I would have joined him but was too focused on my hunger pangs. I had skipped lunch in anticipation of Randi's gourmet cooking.

We drove back to Randi's apartment complex and spent ten minutes hunting for a parking space. It was raining hard now, but she wanted to show me the grounds, especially the recreation room where, it just so happened, there was a crowd. "Oh, a party," she said without sounding surprised. "Let's go in for a minute." Before I could answer, Randi passed through the sliding glass doors. As I followed her, some bruiser in an open shirt with a gold charm hanging on his hairy chest demanded ten dollars. That's ten 1972 dollars. "Guys pay," he said, in a tone of voice you would reserve for an imbecile. I lingered at the door, wondering if Randi would return before this brute shoved me out into the rain. When she re-appeared, she held a half-eaten French dip sandwich from which juice dribbled to the floor.

Randi asked, "Don't you want to stay?"

I stammered, "I thought we were going…"

"I want to go to the party," she interrupted. "We can say good night here." Flakes of French dip clung to the hand that Randi thrust forward. "Good night, young man." All sensuality had vanished from her face, like vitamins going out of stale orange juice. Seconds later, Randi was gone.

My landlord served a free brunch every Sunday. At least ten of us were gorging ourselves on bagels, lox and cream cheese. Someone asked what I had done over the weekend. Randi was worth a story if nothing else, but after three sentences there was an echo: "Ivy League." "Ivy League." "Dinner." "Dinner." "Mirrors." "Mirrors." "Diplomas." "Diplomas."

It wasn't an echo. The words kept coming after I paused. "Bad movie." "Party." "Ten dollars." Someone at the coffee urn across the room was describing to another group of my neighbors what had occurred on his date the night before.

"Excuse me," I asked the owner of that voice. "Were you out with a girl named Randi?"

Indeed he was. Jonathan had been treated to Randi's world of purple walls, diplomas, and mirrors. Like me, he had not been treated to her cooking. Instead—you guessed it—she wanted to see *The Doberman Gang*. Jonathan had gone home without his supper. I respected him because he too had refused to pay the ten-dollar entry fee for the rec room party, and I conceded that Randi must have preferred him over me, because Cornell—his alma mater—actually belongs to the Ivy League.

Thanks to our shared experience with Randi, Jonathan and I became fast friends. We palled around L.A., made some investments together, and double dated with women who actually did want to eat when darkness fell. Ten years later, I danced at his wedding.

Although it's been more than thirty years since we met her, Jonathan and I confess to a lingering admiration for Randi. She was special. Anyone who can sit through *The Doberman Gang* two nights in a row has to possess some unique quality that sets her apart from the rest of us. Woof.

~Anthony J. Mohr

Adventures in Online Dating

Why not go out on a limb? Isn't that where the fruit is?
~Frank Scully

"I'm not looking to meet someone. I have a great life. A man would just mess things up. Besides, if God wants me to marry, don't you think He will bring along the right person at the right time?"

My friend looked skeptical as she eyed me through the steam rising from our cappuccinos. "Did it ever occur to you," she said, "that God wants you to be looking? Sure, you have your teaching career, your house, your Beagles, and your independence. Perhaps a good relationship would add further richness to an already great life."

I filed that last statement somewhere deep in my brain. In the weeks that followed I occasionally took it out, studied it, prayed about it, and then returned it to its hiding place. One day, while in the middle of this ritual, I noticed that my friend's words had increased in size. Taking root, they had spread like mint in a garden and, as such, could no longer be ignored. I was reminded of the Biblical account of Abraham, who sent his servant in search of a wife for his son, Isaac. Abraham did not sit around and twiddle his thumbs, waiting for a young woman to knock on the door of his tent. His plan involved deliberate action.

"Okay, Lord," I prayed. "If you want me to look for a man,

then please tell me where and how to begin my search, as I assume bars, nightclubs, and the underside of rocks are not your preferred venues."

Rewind to 1970. I was sixteen years old and clueless when it came to flirting and dating. The only piece of advice my mother gave me on the subject of boys was, "Don't you ever call a boy on the phone! You don't want him to think you're fast."

Fast at what? Long division?

I heeded her advice, though I disagreed. It was a new era. The 60s mantra of "Free Love" still resonated amidst the disco balls; women burned their bras in Double D-sized bonfires; and Virginia Slims claimed we'd come a long way, baby. Yet there I sat, juxtaposed in time, imprisoned by my pink Princess telephone as I waited for Dream Boat to call. The Pill has been credited with setting women free, but I believe the credit belongs to the microchip. My mother may have told me never to phone a boy; she never said anything about e-mail.

Fast forward back to the twenty-first century. Here began my adventures in online dating, with its freedom to initiate contact regardless of gender. I decided I would not be found sitting in front of a pink Princess computer waiting for a mailbox icon to announce, "You've got male!" I resolved that when and if I came across an attractive profile, I would have no qualms over sending the first e-mail. The anonymity of cyberspace gave me opportunities to communicate with men without revealing my name or address until I felt comfortable doing so, if at all.

I was off, both excited and scared by this self-imposed journey. Occasionally, upon initiating contact, that first e-mail was also the last. This gave me insight into the risk-and-rejection factor that men have experienced for eons. It is not fun. However, taking these risks also brought some fascinating people across my path, which explained why I never met for dinner on the first date. I needed to know I could beat a hasty retreat if we had nothing to talk about, or if he wanted to spend the evening discussing his passion for nude motorcycling in Alaska. For these reasons, and because I love good coffee, I decided to stick with cafés for first meetings. First, however, I established some "Ground Rules." The slightest utterances of "ex-wife," "estranged wife," or "my wife's sleazy lawyer" were grounds for ordering my coffee to go.

I met a plethora of men who could not seem to talk about anything but their broken marriages and messed-up kids, and who had so much emotional baggage they could have used their own personal bellhops. These people were common, but I encountered a few who were downright bizarre. Take the man who, after several e-mail exchanges between us, called me on the phone to chat. During the course of our conversation I mentioned how impressed I was that he was not bothered by our age difference, and by the fact that I was older. His response: "Oh, that's a turn-on for me. Also, you being a teacher really clinched it. You know, it's part of the whole naughty-older-teacher-thing." I mumbled something about having to grade my students' papers and hung up, feeling as if I needed a shower.

Another man, upon seeing the two wood boxes that contain the ashes of my deceased dogs, proclaimed that I was involved in "Satanic animal worship." He added that I could not love both animals and people; I had to choose. So I did. My Beagles and I waved goodbye as he drove off.

One day I came across the profile and photos of someone with whom I believed I had a lot in common, and I sent him an introductory e-mail. Within five minutes I received a reply in which he stated that while I "seemed very nice," unfortunately I was too short for him. (I hail at five feet, three inches.) He was tall and the woman of his dreams had to be at least five foot six. I thought this so ludicrous I decided to write again. By this time my sarcastic sense of humor was running in high gear. "As you seem to be a mature professional, I am rather surprised that you would be concerned with a relatively trivial matter such as height. For a tall person you seem to have some shortcomings." Suffice it to say he sent back a tirade that rivaled Mussolini's speech from the balcony.

As for physical attributes, online dating gave me but a glimpse of someone's true appearance. Some photos were blurred, some revealed only half a face, and others were so morose that they looked as if they were taken just moments before the walk to the death chamber. On the other hand, I viewed bulging biceps, washboard abs, and full heads of hair, only to later encounter clones of George Costanza. I wanted to tell these men that if middle age spread had moved in, and their hair had moved out, look at these changes as signs of experience and wisdom, rather than attempting to begin a relationship under false pretenses. In addition, I wanted to scream, "Please don't try the 'comb-over' in an attempt to look younger! It doesn't work!"

Despite these experiences, I am very glad I embarked on this cyber-dating adventure. I downed a lot of coffee, but that was merely the froth on the cappuccino. In June of 2007 I read the profile of a man who was a committed Christian, lived only fifteen miles away, and who had also never been married. Intrigued, I positioned my fingers over my computer keyboard to send him a message. Then I saw it. He was forty-five years old and I was fifty-three. A full eight years stretched between us. Experience had taught me that men under the age of fifty typically were not interested in women who had crossed that great divide. I decided not to set myself up for disappointment and so did not contact him.

Two days later there was mail in my online box. I clicked it open and received the surprise of my life. "It's that guy!" I exclaimed, although no one but my dogs and God could hear me. "It's the forty-five-year-old-Christian-fifteen-miles-away-never-been-married-guy!" I wrote back and a correspondence began, followed by telephone conversations. One week before my online dating subscription was set to expire (I had resolved not to renew it), on July 30, 2007, we met in person over lattes and scones. We had no trouble recognizing each other, as both of us had posted current photographs. We talked for hours and agreed to meet again; then again; and yet again. We slowly got to know each other as friends. I was taken by his kindness, the respect with which he treated me, and the fact that he liked my dogs. We shared many common interests, yet willingly accepted one another's differences.

On Christmas Day, 2008, he asked me to marry him, and we were wed on April 4, 2009.

All of this transpired because we chose to step out from the familiar and the traditional, to trust God, and to risk walking the fiber optic line of computer dating, gigabytes from my pink Princess telephone.

~Laurel Hausman

14

My Final Date with Veronica

A happy person is not a person in a certain set of circumstances,
but rather a person with a certain set of attitudes.
~Hugh Downs

It was dumb. The dumbest thing I've ever done. Maybe the dumbest thing any human being has ever done. No one at school knew about Thistle. It was a dark secret that had never seen the light of day and I cringed at the thought of anyone ever finding out.

Can you blame me? Thistle was a logging town, a piteous patch of ground where cars were dented, teeth were missing, and haircuts resembled a pre-op lobotomy. It was a disheveled place, a wide spot in the road where lumberjacks drank beer and chopped trees, and sad women with two first names listened to long, complaining ballads about two-timing men and the rocky road of life. The last thing I wanted was for any of my college friends to discover the ugly truth: Thistle was my home.

You might wonder then, why did I tell Veronica? To which I can only reply: I'm not sure.

My girlfriend, Veronica, was attractive. No doubt about it. She was sleek and tall and wore her dark hair in an expensive razor-cut blow-dried unisex coiffure. Oddly enough, though, it wasn't her beauty I was interested in.

She also came from a wealthy family. Veronica had a closet stuffed with Dior dresses and a MasterCard with an unlimited line of credit. Yet I could have cared less about her money.

What impressed me most about Veronica was her mind. She was smart, a straight-A student, senior class president and an avid environmentalist. She used words so big they made me flinch.

So I fell in love with her. For a while there I was on cloud nine. Had I known a little more about Veronica, though, I might have chosen cloud seven.

You see, she had a dark side about her, a sourly intense, pursed-lipped, preoccupied air, and a sometimes rude temper. When angered, she had a way of staring at you that was downright creepy.

But I enjoyed Veronica's company. Night after night I found myself sitting beside her at the library reading literature not just meaningful, or deep, but positively gravid with meaning. Whitehead. Camus. Sartre, for God's sake!

All that liberal cant must have caused a serious time warp in my thinking because that's when I told her about Thistle.

Her "Huh?" was punctuated by a frown. "You're kidding," she said.

"I'm afraid not," I replied.

"Thistle? That sounds almost anthropological, like an African tribe or something."

Obviously Veronica was not simpatico. She arched an eyebrow when I described the tobacco-chewing women and the tow-headed children. Her face puckered with distaste when I told her about the people I knew who had dropped out of school in the seventh grade to attend monster truck rallies.

"You had me fooled," she said. "I thought you were smarter than that."

"It's not that bad," I explained.

"Well, it sounds dreadful," she said. "And I want you to take me there this weekend so I can see it for myself."

Omens and portents were everywhere if only I'd been alert. "Are you sure," I asked? "I mean, it's awfully Middle American."

"Of course, I'm sure. It'll be fun to see how the other half lives."

There was no stopping her. One way or another, I was out to prove Thomas Wolfe wrong: you can go home again, especially when someone is holding a knife to your ribs.

It was a long and dusty drive to Thistle, and Veronica complained all the way. Mom greeted us at the door when we arrived, wearing her usual flowered dress without a waistline and a plain white apron that looped over her head. She pecked me once on each cheek, then held me at arm's length as if to check the merchandise for damage.

"You smell good today, Ma," I said.

"You saying I don't always smell good?" she replied.

"No, I'm just saying you smell nice. You got someone special to come calling?"

She chuckled. "You silly boy."

Veronica kicked my leg. "Oh," I said, "where are my manners? Ma, this is Veronica."

My mother studied her, pursing her lips. "Lord Mercy," she said, "she's a half-cooked little fritter, but a fellow'd have to be coated with Teflon not to let her stick to his pan."

I blushed. "Y'all stop talking like that," I said.

Veronica threw a long measured look in my direction.

"Y'all?" she said. "Did you just say 'y'all'?" I felt the blood vacate my face.

We made our way through the kitchen where supper was cooking. Mom had pots on all four burners, timers ticking, and food covering every inch of countertop.

Veronica, though, was not impressed. The look on her face said, "under this roof lives a family that is one hundred percent pure white trash, probably descended from a long line of cousins."

Our living room was done in a sort of "junkyard" motif. There was a stone fireplace, a coffee table holding copies of hook and bullet magazines, and a mounted deer head hanging above the fireplace. Dad was asleep in front of the TV, out like a side of beef on Thorazine.

"Wake up, Arnold," Mom shouted. "We've got company."

"I'm up," he muttered, pulling his false teeth out of his pocket.

Dad was dressed for dinner. And work too, for that matter. He wore a blue shirt with elbows that looked like they had been dynamited away, Can't Bust 'Em pants, and clunky, black boots—the same clothes he wore everywhere.

I went into the kitchen to check on dinner. When I returned, Veronica and my father were already deep in conversation.

"What do you do for a living, Mr. Hebley?" she asked.

"I'm a logger."

Uh-oh, I thought, here comes trouble. I felt my spirit start to belly over, like the Titanic on its way down.

"A logger," she said. "Is that a fact?"

Dad shrugged. "It's no big thing. I mean it ain't half as excitin' as it sounds."

Mom came out of the kitchen holding a long handled fork. "Don't let him kid you, honey," she said. "That man loves to cut trees. He'd just go on forever, cutting every last tree if you didn't stop him."

Veronica's smile was a fresh wound in scar tissue. "Every last tree, you say?"

"Oh, I love the smell of sawdust," said Dad. "Besides, somebody's gotta cut down the trees before those damn environmentalists put the kibosh on it."

That did it. Without another word Veronica snatched up her coat and headed for the door.

"Wait!" I yelled, but it was too late. She climbed in my truck and sped off, vanishing in the proverbial cloud of dust.

It took a long time for my sorrow to dissipate. Like, say about five minutes. Then I grabbed a beer and sat down in front of the TV. There was a terrific wrestling match on. A fellow in a snake suit was jumping on his opponent's neck. I settled back and smiled, feeling the way a guy does when he knows he's finally home.

~Timothy Martin

15

My Worst — and Best — Easter

Easter spells out beauty, the rare beauty of new life.
~S.D. Gordon

They always say, "You just know, and it will happen when you least expect it," but I never believed them. Especially in L.A. In ten years of living there, dating was among my favorite—and least favorite—of hobbies.

After yet another handful of bad dates—which included a guy who told me he does coke ("but just quarterly"), a guy who said he is getting better in regard to his last break-up ("though we might get back together"), and a guy who proceeded to flirt with everyone except for me at a party I took him to ("I had a great time," he said—little did I know I had set up a speed dating event—just for him)—I had had enough. And that was all in the same week. And, in L.A., this was typical. Quantity, not quality, and I was tired of it. Having grown up in the Midwest, where were all the guys with Midwestern manners? I had the best boyfriend ever before I moved to L.A. and was convinced all these bad dates were payback for my breaking his heart ten years earlier.

"They" also say to meet someone through friends. But guess what? The above three examples prove "them" very wrong.

This last date, the speed dating one, took place on Easter, with a guy from church at a post-Easter brunch. And I didn't think of his behavior as anything more than un-Christian. The previous year, I had given up dating for Lent; now, I wondered why I hadn't this year, too.

Easter night, a group of my non-Christian friends were meeting for dinner as they did every Sunday night. After the above, being in another group situation was the last thing I wanted to do. But since I was all dressed up and had nowhere else to go, I thought, "Why not?"

For the next hour, I sat parked in front of the restaurant, on the phone with my friend Courtney debating whether or not to go inside. At the time, it was more fun to complain about my day and why not to go in.

"I'm not dating anymore," I told her. "It's too hard. I'm just going to focus on my writing," I added. "Yeah, but that's hard, too," Courtney said. "Yet you keep doing it." True, I thought. "Just forget about them, truly forget about them," Courtney added. "You know that everything happens for a reason, and there is someone better out there for you than a flirty guy who wants his ex-girlfriend back and does coke quarterly," she said. I couldn't help but laugh; I knew she was right.

I decided to go into the restaurant, only to realize I had left my driver's license in a drugstore across town, one that was closing in a half-hour. I drove back to get it, then drove back to the dinner, wondering if it was even worth going in anymore, over an hour later.

Outside the restaurant, I saw a guy at the valet, Tyler, whom I had known six years prior, one whom I had had a crush on. He asked if I wanted to go have a drink. Though it was tempting, I knew my friends were waiting for me, and I wanted to see them, so I declined. I secretly thanked God for the ego boost as I stepped inside.

Once there, I saw another guy I knew, Paul, one I had met a couple years ago, one of those people you meet and have chemistry with, yet neither of you are single, so you say you'll stay in touch, but don't. Yet here he was, alone. We talked for a few minutes, and he told me he would find me before he left. Fair enough.

I thanked God for the second ego boost, and finally met up with my friends. After we caught up a bit, a guy and girl whom I did not know joined our table. The guy, David, was sitting next to me, and we soon started talking… and talking… and talking. A few minutes in, I started to like the guy—he was just so… normal, didn't flirt with everyone in the room, and had no ex-girlfriends or coke habits to speak of. I couldn't remember the last time I had clicked with someone so immediately.

However, I had no clue if the girl David arrived with was his girlfriend. I certainly didn't want to talk to him so much if she was, like the speed dating guy had done to me. I asked David about the girl: they were just friends. Phew.

David and I then remembered we had first met eight months prior, at a friend's birthday party. I had even taken a group photo at the party, with him in it. We also discovered that we had been at the same Halloween party months before, yet never saw each other at it (back then, I had a boyfriend, so checking out other guys wasn't on my radar). Finally, David and I realized we shared a best friend, Jeremy.

I suggested we each text Jeremy to tell him we had met. I had given up texting for Lent, so this was my first post-Lenten text. Jeremy wrote right back. I opened my phone for David and I to read at the same time, without reading the text myself first. It said, "Hey, I was thinking of setting you two up. :) He seems like your type." I don't know who turned more red, me or David. "This will be a good story someday, of how we started dating," we said in unison, a little perplexed, yet intrigued.

Jeremy had also texted David, asking how we had met. "J-Date," David wrote back jokingly. The funny thing was, just the other week, I had told Jeremy I was going to go on J-Date, for another Christian girl I know went on and ended up marrying a guy from there. Little did Jeremy know that David was kidding. (If you are reading this now, Jeremy, I guess the secret's out.)

Jeremy then texted me, saying "You're on a J-Date even though you're Catholic? And on Easter? Is that allowed?" "God has a great sense of humor," is all I thought. After all, Easter is a time of rebirth.

Now, hundreds of dates later, "they" were right. You do just know, and when you least expect it. After my long-term, Midwestern college boyfriend, I never thought I would find love like that again. But after meeting David, I realized that I could. And I had. A few months after we started dating, I told David, "Thanks for being at that non-Easter dinner." "Thanks for being," he replied.

~Natalia K. Lusinski

Flour Power

The great doing of little things makes the great life.
~Eugenia Price

Picture this: a slim, tow-headed nine-year-old boy is sitting on a kitchen counter next to a plate of just-baked cookie cutouts awaiting their adornment. The front of his red, footed, fleece pajamas is smudged with flour, as is the tip of his nose. His gray-green eyes look serious as he contemplates the task before him. Standing on a chair nearby is his sister. Splotches of red and green icing cling to the sleeves of pajamas identical to her brother's except they are pink. Her enormous blue eyes glow when she beholds the culinary bounty before her, and her lightly-freckled cheeks are powdered with the confectioner's sugar used to make icing for the stars, bells, trees, and Santas her brother and she are decorating with red and green tinted sugars and multi-colored sprinkles.

A small, dark-haired woman supervises this baking extravaganza, ping-ponging between the two children while offering encouragement and assistance as needed. Decorettes are scattered everywhere. Flour dust permeates the air and settles on the counters, stovetop, and linoleum.

Emanating from the kitchen is an aroma so delectable that a man in gold-rimmed spectacles is drawn to the doorway to investigate the merry, if messy, proceedings. "Dad," his son calls out, "Look what we're doing!"

The man smiles and steps closer to admire the cookies, iced

liberally and gobbed—some to the max—with multi-colored sprinkles. He selects several conservatively decorated ones to munch while he finishes reading the daily newspaper in the living room.

But I'm getting ahead of myself.

Rewind to several weeks earlier, when mutual friends called the man and woman to arrange a dinner party where she, a childless widow in her late thirties, and he, a forty-something widower with two young children, could meet. Though both had nearly given up on finding suitable mates in their small college town—including the university where they taught—they agreed to the setup.

"I'll have to get home by nine to finish grading essays," the woman said before attending the dinner.

"I won't be able to stay late. I have to get the children into bed at a decent hour," the man told the hostess.

At 12:30 A.M., the woman helped the man carry his daughter, now sound asleep, out to his Jeep; his drowsy son followed close behind. "He intends to call," the friends told the woman.

A day, then two, went by. The third day extended past dinnertime with still no phone call. "I guess he's changed his mind," the woman thought with regret, for the man was everything she'd always wanted—children and all.

The phone rang several hours later. It was the man who, amidst an intensely hectic schedule, finally had time to call. The two talked comfortably for an hour before he asked her to dinner at a local Italian restaurant.

They arrived at the restaurant slightly before 7:00 P.M. and ordered wine to sip as they perused the menu. Then they began to talk, really talk, as if no one else in the universe, much less the restaurant, existed. Sometime after 9:30 P.M., they ordered meals. Patrons of the restaurant came and went until the man and woman were the only diners remaining. By this time, their waiter was sipping a beer at the bar.

When the couple detached from their verbal communion, they were astonished to find that the other tables in the restaurant were cleared and empty. Though their waiter assured them they could stay as long as they liked, it was after 1:00 A.M. and time to depart; the man had considerable driving to do before he'd arrive home to relieve the babysitter from her duties. While helping the woman into her coat, his lips met her forehead. At her door, he gave her a real kiss.

The woman entered her dwelling, feeling as if everything around her was electric. Though she'd scoffed when people in love described themselves as "floating on a pink cloud," exactly that was now happening to her. She tried to undress but ended up sitting on the corner of her bed, contemplating the events of the evening.

Her phone rang. It was the man, who declared, "I almost got arrested, and it's all your fault!" While driving home, he'd been so deep in thought that his Jeep kept drifting across the centerline of the nearly deserted highway. A trooper had noticed his erratic driving and pulled him over. The man had talked his way out of getting a ticket by explaining to a sympathetic—and slightly amused—officer that he'd just come from a very intriguing date.

The next day, the man invited the woman to join his children and him at the Sunday matinee of *Ernest Saves Christmas*. The following afternoon, he brought her to his home: a spacious 1940s Colonial furnished beautifully in earth tones and situated picturesquely on five acres of meadowland and woods. So harmonious was the environment that contentment—more like bliss—enveloped the woman. She wanted to sing; she wanted to dance.

After dinner at his house that night, the woman asked if she could bake Christmas cookies with his children.

Which brings us back to the opening scene.

The man reappears in the doorway and scrutinizes the floury footprints crisscrossing the kitchen. "Dad," the little girl pipes up, "Come see this cookie! I made it just for you!" He picks his way across the floor to gaze upon a cookie so covered with icing and decorations that its Santa shape is obliterated. Though inedible by adult standards, it is a six-year-old's dream. The man's eyebrows arch then relax. He turns to his daughter. "Are you sure you have enough sprinkles on that?" he asks.

She giggles. "Doesn't it look good?"

"It's a masterpiece. And you've worked so hard decorating it, I think you should be the one to eat it."

Directly, glasses of milk are poured. Numerous cookies are eaten; dozens more are stored. With bedtime approaching, the children wash up and change into clean pajamas. While the woman tidies the kitchen, the man reads a story to the children. Afterwards, the adults retire to the living room, where a fire dances in the fireplace. Wine is poured, and the man and woman toast the success of the evening. "This is the first time they've ever baked cookies," the man tells the woman beside him on the sofa. "They were too young before their mother died." With arms around each other, they talk—or don't talk—until the fire burns down to tiny embers.

After twenty years of marriage and counting, my husband still maintains that he was set up: somehow I knew that, if I positively wanted to hook him, all I'd have to do was bake Christmas cookies with his children. The ambience created by such a joyous activity made him realize that I was the right woman for him and his difficult years as a single parent were about to come to an end. All he could do after that was completely fall in love with me—and I with him. The rest, as they say, is history.

~Catherine Grow

The One Who Never Was

'Tis better to have loved and lost than never to have loved at all.
~Alfred Lord Tennyson

It was Thursday, around 5:30 P.M. on a perfect spring day; I was sitting in the patio section of a restaurant across the street from a busy train terminal, waiting for Marie to arrive. Every couple of minutes the terminal would unleash a fresh batch of homebound commuters. The seemingly endless waves of commuters served as a good distraction as I continued battling the army of butterflies in my stomach. I am not accustomed to being nervous but it seemed appropriate to feel anxious before my first date with the girl who I didn't want to remember and could never forget.

One week before, I had seen Marie for the first time since graduating college three years earlier. I had finally revealed the truth that had been haunting me since the first moment I ever saw her, a truth I had spent years trying to ignore, a truth which had to be confessed, a truth she deserved to hear, a truth she needed to believe — Marie is the standard against which I measure all other women. Another train pulled in and the terminal started producing a new mob of commuters when Marie called to tell me she had arrived.

The butterflies kicked into high gear as I looked across the street. This wave of commuters contained the woman who forever changed the way I look at all other women. Marie stood out from the crowd like a rose in a barren desert. She wore an unforgettably bright smile and casually walked with an elegance that was as surreal as it was intoxicating. My breath was taken away at the first sight of her beautiful smile. Somehow Marie found a way to make her smile even more alluring when she spotted me from across the street and started walking over.

Little did I know, this date would be the start of an enlightening journey that would ultimately leave me with the knowledge that following your heart will prove insufficient if you allow your fears to create even the slightest bit of hesitation or restraint.

The next two years were a roller coaster. During good times we talked for hours, laughed and enjoyed being together as if our ups and downs and everything else in the world were completely irrelevant. I found myself totally at peace with the job I created for myself—making her feel as comfortable, safe and happy as possible. I thought her eyes revealed that she reciprocated my feelings.

It was not only Marie's physical beauty that captivated me; it was something infinitely more rare and significant. By my standards, nothing can compare to a person who effortlessly exudes an energy that eases the mind of all stress, while simultaneously enabling all that truly matters in life to be displayed with brilliant clarity and joy. The women I had dated in the past all possessed the attributes I wanted (intelligence, humor, physical/inner beauty and compassion) but those characteristics were never enough to make me content—I needed more. I needed a woman with the unique ability to profoundly strengthen and inspire me, a woman who forced me to become a better person simply because I knew she deserved the absolute best I could offer, a woman whose well-being I viewed as being equally or more important than my own.

Eventually we drifted apart, leaving me wondering why the vicious hot/cold cycle had continued for those two years. Was it because I hadn't been assertive enough about what I wanted? Was it because we are both afraid to trust each other with the inherent responsibility that a deep connection like that requires? Maybe my instincts were all wrong and she never felt the same way for me as I did for her. Regardless of what the real reason was, I don't feel any differently towards her or see her in a lesser light. In a strange way I don't care what the reason was; all that matters to me is that she is happy and safe. Regardless of how much I want to be the one to make her smile like no one else can, I'd be content knowing she is smiling and being treated like gold (as she deserves to be) by someone else.

Even though things turned out much differently than I believed they would, I learned valuable lessons from my experiences with Marie. Truth be told, although I have called Marie "the one who got away," the fears and hesitations which I believe to have ultimately kept us apart made Marie "the one who never was" more than anything else.

Even though I would love to go back in time and change how things unfolded between us, I have no regrets. I followed my heart, and although she never truly returned my feelings, she deserved the kindness I gave her nonetheless. I learned that when a person as special as Marie comes into your life you owe it to yourself and to her to follow your heart and put it all on the line. Otherwise you'll allow your fears to restrict your future, leaving you with nothing but memories of "the one who got away" or even worse, memories of "the one who never was."

~Jeffrey Nathan Schirripa

The Rainbow

And as he spoke of understanding,
I looked up and saw the rainbow leap with flames of many colors over me.
~Black Elk

1995 was a bad year; my husband of forty-eight years died in August, then four months later my mother died. What was I supposed to do now after caring for him for ten years, and helping with Mother's care? Lonely days and nights stretched endlessly. Dark and dreary thoughts constantly filled my mind. If I slept at all, I had nightmares. One day my pastor invited me to his Grief Support Group and I went, reluctantly, and met others who shared their feelings, how they coped. Finally, in an effort to dispel the depression that threatened, I resolved to turn my mind to other things, to seeing the beauties of nature, beginning with my first ocean cruise. I was hesitant to travel alone, so I invited four of my teenaged granddaughters for company. On a lovely sunny day in June we boarded Holland America's *Nieuw Amsterdam* in Vancouver and headed for Alaska. The two older girls, sisters, shared one cabin. The other two bunked with me.

Each morning I awoke before the girls, walked the decks, and savored the sights, smells, and sounds of the ocean. The girls and I took in all the shows, went on three shore excursions, marveled at hundreds of bald eagles in the wild, and even walked on the Mendenhall Glacier. When they were occupied with teen activities, I relished my moments on deck and tried to banish the dark thoughts and nagging concerns. Watching the soothing waves helped.

For weeks I had debated and prayed about what was happening in my life. My greatest concerns were about the nice widower I had met in the Grief Support Group. I saw him at church each Sunday. He phoned occasionally to chat. We went to dinner and a movie once, riding in the red Firebird he was so proud of. He tolerated my depressed moods and bouts of tears and even managed to make me laugh a few times. But was I being fair to take up so much of his time? I couldn't forget that my husband had been dead less than a year. What was I doing? I was almost seventy. What would my children think? I needed a sign, but the rolling waves of the Inland Passage never showed me any.

The morning our ship sailed into Glacier Bay, I dressed quietly and hurried to the Promenade Deck. Alaskan time was four hours earlier than at home, so despite the ship's clock saying it was 4:00 A.M., my built-in clock insisted it was 8:00 A.M. I walked briskly around the deck and watched the ocean and the lightening sky. On my first turn around the bow I spied a brilliant rainbow spanning the western sky. I was almost afraid to hope, but I couldn't help wonder if this were the answer to my prayers.

Martha, another widow, joined me on my next lap. She also had a knotty problem: deciding whether to surrender her independence and move in with her lonely sister, who had recently lost her husband. We had discussed our respective dilemmas two or three times on previous days without coming any closer to conclusions. Now as we rounded the bow, we admired the intense colors of the rainbow.

"Martha, I wonder—do you think this could be God's sign for us? You know, like when he showed the rainbow to Noah?" I asked.

"I don't know," she said, "but if it's still there on our next lap, I'll consider it."

Our rainbow continued to brighten the sky on subsequent laps, fading only when we went inside for breakfast. We ate in silence, but I felt more relaxed and at peace than I had in weeks.

I spent the entire day on deck, drinking in the glaciers, the blues and greens of the ice, each from different decades, even different geological ages. The summer day was warm, the sky a clear cerulean, the water a mirror, as if posing for reflecting pictures and broken only by the occasional otter splashing playfully in the ocean. Ice walls towered above the ten-story deck, their beauty demonstrating once again God's majesty.

When we docked in Ketchikan, I phoned my widower friend, Cal, but didn't mention what had happened. He was cordial and offered to pick me up at the airport on my return. Cal is a retired engineer, an avid woodworker, and a bicyclist who loves to travel. He and his late wife had not been able to do so during her many illnesses any more than I had been able to travel during my husband's illnesses.

When I returned from our cruise, he visited my house often and I soon realized I was developing strong feelings for him. But I never put a name to our relationship until the night my daughter phoned. When I mentioned I had been out to dinner with Cal, she exclaimed, "Mother! You never told me you were dating!" She sounded happy.

During the rest of that year we attended plays and the ballet and took day trips to state parks in the area in his Firebird. He often brought me flowers; he became very affectionate. In January, Cal knelt down on one knee and proposed marriage. I accepted. After consulting with our pastor, we set a date in April, sold our homes and bought one together. Our wedding arrangements were overseen by the watchful eye of the congregation, some of whom even threw us a shower. In our joy, we invited the entire church membership to attend the ceremony.

Tennessee's spring in 1997 was at its most glorious. The redbuds and dogwoods put on a spectacular show for our northern guests while Southern magnolias and azaleas burst with crimson and white blossoms. All seven of our children flew in from distant parts of the country to participate; his sisters and their families drove down from the Midwest; two of his cousins came from Ohio and Missouri. My late husband's brother and his wife drove in from across the state.

On the day of our wedding, it rained lightly at intervals, but the sun finally showed itself in time for our evening ceremony. When n̖ brother arrived to escort me to the church, we both marveled at the glorious rainbow in the eastern sky. I may have had doubts that the rainbow I saw in Glacier Bay was a sign, but I firmly believe that this one on our wedding day was showering God's blessing on us.

Cal and I have been married for twelve years now and each day our joy and love grow deeper. He still brings me flowers. No more dark thoughts plague me.

We spent our honeymoon on a Caribbean cruise, trying nightly to count the millions of stars and watching the Hale-Bopp comet process regally across the sky. Together, we experienced both the rough Atlantic and calm Pacific oceans on our recent voyage through the Panama Canal. On the last night aboard, we had the rare pleasure of viewing a full lunar eclipse away from all city lights. One year we plan to share the beauties of a different Alaskan cruise. God has been good to us.

~Elsie Schmied Knoke

Go for It

You come to love not by finding the perfect person,
but by seeing an imperfect person perfectly.
~Sam Keen

In 2007, I turned fifty, was recently divorced, and had been disabled since age thirty-six. "Well, Debbie," I said in a pep talk to myself, "you still wear the same size jeans you wore decades ago. Age has made you interesting. Maybe someone will develop a romantic interest or take a second look."

Who was I kidding? I was middle-aged and disabled... unworthy, damaged, broken, a burden. How could I socialize, let alone explain my bizarre disability? Did jeans really matter?

In 1994, I was diagnosed with a rare neurological disorder, Stiff Person Syndrome (SPS). It occurs in one in a million people. My compromised neuroinhibitory system has a heightened response to external stimuli, i.e., touch, sound, emotion, and movement, eliciting severe body spasms and frozen rigidity, predisposing me to injury from unprotected falls.

Turning on my computer, my spirits lifted at an e-mail from John, my best friend. I lived in Colorado. He lived in Florida, but we were close. Telephone and e-mail communications with him were stimulating, fun, and deep. Candidly, I shared my insecurities with him in a phone conversation.

"John, nobody will want me. I am very limited in what I can

do. It wouldn't be fair of me to ask any man to take on my physical baggage."

"Debbie, I believe God will have someone for you. You still have so much to offer," he replied in an attempt to boost my confidence.

"I just don't think so. I want to live my life alone. I can't go through another divorce. I'd rather be alone by choice than lonely in a marriage," I sighed.

John reminded me about his late wife, Donna. "I wasn't looking for anyone when I met her, content living alone and occupied with my business. Donna poked her head into Sunday school class one day. Obviously, God had plans for us. It was a good marriage. Trust me, it is possible for you."

Pondering his encouraging words, I still had serious doubts, especially considering the uncertain and frightening possibilities of my SPS diagnosis.

During my next phone conversation with John, I told him my daughter, Jaime, and I had tentative plans to go to Clearwater and Disney World. "Let me know when you are sure and I will help you book arrangements. I think I can schedule a free day to come and have dinner with you and Jaime," he offered.

A few months later, Jaime and I were waiting at our Disney World hotel to have dinner with John. After months of phone conversations, Jaime and John had become close and were anticipating meeting one another. Jaime understood my nervousness over John seeing my disability for the first time. When he phoned to let us know he was in the lobby, I asked my daughter for a few minutes alone with John, leaving my walking stick in the room.

Thoughts of seeing John excited and intimidated me. Talking about a disabling condition is different than actually seeing the reality. Would he think differently of me when he saw me?

The elevator doors opened to a paparazzi flash, John taking my picture. Aside from the shock on my face, the picture is of a seemingly normal woman with dark brown hair, black capris, and a stylish print shirt.

I absorbed every detail of John: receding hair, portly build, twinkling blue eyes, black pants, white shirt… and his cane, since John has SPS too. Taking a seat on a nearby settee, we looked into each other's eyes for the first time and embraced. Inhaling the subtle masculine scent of his cologne, I was surrounded by his warmth.

After the Florida trip, our phone conversations became five-hour marathons, a couple of times a day, every day. Our friendship had evolved into something so much deeper… and so very complicated. John is almost fourteen years older than me and has other major health issues along with Stiff Person Syndrome. I have insulin-dependent diabetes with my SPS. We discussed our feelings versus the reality. Should we?

I became Mrs. John Crawford in 2008 and relocated to Jacksonville. Our life is rich, full, and unique. Reality stalks us but experiencing wonderful is worth it.

~Debra A. Crawford

Another Forever

For it was not into my ear you whispered,
but into my heart. It was not my lips you kissed, but my soul.
~Judy Garland

I sat at my desk on the third floor of our office building. My desk was covered with promotional materials and items that called for my attention as the associate director of public relations for our large denomination. There were two new roles in my life now—widow and public relations specialist.

After serving nearly fourteen years as a missionary in the Caribbean, my husband's untimely death from cancer had certainly changed the direction of my life. Left with my youngest son to finish high school, living and working in Atlanta was a far cry from our ministry amid the simplicity of life on the beautiful island of Grenada!

Focused on my latest project, I was interrupted when a secretary from one of the departments walked into my office and tossed a professional resumé on my desk. "You'll be interested in this," she smiled. "Our newest guy—he's a widower!"

I was courteous, but miffed. One thing I did not need was the concerted interest that had been shown in my "aloneness." At age forty-seven there was certainly, in the back of my mind, the idea that I would not remain single forever; I had enjoyed a good marriage and considered that "someday" that might be my pleasure again. But not right now!

As I opened the folder to consider which news sources would get the latest press release that I would prepare, I glanced at the profile. What? Coming to Georgia from Oklahoma was Ed Onley, age fifty-one, with… six children!

Forget that one! What in the world was my friend thinking? I had three sons, all spaced an orderly four years apart.

In the following two weeks I did my professional duty. I interviewed "the widower" and sent the proper media outlets his most impressive work history, extolling the benefits of his having left his home missions assignment to join us. I admit that I was readily impressed with the native Virginia accent that he had not lost while he established community ministry centers, medical care clinics and chaplain programs in Mississippi, Arkansas and then Oklahoma. I cheered him on as he began to do the same thing in Georgia.

Then it happened.

One day Ed stopped me on the balcony walkway as I was leaving the director's office. With a strange combination of shyness and boldness, he asked if I had just a minute. I stopped, and he posed his first non-professional question to me: "I was just wondering… have you come to the place in your life where you would care to go to dinner with a gentleman?" He must have seen the surprise on my face, as he quickly added, "And that gentleman is me!"

That day in January was the beginning of a sudden, unexpected and delightful friendship that soon blossomed into much more. I found underneath my superficial judgment one of the finest and most loving men I had ever known. An example of his goodness was expressed as he let me talk about my personal loss, and he shared openly about his own marriage. In conversation with him I found that I did not have to put my twenty-seven years of marriage out of my life, and he could continue to nourish the thirty-one years he had with his late wife.

Just one example of his generous spirit was shown after he heard me complain about not being able to get any grass to grow on the gravesite where my late husband was buried in a country churchyard. Unbeknownst to me, on one of his days off he drove some thirty miles to the site, tilled the surface and laid sod. He would show it to me later when we made a visit to the cemetery.

After only a few months of dinners and walking the various malls together, it was obvious that we two adults with such similar ministry backgrounds had much more going for us than "friendship." But how could we move from one level to the ultimate when we had such wonderful histories with our separate families?

That was resolved one evening when, after dinner at a favorite Atlanta restaurant, Ed looked at me with what I had come to call his "baby blues"—eyes that reflected honesty, care, and love. With what he still says was an uncommon courage, he took my hand. "I know that you had a wonderful husband, and that you loved him very much. I know that you promised to love him forever." He paused, then continued, "I was just wondering, do you think that maybe you could love me for another forever?"

He was not asking me to forget my first love, but asking that I consider extending my love to include him. I did not hesitate. I said yes.

Less than six months after that first encounter on the balcony when I agreed to "go to dinner with a gentleman," Ed and I were married, surrounded by family and friends who celebrated the gift of our unexpected union.

So, here we are, nearly twenty-five years later, a blended family of nine children and fifteen grandchildren. We have walked through valleys, celebrated mountaintops, experienced joy and tears, gains and losses—all that have served only to make us stronger.

And we keep on walking together—for another forever.

~Elaine Herrin Onley

21

The Frog Prince

I'd kiss a frog even if there was no promise of a
Prince Charming popping out of it.
I love frogs.
~Cameron Diaz

To all the single girls out there who want to find their prince, I want to let you know it's possible to find him. All you need is a frog. Seriously. Pretty much any kind of frog will do. Let me tell you about my frog and how he led me to my prince.

One Saturday morning I was shopping at my favorite garden store. I was wandering through the section that housed the garden statues. I hadn't dated anyone in quite a while and was feeling sorry for myself. I was in my thirties and desperately wanted to meet the man of my dreams and have a family. However, there were no prospects in sight.

I was about to leave the area when I saw him. He was short and squat and wearing a crown. My frog prince. That's right, a statue of a frog with a crown. I reached down to pick him up and started to chuckle to myself. I wondered if this was a practical joke God was playing on me. Was this my Prince Charming? Somehow, he cheered me up and I decided to buy him as a reminder to not take myself and life so seriously.

He went outside in one of my flowerbeds and I smiled every time I saw him, thinking, "Someday I WILL find my prince." He was my little secret, my hope for what was to come. I eventually met someone and we began dating. I wondered, "Is this my Prince Charming?" Eventually I realized he wasn't the one I was looking for and the search began anew. Meanwhile, I kept accumulating frogs. You see, I had broken down and told my family about my secret frog prince and soon I was getting a frog from my mom for each birthday and Christmas. She had high hopes for me as well.

After a while, I decided that I needed to step up my efforts to find Prince Charming so I put a profile up on Match.com. I went on a lot of first dates and even kissed a few frogs along the way. Meanwhile, I never gave up hope that I would find him. Then it happened.

My brother and his fiancée gave me a special ornament for Christmas. It was a very small but ornate frog wearing a crown. Since I received it at Christmas and it was almost time to take the tree down, I didn't put the ornament on my tree that year. The following year, I put my tree up the day after Thanksgiving as I usually do. It was also the day I updated my profile on Match.com with a new picture. On Sunday, I realized that I had forgotten about my new frog ornament that my brother and my now sister-in-law had given me. That night, I placed it at the top of the tree, right under the star.

The next day I checked my profile on Match.com and I had received a wink from a guy who sounded really interesting. The rest, as they say, is history. After two months we were engaged. No, Mom, I wasn't pregnant. We both just knew that we were meant to be together. We have now been married for five years and I have three terrific step-kids and a three-year-old son with my husband.

A little while after Steve and I got married, a single friend of mine had a birthday. I couldn't figure out what to get her. I was wandering through the Hallmark store when I saw him, a stuffed frog. I decided to pass on the frog prince to my friend. I figured that if it worked for me, it might work for her. On her birthday, I gave her the stuffed frog and told her the story. The frog sat on her bed for a couple of years, but last year she met someone.

I could tell from how she talked about him that this was some-one special. She recently called me to tell me that they are engaged and will be getting married this summer. She asked if she should keep the frog. I told her that she should pass it on to whoever she felt was ready to open her life to love. Maybe there's something to this frog thing after all.

~Laurie Ozbolt

Chapter
3

True Love

Meant to Be

True love stories never have endings.

~Richard Bach

22

Mr. Brownlee

There is no instinct like that of the heart.
~Lord Byron

One Friday night, my senior year in high school, my boy-friend was driving me home from the basketball game. I told him that I knew who I was going to marry. I felt him tense up.

I said, "Don't worry. It's not you, it's Mr. Brownlee. I had a dream last night and when I woke up I knew that Mr. Brownlee was going to be my husband!"

Dan almost wrecked the car laughing.

Mr. Brownlee was a young, good-looking, accounting teacher and basketball coach at our school. Nearly every girl in town had a crush on him. And he certainly wasn't interested in me.

Not only was Mr. Brownlee attractive, he had a very magnetic personality and carried himself with confidence. Many people thought he looked like Clark Kent from *Superman*. There weren't many men like him from our small farming town and the local women wanted to be his Lois Lane!

It wasn't long before my dream about marrying Mr. Brownlee became a joke among my friends and their parents.

I went to college, got a job, and married a man who I met at work. We divorced after five years of marriage and one child.

After three years of being a single parent, I booked a trip to

California for my son's Christmas present. The day after Christmas, Nicholas and I flew to Orange County and enjoyed a nice vacation.

Then, on New Year's Eve we headed back to Dayton, Ohio. Our flight was from Orange County to Pittsburgh and, after a two-hour layover, from there to Dayton.

In Pittsburgh, we waited for our flight at the gate. I read and Nick played his handheld video game. Looking around, I saw Mr. Brownlee leaning against one of the columns! He still had that Clark Kent look! I sat paralyzed for a second. Then I decided to talk to him.

I approached him and said, "Excuse me, are you Mr. Brownlee?"

He looked at me and said, "Yes. Do I know you?"

Rather uncomfortably, I said, "I'm Sheryl Hafle."

He said, "Yes, I do remember you, because you were one of my first students. How have you been and what are you doing here?"

I said, "Come sit with me, meet my son, and I'll tell you."

I told him where we'd been and he said he was returning from playing golf in Florida.

He asked me if I was on the 5:35 flight and where was I sitting. I told him row 35, seats B and C. He showed me his ticket and he was assigned to row 35, seat A.

I felt a chill go down my spine.

We boarded the plane and talked all the way to Dayton. That's when I found out he wasn't married, engaged or dating anyone. He was teaching high school in a larger district and still involved in basketball and golf. The forty-five minute flight was way too short.

Once in Dayton, I handed Mr. Brownlee my business card. I told him that I worked for a radio station and got free tickets to events. If he was interested in something, he could call me and I'd see what I could do.

He looked at my card and said, "Okay, I might." He got his bags and hailed a taxi.

While we were talking, we realized that we had a mutual friend. A couple days later, I ran into her and relayed my story.

She said, "Rick will never call you, but you need to call him." She gave me his number.

I dialed Mr. Brownlee's number and he answered. I told him that I was wondering how much his cab fare was. He said, "Twenty-seven dollars and I left a three-dollar tip."

I said, "Wow, I never imagined it would be that much in Dayton."

He said, "Don't you think it's weird that we were seated by each other?"

I said, "Yes."

Then he said, "I'm watching the game and I need to go."

We hung up and I felt like I'd made a fool of myself.

Our mutual friend called me a few days later and asked what happened. When I told her she said that I'd have to call him again.

After much persuasion, I called Mr. Brownlee again. I told him that I had free concert tickets and asked if he'd like to go. He told me he wasn't interested.

I was embarrassed and said that I had to go. He asked me if he could call me sometime and all I said was "Whatever."

A couple of days later, Mr. Brownlee left a voicemail on my work phone asking for my home number.

That evening we talked for over two hours about everything. We realized that we had a lot in common. We spoke nightly for two weeks and he never asked me out. Finally, one evening, I asked him to a Dayton Flyers basketball game. He gave me some lame excuse. That's when I decided that I was too old to continue talking to my high school teacher who wasn't interested in me. I said, "I have no idea what is going on here, but I'm thirty-three and you're forty-one and I'm not participating anymore. I'm hanging up and ending this game."

Mr. Brownlee said, "Wait, so that's what's going on here? I wasn't sure! Actually, I'd like you to go to Friday night's basketball game with me."

Mr. Brownlee picked me up Friday night; we went to the game and had a great time. After the game and dinner he said to me, "Look,

I'm not into dating, so if you're not working towards marriage then I think I should just drop you off and forget it."

I realized then why a great man like Mr. Brownlee wasn't married.

We dated a week. Then he told me that he loved me and said, "Tomorrow let's go to the Justice of the Peace and become Mr. and Mrs. Brownlee."

I said that I'd always loved him, but that we should date a while.

Six months later Rick Brownlee and I got married on the porch of the Island House on Mackinaw Island, Michigan.

~Sheryl Brownlee

Somehow I Knew

Nothing in life is to be feared. It is only to be understood.
~Marie Curie

The yellow cab was stopped at a red light. Sitting in the back seat on a second date with a man named Ted, I was checking my calendar. He had asked me when I was next free. I opened my date book to the week of July 7th and skimmed the days. "First anniversary" was written in big blue letters on Saturday, July 12th. Silently I cursed. Ted had seen it too.

"What's the anniversary?" he asked.

My mind fought for a quick, appropriate answer. It failed.

"You know what?" I said. "I'll tell you about that later."

Ted and I had met the week before on a blind date. Set up by Julia, a co-worker of mine, she had met Ted backstage after a play. The lead in the play was Julia's roommate and a friend of Ted's from high school.

For the first date we met near Ted's office in Tribeca, a hip area in New York City. He worked long hours and he had a short break for our dinner date.

I wore black Capri pants, flats, a white short-sleeved oxford shirt, and a jean jacket. I wanted my personality to be rated before my breasts and hips. Ted wore a gray shirt, which matched his pallor, and an ugly tie. The man was clearly single. But it didn't take me long to realize that he was funny and smart—my top two requirements. Dinner was fast and fun.

Our second date was the Marathon Date. We had each passed the other's first inspection, and we wanted to spend time getting to know each other. The date was on a Friday night, and we were meeting at the Metropolitan Museum of Art to see a Winslow Homer exhibit. After the Met we were going to have dinner at the Yale Club, where he belonged. And after that, if all continued to go well, we would head down to Alphabet City to see my friend perform in an improvisational comedy theater group.

On the second date I decided to highlight a physical attribute or two. I wore a yellow sundress that cut a little low on the neckline and pinched in at my waist. As I walked up the steps at the entrance to the Met—a perfect five minutes late—I saw Ted on the top step in an ocean blue shirt that matched his eyes, looking at me, smiling a great big smile.

We toured the busy exhibit, and every time I looked for him, I found him looking at me. It was clear that neither of us was taking in any of the art. Soon we headed south on the subway. We ate burgers at the Yale Club and enjoyed effortless dialogue. I had never met a man filled with such kindness and gentleness who was able to be strong and confident at the same time. He was smart without being cocky and somehow made me laugh without having to say anything mean or negative.

It was in the taxi ride to the comedy show that Ted asked about the next date, raising the dreadful anniversary question. What I didn't want to tell him was that on July 12th a year before I had been raped. The trial that put my attacker behind bars had ended in April, just a few months before our first date. I knew that this was information Ted might need to know at some point, but I didn't know how he'd react, and I feared its effect.

After I avoided answering his question, the date chugged along. We discussed our plans for the weekend. Ted was going to crew on a friend's sailboat in a two-day race on Long Island Sound, and my college roommate was flying in from Boston for a visit. We laughed a lot during my friend's show, and everything was as easy and comfortable as it had been from the beginning—five-and-a-half hours and counting.

At twelve-thirty, in yet another yellow cab, this time pausing in front of my building to let me out, I leaned over to give Ted a kiss. It seemed like the right thing to do. I aimed for his lips, made it quick, and fled the taxi—ending a date was never my forte.

The next day I woke up to the news that Hurricane Bertha was going to hit New York. Her winds were high, her rain would be fierce, and all flights in and out of the city were cancelled. My friend called to say she couldn't make it in. My thoughts jumped to Ted's sailboat race. I considered calling him, but too nervous, I decided to grab a bagel and coffee around the corner instead. Walking home I decided that I would call him. Why not? When I opened my front door I saw my answering machine's message light blinking. I knew he had beaten me to it.

We took a wet walk through Central Park and he tried to impress me with his knowledge of tree varieties. I grinned often since many of the trees were labeled, and his data and the labels often disagreed.

We went back to my apartment, where I made my famous black bean soup for lunch—by opening the can, heating it, and serving it. Seeing that he was perfectly happy with my offering, I decided that now was the time. If this guy was going to have a problem with my history, I needed to know. If he was going to run because I was dirty and used, I didn't want to keep feeling the way I was feeling.

I spoke as I passed him his cup of black bean soup.

"I want to tell you about the anniversary that you noticed in my date book," I said.

Along with a punch of nausea, I could feel anxiety creeping up my neck. I took a deep breath. Although I saw his soft eyes steadily watch my face, I couldn't look back.

"The anniversary that you saw on July 12th is the day I was raped." I waited a moment for it to sink in. "Last year a man came into my apartment and raped me." I couldn't control the tears that fell. "I didn't know if I should tell you, but I think it's important that you know."

"I am so sorry," he said. He put down his cup of soup and spoke slowly. "Will you come here so I can I give you a hug?"

I walked to him and he folded me into his arms, holding tight. Finally he released me and looked right into my blotchy, tear-stained face.

"Somehow I knew," he said. "I knew right away that you were raped, Jen. I knew when you said you couldn't tell me. I don't know why, but I did."

Today, Ted is my husband. We've been married only ten years, but we'll be together for a long time.

Somehow I know.

~Jennifer Quasha

Destiny on Two Wheels

Every man has his own destiny:
the only imperative is to follow it,
to accept it, no matter where it leads him.
~Henry Miller

There was a time when hitchhiking was considered a safe mode of transportation. In fact, in the 1970s, Vancouver, BC's bus drivers were on strike and the government actually encouraged pedestrians to hitchhike and drivers to give them rides.

But I had stuck out my thumb because the insurance on my car had run out and, being a student at the time, the money for it needed to be spent elsewhere. I knew that King Edward Avenue was a notoriously difficult road on which to hitch, but I was scheduled to write a French exam and there was no option.

Few cars passed and the drivers in those that did, ignored me. I was enjoying the sunny, warm day in late September, but getting concerned that I might end up missing my test.

Finally, a Volkswagen began to pull over and I sighed my relief. The next thing I knew, a motorcyclist cut the Volksie off and encouraged the driver to be on his way. As the latter left, shaking his head, I found myself getting very angry. Thinking that the motorcyclist was simply parking I couldn't believe that he'd done so by getting rid of the only ride I could get!

The motorcyclist reached behind him and grabbed a helmet. "Ever been on a bike before?"

Squinting, I took in the scene: he was a tall man with a white, full-coverage helmet sporting a dark flat shield, hiding the face but allowing a beard to show below; a black leather jacket, black gauntlets, black pants and black boots. As any young woman of that era would do, I replied, "Are you kidding? I used to own a bike!"

"Great! Hop on."

Later, I'd discovered that he had ridden the hour and a half to the town of Hope for breakfast and was heading home when he saw me on the other side of the boulevard. He'd rushed home to retrieve his spare helmet and came back, in hopes that I'd still be there. He wasn't about to let that Volkswagen pick me up.

He drove me to my destination, and we talked briefly before I went in for my test. We didn't even exchange names as we parted ways. That night he went to a party and told his good friend, Laurie, about the girl he'd picked up. "Did you get her phone number?"

"No."

Laurie, always trying to set him up, chastised, "You idiot!"

"Don't worry," he said. "I'll see her again."

The next day I needed another ride. My mom, who supervised the daycare center at a local college, and I had planned on meeting for lunch. So I walked up to the main crossroad and again, extended my thumb. I couldn't believe it when I saw the motorcyclist riding my way. But he was intent on turning left into the service station and didn't see me. "I bet he'll give me a ride," I thought as I crossed the road.

He was in conversation with the attendant, an old friend, as I came up from behind. But, as he turned around and our eyes met, it was as if the attendant had transferred to another dimension. The latter quickly left as he became aware that he had no part in whatever was now taking place. "Hi!" the motorcyclist said.

Of course he'd give me a ride! It was another banner day and the ride was wonderful. We discovered each other's names, Harry and

Diane, that we'd gone to the same, large high school (two years apart) and that he knew my older brother.

Once at the college, Harry asked me for a date, took off his gauntlet and wrote my name and number inside.

Within five weeks (it took four weeks to find a place that would allow all my animals) we'd moved in together and a year later we were married.

Our lives have been filled with many joys, including two living sons, and many sorrows, including twin sons who died shortly after birth. But we've weathered the storms, celebrated the calms, have maintained and grown our extraordinary love for each other, and continue to share all aspects of our individual lives, together.

And Harry, a sentimentalist at heart, still keeps the gauntlet....

~Diane C. Nicholson

Change of Address

There is no such thing as chance;
and what seem to us merest accident
springs from the deepest source of destiny.
~Johann Friedrich Von Schiller

After being "on the bench" and not dating for quite some time, with the exception of one disaster, I decided that marriage wasn't for me. As I drove home from work one evening, I suddenly found myself briefly looking towards the sky through my windshield and telling God, "Lord, I'm not getting married." Afterwards, I felt a huge sense of peace and continued making my way home down Los Angeles' 101 freeway, feeling sorry for all those other women in their forties who were practically howling at the moon every night because they wanted a husband so badly.

Two years later, my life had changed quite significantly. I was making less money and had just moved to an apartment in Burbank after selling the beloved condo I had lived in for nine years. I simply couldn't afford it any more. If that weren't enough, the oldest of my three cats, Risqué, had just been put to sleep. She had cancer and I didn't even know it. I was exhausted from all of the crying. I missed her so much. And, as if my heart wasn't already broken enough, it would break a little more every time I saw my two remaining cats, Esther and Joseph, looking for their sister.

After I had unpacked the last of the boxes, it dawned on me that while I had notified all of the appropriate parties regarding my change of address, I had yet to notify Bed Bath & Beyond. I needed some stuff for my new place and didn't want to miss getting any coupons they would be sending out in the near future. I called and was greeted by a very friendly voice. "Thank you for calling 1-800-GO-BEYOND. This is Jason. How may I help you?"

Jason proceeded to assist me with my change of address, but couldn't hold back his response when he heard the name of the street was I now living on. "Screenland Drive? Sounds like you live near a bunch of movie theaters," he said.

I quickly responded, "Oh, actually, I live by all the studios, like Disney, Warner Bros. and NBC."

"Well," he said. "I work here during the day, but I'm actually a musician. Would you like to see my website?"

I seized the opportunity to drum up some business for myself. "Sure! I'm a freelance writer, but I work a full-time day job for steady income, so I completely understand where you're coming from. As a matter of fact, if you're a musician, I can help you with your bio. Would you like to see my website?" Jason and I exchanged our website information and he completed my change of address request.

When I got home that night, I had completely forgotten about my promise to check out Jason's website. That is, until I logged into my e-mail and found a message from him. "Ah!" I thought to myself, "I forgot to check out that dude's website." I typed the URL into the address bar. Alright, so he was handsome and I noticed. The photo I was looking at was the cover of his latest CD. I then proceeded to read the page, which by the way, was written very poorly.

I could see that Jason was based in New Jersey and as it turns out, is a vibraphonist who was mentored by Lionel Hampton. I was familiar with his music. Jason also had a couple of Grammy ballot nominations under his belt. Quite impressive, but the guy really did need some help in the writing department. His website was a mess.

I responded to Jason's e-mail and complimented him on his accomplishments. I then closed my message in a businesslike manner, stating that I was looking forward to possibly serving his writing needs in the future.

The next night, there was another e-mail from Jason waiting for me. This time, he asked me if I was married with children. I started typing a response. "If you read my bio then you saw that I am studying to become a licensed minister, which is something I take very seriously. So, if these e-mails become inappropriate, I will let you know! I am not a desperate woman." My keyboard was practically smoking! Then my phone rang.

"Hello, Anji. This is Jason Taylor. I just sent you an e-mail, but I thought I would go ahead and give you a call. I know you know the Lord. That's why I wanted to talk to you. I know we were discussing you doing some writing work for me and I still intend on having you do that, but there is something else I want to talk to you about." I couldn't imagine anything this guy would need to talk with me about besides writing. So, I braced myself, ready to hang up, if necessary. He began to speak. "I don't know how to say this, so I'm just going to say it. I went to your website last night, and after reading your bio, I do believe you're the woman I've been praying for." Jason then began to speak in a language he knew I would understand—scripture. "Don't limit God, Anji. Because with God, nothing is impossible." Those words immediately warmed my heart and in spite of the way I felt about marriage, I was willing to listen to what he had to say.

After a few conversations with Jason, he and I decided to give a long distance relationship a try. Because of the distance, he jumped through a lot of hoops and met a lot of people who were interested in my wellbeing. We all needed to make sure he was the gentleman he presented himself to be. After we got married, I moved to the East Coast, making it necessary for me to change my address again.

~Anji Limón Taylor

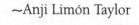

26

Searching for a Soulmate

There are two kinds of sparks, the one that goes off with a hitch, but burns out quickly. The other is the kind that needs time, but when the flame strikes... it's eternal, don't forget that.
~Timothy Oliveira

My husband and I met in driver's training class when we were fifteen. We've been best friends ever since. How corny is that?

Friendship doesn't always lead to romance, however, and for us that leap didn't come until years after we'd declared our best-friendship.

During the time after we met, but before we started dating, we helped each other out in the romance department. I set him up with my friends. He provided comfort when an unbelievably stupid boyfriend broke up with me. I often criticized his choice in women; he hardly ever liked the guys I went out with.

Each year, on our birthdays, we'd go out on a "date." And on New Year's Eve, if neither of us was in a relationship, it was agreed that we'd celebrate the night together. You know, sort of like best friends would do.

All the while I was in search of Mr. Right—my soulmate. The mere thought of him made me sigh with anticipation. I knew he was out there—somewhere—the guy who was born just for me, and I him.

Trouble was, this soulmate of mine wasn't making himself easy to find. He had no distinguishing characteristics that I knew of. I couldn't tell him from a hole in the wall, or a best friend.

A funny thing happened on my search for a soulmate. One summer, my best friend and I began to see each other in a new light. The air around us changed and was charged with an energy we couldn't ignore.

By this time, we'd been friends for so long that we already knew almost everything about one another. A romance like that is brief. We were engaged after just weeks and married within the year.

I'd been searching for my soulmate and he'd been right there beside me the whole time! Or so I thought.

It wasn't long after our honeymoon, when I looked at him lovingly and posed the hypothetical question: "Do you think we're soulmates?"

His answer was not what I expected. "What's a soulmate?" he asked with the innocence of a newlywed.

I was stunned. How could he be my soulmate if he didn't even know what it was?

Thing is though, I was in love with the guy. Soulmate or not, I was committed to him for better or worse. So for us, life went on—together. I tried to quit worrying about silly ideals like soulmates.

Through the years we've learned that in many ways we are more different than alike. I am a bargain hunter; my husband is an impulse shopper. I read poetry; he scans the front page. He hunts; I knit. He prefers spicy hot barbecue; I'm a cool ranch fan. I believe in soulmates; he doesn't know what they are.

But as different as we seem to be, we've managed to keep each other interested (and at times entertained) for more than twenty years. Despite the fact that I tend to hog the covers and he (occasionally) snores, we've found a weird sort of rhythm that works for us. There is a happy cadence to our days.

Each night, I get the coffee maker ready for the next day. And each morning, he brings me my first cup, poured just the way I like it with the right amount of cream. One evening, I was tired, and said, "It's late. I don't think I'll make the coffee tonight."

His answer wasn't what I expected. "But then I won't be able to bring you your cup in the morning," he said. "And that's what I do." His words had a certain tenderness that can only be earned after years together.

Needless to say I made the coffee that night.

I haven't forgotten about finding my soulmate, except my definition has changed. I no longer think a soulmate is someone born for me. I realize that would be way too easy. A soulmate is someone you grow with and into over time until the day comes that something as simple as cup of coffee illustrates feelings so deep that they bring tears to your eyes.

That is what my soulmate—and best friend—does for me.

~Jill Pertler

27

When You Wish Upon A Star

We were written in the stars, my love, all that separated us, was time,
the time it took to read the map which was placed within our hearts,
to find our way back to one another.
~Source Unknown

I was a fourth grader in love. Our families were friends and our moms thought it "cute" that I had such a crush on the neighbor's son, who was five years older and entering high school. But, to me, it was real love from the first moment when he gently smiled and looked at me with his soft hazel eyes.

Each night as I lay in bed, I quietly half sang and half recited, "When you wish upon a star, makes no difference who you are... anything your heart desires will come to you." I was sure that Walt Disney had gotten it right. Did it really matter that I was in my awkward stage, with buck teeth, and that he was in high school and didn't know my name? Not really, I decided, because somehow marrying my fourth grade crush was going to happen.

As the years slowly passed, I still "wished upon my star," yet reality was slowly creeping in. He was in college, had a serious girlfriend, and life beyond college would be starting soon. I reluctantly tried to move on, but each young man I dated unknowingly shared some similarity with the boy that I "wished upon a star" for—the hazel eyes, soft smile, tall and slender frame, or a gentle and kind heart. Yet no one I dated was him—not even close. In my heart, as strange as it seemed, I couldn't let go. Was it because I had fallen hard for my first crush, or did I really know something? Such a simple question, but one that I truly couldn't answer. Maybe one day my heart's question would be answered honestly.

The summer I graduated college was the summer my brother got married. It was a small and intimate wedding with just family and close friends. "He's probably not coming," said my mom, when I asked if my crush would be there. He was moving and his life had become busy with work and weekend plans. "His parents will be there though," she added. It would be nice to see them and find out what had happened to the boy I had once known. I quietly "wished upon a star" as my heart fluttered. Maybe he would come after all.

A few days before the wedding, my mom found out that he in fact would be coming. It was one of the few weekends that he had free to come home to spend time with his family. And, since there was a wedding of a longtime friend, this weekend seemed like the perfect time. As excited as I was to hear this, it only complicated things though as I had refused to go to my brother's wedding alone. A college friend had accepted my invitation as my date and it was obvious that he hoped for a more serious relationship despite my desire to only be friends.

My heart skipped a beat as I entered the church in front of my soon to be sister-in-law. I scanned the backs of the guests as I walked down the aisle. I spotted him almost instantly—and he was just as I had remembered him. As I led the wedding procession past his pew, he looked at me with astonishment. Goodbye to the pigtails, braces, and buck teeth. I was no longer "Jeff's sister" as he finally noticed me for who I was. As our eyes met, his head gently nodded towards me and he smiled the tender smile that I had loved for so long.

It was the longest twenty-minute wedding I had ever attended. "Where is he?" I asked when the service was over. "I don't know," said my mom as she greeted every guest with hugs. "He'll be at the house, I'm sure," she added. My heart continued to leap, skip, and jump. Even though I was a college graduate heading off to a new life in two weeks, I tingled while thinking of reuniting with my fourth grade crush at the reception.

"Why did I ever invite a date?" I wondered. Conversations I hoped to have with my crush were definitely going to get complicated. As the reception began, I found myself sitting between my date and my crush. My crush was just as anxious to get to know me as I was to see if this was a crush or if this could be true love. We snuck in moments away from the wedding guests and my date to quietly catch up on the years that had separated us. The wedding reception quickly became a blur; an instant friendship, gentle love, and admiration for each other quietly began that day.

Two weeks was all we had before summer ended and I moved to Maryland for my dream job. The summer was ending too quickly and I found myself wishing I could stay at home, but I had no choice. We constantly dated yet I always found myself wondering if I was living out my girlhood dream or if it was true love.

On one of our last dates, he gently took me in his arms as we stared up at the stars in the night sky. "Susan, would you ever consider marrying me—if I asked at some point?" He had taken my breath away again. "Yes, I think that could be very possible," I quietly replied. My heart was leaping as I realized that it was true love that we shared. It had taken awhile for us to find each other, but all my wishes had come true.

Three months later, during one of his visits to Maryland, we headed to the Eastern shore. Soft breezes, seagulls, and the gentle lapping sounds of the waves relaxed us as we quietly sat down to a picnic on the beach. Nestled in his arms, I watched a couple walk by hand in hand and I smiled, knowing that I had also found such happiness, friendship, and love. As I turned my head to look up at him, my dream became real. "Susan," he began, "will you marry me?" My heart's question was finally answered as he slipped the ring on my finger.

After almost seventeen years of marriage and children, my husband is still the boy I fell in love with thirty years ago, but even better. Yet one thing remains the same—my heart still skips a beat every time I know he's coming home. The star that I wished upon so many years ago is brighter than ever.

~Susan Staunton

One Little Word

Sometimes new love comes between old friends.
Sometimes the best love was the one that was always there.
~Author Unknown

I am not one of those people. You know the ones who have houses full of "treasures." The people who cannot get rid of anything. A napkin, a ticket stub, a crumpled up old leaf. Some people call it junk, but to the person who owns it, it holds value because of the memory attached to it. I admit I do have one of those items. It is small and simple but oh so important to me. It measures only two inches by three inches and contains one little three-letter word. It's not a romantic word, and anyone reading it would surely wonder what it meant. What is the word? Well I think I should start at the beginning....

I grew up like many other little girls dreaming of my big wedding day with visions of my Prince Charming dancing in my head. I even wrote one of those lists. Oh, admit it; you know the list. The list of all the traits of that wonderful person you would surely one day meet. A sense of humor, romantic, blue eyes. I've always been a sucker for blue eyes. But somehow in my twenties that list was forgotten. The guys I dated were promising, but then the real frog would emerge and it would become evident they were certainly not my Prince Charming. And so I began what would be a long journey of disappointment in love.

By the time I reached my thirties, still single, I wrote off those dreams as the whimsical ponderings of a little girl. I chose a different route and decided to become self-sufficient so no man would be required. It would just be easier. I would often be heard saying things like, "It is so great to be single and do whatever I want" or "I just don't have time to date with my busy schedule." I wonder if I ever actually convinced anyone.

So men became my friends. It seemed perfect. And guess what? I found out guys could be really great friends when I wasn't expecting anything from them. I became really good friends with one man. A fellow single thirty-something-year-old. We talked and laughed and swapped dating disaster stories. It put a lot in perspective! It was a perfect friendship. But then the evitable happened when a single man and woman are friends. We've all analyzed the *When Harry Met Sally* movie and know the risks. And so it happened to us.

It was a lovely day in May and we were out golfing together. We were doing the usual talking and laughing but then it changed. The teasing took on a new tone and sounded more like flirting. The casual hugs lingered a bit longer. It was a magical out-of-control day. The unwritten rules were being seriously disobeyed. But we could've cared less. Or so I thought.

When I got home that night and was alone the freak-out set in. I was an expert on freaking out because I spent most of my adult life doing that. Over-analyzing every conversation with every man I ever dated. I would ask my girlfriends, "What do you think he meant when he said I'll call you later?" "Do you think he was trying to make me jealous?" "Do you think I should call him?" And on it would go.

But this time it was different because I really knew this man. This wasn't some guy I could just ignore and eventually he'd go away. This was my dear friend. And he really knew me too. The real me. Then insecurity decided to pay a visit with its comments. "You were imagining it. He doesn't really want you that way." Maybe I was making something out of nothing. I was so, so scared of falling in love and getting hurt again. And he knew that. Why is it all so complicated? I went to bed with this whirlwind of emotion in my head and heart.

The next day at work I went to open my e-mail with a good solid mix of excitement and fear. What would he say? Would he suggest getting together for "the talk?" I went to my inbox and cautiously hit enter and… Empty. Great. Now what?

Within an hour, I had a delivery of beautiful flowers. In the envelope was a small piece of paper. It had one little word on it. My heart melted and every insecure thought and fear fled. With just one word this man knew me well enough to express to me his love and understanding. His understanding of my fear of love. He won my heart and everything became crystal clear with that one silly word: "BOO!"

The rest of our story is magically simple. I fell in love with him with no fear. There were no hurts or disappointments. I found out how love should be. It was so easy. It was just meant to be.

We have been married almost six years now. I still adore this man. Our love is simple and pure and good. It is so much more than that little girl could have ever imagined. Oh yes, and by the way, he does have beautiful blue eyes….

~Linda Baskin

29

Amore

A man is not where he lives, but where he loves.
~Latin Proverb

I was born and raised in Canada, by parents who both emigrated from Italy. A typical Italo-Canadian, I grew up with Italian ideals but lived a Canadian lifestyle. I am ashamed to say I didn't even speak Italian when I was young. Nevertheless, I made my first venture to see our glorious mother country with my family when I was ten years old. A shy, reserved child hiding behind bulky glasses and a bad haircut (which I still regret), I had no idea what I would find there.

In the piazza of my mom's town, Mignano di Monte Lungo, was the most gorgeous, confident thirteen-year-old boy I had ever seen. His name was Ludovico. He cruised around on his bike, suave and sweet with a genuine smile that lit up his whole face. He seemed like such a man. One day he bought me gelato (with his own money!). My heart raced every time he came near. I could barely look at Ludovico, so great was my crush. Of course, I could tell no one of my feelings—not my mom, not even my cousin! It was too embarrassing… besides, I didn't understand a word he said (but it sure sounded good to my ears). I left Italy after a month, sad to leave behind the new world I had discovered, and the boy who made my heart beat fast.

Time passed, and I didn't think much about Mignano during my teenage years, but for some reason, I wanted to learn Italian. I took a few courses at school and spoke horribly, but was able to spit out a few words in the beautiful language… which prepared me for my next adventure.

When I graduated from high school, my mom and I planned an extensive trip to Europe that would include a return to Italy. On the plane ride there, I thought of the people I hadn't seen in years. The cousins, relatives… him. I felt a tingle in my stomach at the thought of Ludovico. Would he find me pretty now that I had grown up?

I still remember the exact moment he pulled up behind me on his motorcycle on our return visit. I was wearing a denim miniskirt, overwhelmed by the midday August heat. My mother and I had been exploring the streets of her hometown. Everyone who lived there was resting, it seemed, hiding from the blazing sun. Except for him. I turned around to see him straddling his bike on the edge of the road, grinning behind his sunglasses.

"Do you remember this young man?" my mother smiled.

Of course! I wanted to scream… he was still SOOOOO BEAUTIFUL.

I felt like I had been struck by lightning. Thankfully, this time around, he felt something, too, because he mysteriously showed up everywhere I went in the next few days.

Finally, Ludovico and I had an opportunity to be alone. He took me on a breathtaking tour with his motorcycle, introduced me to all his friends, and ultimately, told me how he felt… that he was in love with me and wanted me to return quickly to Mignano. I said, of course, that I would and that I loved him, too!

We enjoyed that feeling for another day and then, regretfully, I had to leave. I felt like my heart was being ripped from my chest. To make things worse, my mom had clued into what was happening, and tried to discourage this long distance affair… it was torture! I told him I would be back soon, and he said that he would wait for me.

I cried so hard when I got back to Canada. My parents kept trying to console me.

"If it's meant for you, it won't go by you!" they would tell me. A silly cliché meant to calm me down. I don't think they really believed those words as they do now.

Ten years passed and I was twenty-eight years old when it happened again. I'd had my share of relationships, but never quite found the man I wanted to marry.

One day my mother announced casually that Ludovico from her town was coming to Canada for two weeks to confirm his nephew and that we should have everyone over for dinner in this Italian's honour. I was stunned.

"I don't want to see him," I told her adamantly.

"Why not?" She was shocked. Did she forget what had happened?

I tried to tell her how I felt. "I am way too embarrassed… the last time I saw him, we said we would wait for each other, and now ten years has passed… how humiliating."

What I really felt, however, was that somehow my life would change. That he would awaken something deep inside. I didn't want to feel such immense sadness again, the pain that came from loving someone so far away.

Some things are unavoidable. The moment we laid eyes on each other, it was as if not a day had passed since our last encounter. In my mind I was eighteen again, he twenty-one, the feelings as strong as ever and we were both a little shocked at the enormity of it. Suddenly he had to leave again, and this time he said, "I don't want to wait another ten years, this time we will be together."

And, after many sacrifices, tears, trials and tribulations, he moved here to marry me the following year… proof that dreams do come true, and that we can never escape our true destiny!

~Sylvia Suriano-Diodati

30

Unforgettable

Never, never give up.
~Winston Churchill

Divorced and living the life of an empty nester in Dallas, I wasn't interested in marriage, and I had given up on finding a good man to date. The best relationship I could recall was with Gary, my college sweetheart thirty years earlier. He traveled from Massachusetts to school in Texas because of a football scholarship. Like many love-struck college students, we talked of marriage.

However, a back injury forced Gary to return to Massachusetts for surgery, and he lost his scholarship in Texas. Without low airfares, continuing our relationship seemed impossible. His whole future was in question since he wanted to get his teaching degree and coach the sport he loved. Our world was turned upside down, and in great emotional pain, I ended the relationship before Gary left. We talked on the phone once after he returned to Massachusetts, but the 1,750 miles between us was too big a hurdle to conquer—at least in my shortsighted vision.

Over the next three decades, I thought of Gary periodically and looked through my scrapbook that held newspaper clippings of his athletic achievements. I always wondered what became of him. He was tall, handsome, and had a terrific sense of humor bolstered by his Boston accent. My mother loved him too, and she was sorry when I ended our relationship. My dad, on the other hand, feared Gary would take me far away to New England. Consequently, my father painted a bleak picture of life in the cold Northeast. I later realized Dad's comments were self-serving, but at such a young age, I might not have undertaken a big move to Massachusetts even without his cautionary statements.

Once my own daughter left for college, random circumstances brought Gary to mind more frequently. Whenever I heard Barry Manilow's song "Weekend in New England," thoughts of Gary drifted my way. When I switched to country stations, Reba McEntire belted out "Whoever's in New England." Recurring questions rambled through my head. Had Gary's surgery been successful... so much so that he was drafted and sent to Vietnam to die like so many men of our generation? Or did he graduate from college and became the coach he talked of being? If so, I assumed he was married with a large family like the one in which he was raised.

One weekend in March, I went to dinner with a neighbor, and we met a man from New Hampshire. Gary came to mind. The next night, I came home and turned on a televised Bee Gees concert just as they sang "Massachusetts," which was popular when we dated. On this night, the Bee Gees song hit me like a ton of bricks, and I raised my hands to the heavens saying, "Okay... enough. I'll try to talk to him."

I knew when Gary left Texas, he felt I didn't care about him, and I had a long-overdue need to explain my actions. I also needed to know how things had turned out for him. I wanted to find him alive and well.

I dialed Directory Assistance, and the operator relayed the only listing she had in the Boston area for a Gary Bogart. As his phone rang, I wondered what in the world I was going to say. What if his recorder answered? Should I leave a message? What words were appropriate after thirty years? What if a wife answered?

I didn't know why thoughts about calling Gary had been hounding me. All I wanted to tell him was why I ended our relationship when he was struggling to keep his world together. My father had colored my thinking to a great degree back then, and I just didn't see how we could achieve our dream of being together with all those miles between us. After all, neither of us had any money.

After a few rings, I heard a routine "Hello" from a man's voice.

"May I speak to Gary Bogart?" I asked.

As one might guess, he responded, "This is he."

I muttered, "Is this the Gary Bogart who attended college in Texas?"

He later told me that, at that moment, he knew the voice was mine. I hadn't realized the time was after 10:00 P.M. on the East Coast. Thankfully, Gary was home alone sleeping, and he told me he sat up like he'd been hit by a bolt of lightning when he recognized the voice on the phone. He had been divorced for eight years.

I finally had the chance to explain the thoughts that led me to end our relationship in 1968. He said my call healed something inside him, because he never understood why I turned away from someone I proclaimed to love. He always suspected there was another guy in my life—possibly an old boyfriend—and nothing could have been further from the truth. He had never forgotten how much we meant to one another, and he also wondered where life might have taken us if we had stayed together.

We talked for forty-five minutes before I said I had to hang up. I had achieved my purpose in calling, and I was elated to have been able to answer the decades-old questions that lingered in his mind. For the second time in my life, he asked for my number. After six weeks and many long phone conversations, we met in Florida. It was surreal, as if three decades had suddenly disappeared. I worked for an airline, which allowed us to spend lots of time together that year.

Dozens of flights and nine months later, Gary and I married on the beach at Sanibel Island, Florida. The sun was setting as we became husband and wife, and the onlookers included two dolphins that swam unusually close to shore. One passer-by proclaimed the dolphins' presence to be a spiritual blessing. That may have been so, but all we knew for sure was we were ready to fulfill the dream that fate had suspended for us.

Two nights after we married, we attended a Bee Gees concert

where Barry Gibb made a surprising announcement before they sang "Massachusetts." My best friend had let them know about their role in our rekindled romance, and Barry dedicated that song to "Gary and Betty" before beginning its enchanting melody.

I finally made that once-foreboding move to Lynn, Massachusetts, where we lived for several years before relocating to Florida. As we celebrate ten years of marriage, we are grateful we can be together at this point in our lives.

~Betty Bogart

31

We'll Manage

Live the life you've dreamed.
~Henry David Thoreau

As the young bride and groom walked slowly down the stairs, their faces displayed a solemn expression that belied the joyous spring to their steps. They took this momentous occasion in their young lives very seriously.

The bride wore a simple dress buttoned up to her slender throat. White ankle socks accentuated a pair of her mother's black high-heeled shoes. A lace window curtain was on her head, the "train" flowing several feet behind her.

The groom wore starched jeans, a Roy Rogers T-shirt, and a pair of brown cowboy boots. He held her closely, supporting her down each step, as she placed one foot unsteadily before the other. Her arm was wrapped around his and their hands were clasped tightly together as he looked down at his bride with pride in his eyes and love in his heart.

They didn't care that there was no wedding party, no flowers, nor even the traditional Wedding March, but both were humming the tune softly together. It was a simple ceremony because the groom was six years old and the bride was four.

It was Valentine's day of 1945.

Lynne's mother met us at the bottom of the stairs. She was my mom's best friend. Her eyebrows rose questioningly and the beginning of a smile formed upon her lips.

She turned toward the kitchen. "Viv, look at this," she called.

When my mother saw Lynne and me, her hand flew to her mouth in an evident effort to suppress her laughter.

Letting go of Lynne's hand, I hesitantly approached her mother, looked into her eyes and said, "Em, when Lynne and I get old enough, can we get married?"

Em knelt in front of me, placed both hands on my shoulders, then looked steadily into my eyes. "Gary, when you're old enough and have a good job, if you still love each other, then the answer will be yes. And I'll buy you a set of dishes as a wedding present."

Lynne and I then went happily into the kitchen for some Jell-O topped with whipped cream.

A couple of years later my parents and I moved away.

I had been several years in the army, stationed overseas, when my mother wrote that Lynne was very sick with mononucleosis. That Valentine's Day of 1945 was far in the past, and I'd almost forgotten about her. Nevertheless we began writing regularly, getting to know each other all over again, and soon we exchanged pictures. It was the first time I'd seen her face since I was ten years old. Looking back at me was a now beautiful young woman of nineteen with the bluest eyes I'd ever seen. I was in love all over again.

As we wrote, the time passed very slowly. I couldn't wait to see her, and over the months our letters had become more intimate and it was as though the passing years were inconsequential. Two years later I came home on leave and flew to Portland to see her. She was standing on the tarmac as I approached the top of the ramp. We stood looking at each other silently for long moments until a cough behind me got me moving. I bolted down the steps, took both of her hands in mine, looked into those gorgeous blue eyes, then took her in my arms and kissed her. We were soon engaged. It was Christmas, 1962.

On Valentine's Day of 1963 I was at Fort Bragg, North Carolina getting ready to undergo Airborne training with a small group of candidates. At one in the afternoon I was called into the orderly room and handed a telegram.

"Arriving at 3:00 P.M., February 14 at Piedmont Airport, Fayetteville. Can hardly wait. Love Lynne."

I had no idea she would be coming this soon. We had agreed that we would wait until my training was complete. She told me later that it was my letters and phone calls telling her I missed her so much that convinced her to come early. Besides our mothers thought it would be a wonderful Valentine's present for us both.

In those frantic two hours, I rented a small trailer and bought what we would need at a local pawnshop. The only things new were the linens. With twenty-five dollars left and payday two weeks away I'd forgotten about food.

Luckily a general and his aide had to be taken to the airport and, because of Lynne's pending arrival, I was allowed to replace the regular driver for that trip.

At 2:45 we pulled up in front of Piedmont Airport. I took the general's bags to the ticket counter and was dismissed. I was just in time to greet Lynne at the arrival gate and soon she was in my arms. What a wonderful Valentine's Day! The hassle of the past several hours made it all worthwhile.

Lynne saw the unfurled flag on the staff car waiting at VIP parking. "Wow!" She smiled.

"We're lucky to have this car, Lynne. But this is just for today. The only transportation we're going to have is what I can borrow. And," I said sadly, "I have to report to jump school at Fort Benning in a little over a week."

I could see disappointment on her face but then she said something that was to be the hallmark of her outlook whenever difficulty arose in our lives together. She placed her hand on my arm and smiled bravely. "We'll manage."

One week later, on February 21st, we were married in Post Chapel 21. Like our earlier "marriage" it was an informal affair and we wanted it that way. My best man and I were the only ones in dress green uniforms. The rest of the unit, some forty men together with the chaplain, were in the duty uniform of the day (fatigues). My commanding officer gave her away.

One of our wedding presents was the set of dishes Lynne's mother promised us so many years ago.

Our marriage has occasionally been difficult for Lynne, especially since I made the military my career. There have been assignments in underdeveloped countries where she had to soak vegetables in water and bleach to avoid intestinal parasites and diseases. Many times our only transportation was a horse and cart in Africa or a smoke-belching motorized pedicab in Thailand. She endured martial law in Turkey and witnessed the bombing of a neighbor's apartment that narrowly missed killing our friend and her three-year-old child. In spite of it all, Lynne looked upon each setback as a challenge. And each and every time, Lynne's response was like the first time. "We'll manage."

One day we came across a picture of us that her mother had taken on that long ago day when I first asked for Lynne's hand. We were amazed that the dress she was wearing was almost an exact duplicate of the one she wore at our wedding all those years ago.

Now some forty-six years later we're still just as much in love as that six-year-old boy and four-year-old little girl in 1945.

And through it all, "we've managed."

~Gary B. Luerding

"I still love you as much as I did back then. I always had good taste ... and style!"

32

Hello Again

The more faithfully you listen to the voice within you,
the better you hear what is sounding outside of you.
~Dag Hammerskjöld

ight years after I'd placed the scrap of paper into an old address book, it was still there. I smoothed it across my thigh to get the tiny wrinkles out and, thankfully, I could still read his phone number. At least it had been his number in Chicago almost a decade ago. Now there would be no more hesitating. No more driving myself crazy that perhaps I had cavalierly tossed aside something worthwhile.

My mind worked furiously, preparing for all sorts of contingencies. If I called the number and if it was disconnected, I would resign myself to never really knowing what happened to him. If it was no longer his number, I would apologize, hang up, and be done with it. If a woman answered, I'd silently hang up and, with my Dallas phone number, she'd suspect nothing. Believing I'd covered all scenarios, I dialed the phone with a shaky hand.

"Hello?" It was a male's voice.

OmiGod! In all my planning, I hadn't even thought of what to say if he answered. We'd known each other fifteen years, but fueled by my romantic wanderlust, we hadn't spoken for the last eight of those years.

For a second I thought about hanging up. Coward! Instead I swallowed and croaked, "Hi, Greg."

He responded as if we'd just spoken yesterday. "Hi, Carole."

My eyebrows shot up. "You don't sound surprised."

"I knew I'd hear from you again someday," he explained, as if an old flame calling out-of-the-blue was a natural occurrence.

We chatted for a few minutes. He sounded welcoming and relaxed. I was perspiring.

"Carole, I'd like to talk more, but I was just going out."

I didn't even think about it being Saturday when I called. He had a date. I didn't.

I giggled nervously, "Oh, I'm sorry. I didn't realize…" My voice trailed off, hoping I didn't sound like a dateless loser.

But he rescued me. "Can I call you tomorrow?"

Yes! I forced my voice down an octave. "That'd be fine." I gave him my number and hung up, feeling like a strand of spaghetti left to boil way too long.

The next day, I told my friends what I had done.

"How exciting!" Cindi, my kind friend exclaimed.

Dora, my worldly, cynical pal, didn't say a word at first. But I knew by her scowl, she disapproved. "Men are never as good as we remember them. You should have let sleeping memories lie."

I shrugged, refusing to let her doubts become mine.

He kept his promise and called that evening. The conversation flowed smoothly. Then he asked me the question I hadn't the courage to ask him.

"So… are you seeing anyone?"

Be coy. "Oh I'm dating several guys." I swallowed hard and forced my voice to stay level. "What about you?"

He was seeing someone.

My heart sank. I knew he wouldn't be pining for me. But at least he wasn't engaged.

He called once more and then without warning, stopped. I was disappointed and my fingers itched to dial his number, but I refused to scratch.

"At least I tried," I explained to Dora and Cindi. "Anyway, he's still in Chicago. I'm in Dallas."

Dora harrumphed. Cindi looked at me with such pity you'd have thought I'd lost both arms in one single, tragic accident.

A few months later, Greg left me a message, apologizing for disappearing and asking me to call.

I smiled from ear to ear, but decided not to call him that night. He could wait, as I had. But the next evening, I dialed his number, hoping my excitement wouldn't travel across phone lines. This marked the first of many calls. They were a bright spot and during them, my road-warrior job stress melted away.

On in-office work days, my travel planner, Jay, and I talked about my phone relationship. He asked when Greg and I planned to get together.

I answered vaguely, "Someday." I was comfortable with the phone relationship. Even though I'd initiated the contact, I didn't want to face the possibility that Dora was right. Memories were pliable and were often better than reality.

Soon after, though, Jay slapped the tickets for my next business trip on my desk and with a wicked grin told me, "They're non-refundable."

The flight itinerary included an eight-hour layover. In Chicago. Before I could say anything, this office Cupid folded his arms and insisted, "Call that man and tell him to meet you."

I called Greg, trying not to sound like a prepubescent girl with a crush as I told him about my trip. To my relief, he laughed and told me to thank Jay for him.

Then I blurted out, "I'm blond now, and I've put on a few pounds."

He snickered. "That's fine. I look about the same except I've got less hair."

"Okay, neither of us will be surprised." But I knew that descriptions never quite matched reality.

Thankfully, I was very busy and it wasn't difficult to put our meeting out of my mind. Until I stepped on the plane to Chicago. I boarded with an extra carry-on—butterflies in my stomach.

My legs shook as I waited to deplane, and I berated myself for letting this happen. I was going to kill Jay for setting this up.

In those pre-9-11 days, Greg stood waiting at the gate. Our eyes locked as we instantly sized each other up. We both smiled broadly.

He planned the whole day. It was great, but the best was when he took my hand in his as we walked. After dinner, he leaned back in his chair and asked, "Should we give this another try?"

My cheeks ached from grinning. "Definitely."

I'm not sure why, but things were different this time around. As far back as I could remember I was attracted to men who were opposites of me. However, I discovered that these differences made the relationships ultimately impossible. Before, it had irritated me that Greg and I were so similar, Now, I was thrilled to be with someone who understood and liked me for being me. When we were together, I felt cocooned in a warm, familiar place. I didn't think it could get any better. But it did, that July 4th.

I had flown in early that morning and I was tired, so begged off seeing the fireworks that night.

"Come on, you'll miss the best part of the day."

With a soft moan, I gave in and we lugged two lawn chairs up the hill to watch.

As soon as the first glare burst in the sky, I knew he'd been right. The display was spectacular, with its greens, reds, and silvers. I squeezed his hand. "Thanks for talking me into this. I really love fireworks."

He leaned close. "We could have fireworks the rest of our lives if you'll marry me."

The fireworks in the sky dimmed as the stars in my eyes grew brighter.

We've been married for eight years now, and I've learned that sometimes, making new memories is a lot better than polishing old ones. The trick is: you've got to try.

~Carole Fowkes

Chapter
4

True Love

The Proposal

We love because it is the only true adventure.

~Nikki Giovanni

33

Understanding the Rules of Engagement

It was so much fun, we proposed to each other all day long.
~Melissa Errico

It was a warm May afternoon in Buffalo Grove, Illinois, and my girlfriend Joanna carefully opened the presents that were on her lap. All eyes were on her... after all, it was *her* birthday party. Unfortunately, I wasn't able to be with her on this day because I was deployed to Afghanistan with the United States Army. But even though I wasn't present, many other loved ones were, including Joanna's best friend who flew in from Arizona and my best friend, Matt. In fact, it was Matt who had really orchestrated the gathering: months ago, he suggested that the group should throw Joanna a birthday party this year to cheer her up; to let her know that even though I wasn't with her, she wasn't forgotten. And thus came about Joanna's birthday.

Joanna finished opening the last present and got ready to thank everyone for the gifts, but not before Matt approached her with a card in his hand. He offered it to Joanna, explaining that I had sent it to him to give to Joanna at her birthday party. Intrigued, Joanna opened the card.

Joanna, I know I already gave you presents for your birthday, but I didn't want to leave you empty-handed at your party...

which is why you need to report directly to the secret hiding spot.
Love, the Boy Toy

Joanna knew exactly what hiding spot my card was referring to. There was a spot in her house where I had hidden countless presents before: it was a small closet on the top floor in her house, just across from the guest bedroom. So, Joanna marched herself upstairs to see what the closet held.

In the closet, Joanna found a DVD waiting for her. It had implicit instructions to be immediately viewed, so Joanna popped in the DVD for everyone to see.

The DVD was a short video: the setting was the chapel in Gardez, Afghanistan, which was the chapel that I worked in as a chaplain assistant. Just a few seconds into the video, there was footage of me walking through the chapel door and strolling up to the camera to hold up a sign.

You have a surprise waiting for you in the spot we first met. Go get it before someone walks off with it! Bring everyone along.

Joanna knew instantly the "spot" that the video was referring to: it was the playground of Joyce Kilmer Elementary School. Not only is that where we first met in the sense that we went to kindergarten together there, it was also the spot that we decided to officially meet each other as adults in February 2006 when we were reunited by a series of very unusual events.

Within minutes, everyone found a car to jump into, and a convoy was headed to Joyce Kilmer for whatever it had in store for Joanna.

Everyone parked in the school parking lot and started speculating: "Isn't today a school day?" "What could be hiding on the playground?" "What if we misunderstood the DVD?" "What do you think this could be about?"

Within moments, these questions were answered for everyone. As Joanna walked up to the playground, she immediately saw and recognized what the surprise was for her on that warm day. On one of the playground's slides was the bright silhouette of a uniformed soldier.

In disbelief, Joanna neared the slide as my silhouette began to move. I slid down the slide, as I had done with Joanna so many years ago on that same playground when we were children. I emerged at the base of the slide and walked up to give a hug to a very weepy Joanna.

Joanna didn't say a word and simply dug her fingers into my side and cried her tears on my shoulder. I gently whispered in her ear, "I love you."

Shock began to set in for everyone else. They were personally witnessing the presence of a deployed soldier hugging his girlfriend on the playground, and yet it seemed all too surreal to be authentic. All of a sudden, I was no longer in the middle of a war; instead, I was in the flesh and blood right before them. It seemed a fantasy — a fairy tale too good to be true.

I gave a round of teary-eyed hugs and then began to explain the circumstances of the day: I had been given fifteen days of mid-tour leave, which is how I found myself before my loved ones on this day. Slowly, things began to make sense for those still seeking clarification of the situation.

To even further enhance the surprise for Joanna and me, our old elementary school faculty members emerged from the school to witness the event. They were our original teachers and principal who had guided us so many years ago, and now they were gathered again to see us through on such a joyous event.

But that wasn't all. I began to reason aloud that I had originally thought this opportunity would be a great time to formally propose to Joanna, but I had instead made a promise to her a long time ago that I would only propose after two conditions had been met: one, I had to be physically present for the proposal (which, in this rare case, was a standard that was met), and two, I would have asked my future father-in-law, Chuck, for his blessing of the marriage.

At that moment, when I announced the stipulations for such a proposal, Chuck knew something that the others didn't: I *had* already gotten his blessing last Thanksgiving, during a four-day pass home just before I deployed. And so, it came as no surprise to Chuck when I looked into Joanna's eyes, got on one knee directly before her, and pulled a diamond ring out of my pocket and uttered the words, "Will you marry me?"

Joanna's eyes swelled with tears, barely able to muster a "Yes." And in the sight of our loving family and loyal friends, in the sight of our first teachers and beloved principal, and, most importantly, in the sight of God, we became a couple engaged to be married in the near future to live a life of love and joyfulness.

I slipped the engagement ring onto the finger of my fiancée, and then the two of us began hugging each other once again, holding onto each other for dear life as if this would be the last time we'd ever see each other again. But in fact, this was only the beginning of a life in which we would be with each other forever more.

Only, unlike every other moment up to this point where we saw each other as boyfriend/girlfriend, we would soon be seeing each other as husband/wife, just as God intended.

~Sgt. Nate Danger Geist

"I'd marry you even if you were a mirage!"

34

Love or Success?

The loving are the daring.
~Bayard Taylor

uenos Aires is famous for its magnificent European archi-
tecture, its exceptional Malbec wines, and its status as the
birthplace of the tango. But the city's most distinctive char-
acteristic is its people, who have an unrivaled passion for living life
to the fullest, evident in their spirited three-hour conversations over
dinner, the nightlife that starts at 2:00 A.M., and the couples sharing
a kiss on any street corner or park bench.

It was on a humid April evening in this Latin capital that I first
laid eyes on Natalia, a tall, olive-skinned brunette whose appetite for
life was exceptional, even by Buenos Aires standards. When I saw her
across the dance floor, she hypnotized me with her brown eyes, silky
shoulder-length hair, and full lips framing the most lovely smile I'd
ever seen. She glanced my way and our eyes made contact, just for a
brief, intense moment. She had a confident air that both drew me to
her and gave me butterflies in my stomach.

Overcoming my natural shyness, I approached her and we talked.
Despite my limited Spanish, she patiently conversed with me as if I
spoke fluently. I explained that I was an American studying abroad
and she said she was a student at the local university. We talked and
danced well into early morning.

Our conversation continued the next day, and the day after that.
And within a week, I was hopelessly falling for her. We spent every

waking moment together, exploring the city and losing ourselves in conversation, often finding ourselves sharing a kiss, as the Argentine tradition goes, wherever the urge arose.

Then, one afternoon, Natalia broached the taboo topic we had avoided discussing for two months. My time in Argentina was almost up, and I had to return to college in the U.S.

"What do you want to do about us?" she asked, looking me in the eyes and trying to see the answer in my face. "Since you're going back to your country in a few days, do you think it's worth it to stay together?"

"Of course," I said without hesitation. "We'll make it work." I took her hands in mine. "It's too early to give up on us. I'm too in love with you. I'm not ready to say goodbye. If it is meant to be, it will work out, no matter how far apart we are."

Despite my confident words, I was just as scared and uncertain as she was. I didn't know when or if I'd ever return to Argentina. But we were young and in love, and we listened to our hearts. We decided to go for it. And we sealed the deal with a kiss.

Over the next several months, we spoke every day on the telephone. Weeks flew by, then months. Each afternoon, I called to share my day with her, and she called every evening to say "buenas noches." Her sweet voice put a smile on my face every time she answered the phone. Aside from the 7,000 miles between us, we had a pretty enviable relationship.

But after a year and a half, the separation was wearing us down. We were both tired of the lack of intimacy, the dinners alone, the increasing questions from our concerned friends and families.

"When will we be together?" Natalia began asking with increasing frequency. "I don't know how much longer I can wait…."

For the first time, I felt I might lose her. The "I love you" and "I miss you" that had been so frequent in earlier conversations became "How much longer?" and "When will I see you?"

As a result, I found myself faced with one of the most difficult decisions of my life.

It was my senior year of college, still seven months from

graduation, and I was determined to get into law school. I had sacrificed for years in pursuit of that goal. While my classmates socialized, I studied. And my sacrifice had paid off; I carried a 4.0 grade point average. At that point, I was just two weeks away from my next final exams, which would be crucial to my law school applications.

But I could feel Natalia and I slipping apart. I knew if I didn't see her immediately, our love would fizzle out. And I could lose her forever.

While studying one evening, I asked myself whether I should stay and study, or whether I should go to Natalia. Success or love? If I stayed, I could finish up another perfect semester. If I left, I might save our relationship and have a chance to build a future with Natalia.

The answer was easy. I dropped the textbook I had been reading and hurried to my computer. Within five minutes, I had purchased a ticket to Buenos Aires.

Two days later, unbeknownst to Natalia, I made the twenty-hour trip to Buenos Aires. When I arrived, Natalia was at work. I asked Deby, a friend of Natalia's, to help me organize an unforgettable evening for Natalia, and she agreed.

That evening, Deby and some other girlfriends took Natalia to a Mexican restaurant where she and I had shared a romantic evening. I waited outside the restaurant, nervously rehearsing what I would say. My heart raced and I was shaking, a million thoughts running through my head. After so much time, would it be like before? What if she had changed? What if I had changed? It had been a year and a half, and I had just come halfway around the world to surprise her. Was I crazy?

After a few minutes, as planned, mariachis approached Natalia and began serenading her with a famous ballad that says "señorita, I'll give my heart to you…" but they replaced the word "señorita" with "Natalia." Hearing her name caught her off guard, and she looked up at the mariachis, wondering if it had been her imagination. Then they sang the chorus again, "Natalia, I'll give my heart to you…" Natalia couldn't believe her ears. She looked at Deby, searching for a clue as to what was going on.

At that moment, I walked over to her with a dozen red roses, handing them to her as she looked at me wide-eyed and speechless. I took her left hand in mine and got down on one knee. "Natalia, you are the love of my life," I told her. "My feelings for you have grown stronger every day we've been apart. I'm tired of missing you and I want to spend the rest of my life with you. Will you marry me?"

She took a deep breath, her eyes tearing, her hand trembling slightly. And with one word, she erased the doubt, the fears, and the questions, she closed the distance between us and made the eternity we'd spent apart a distant memory.

She said "yes."

~Wes Henricksen

Editor's note: Although Mr. Henricksen's grades dropped slightly and he lost his 4.0 GPA on account of his spontaneous flight to Argentina, he was nonetheless accepted to law school and is today a practicing attorney in southern California. He and Natalia are very happily married.

35

Perfect Timing

Love is the greatest refreshment in life.
~Pablo Picasso

I wriggled out of my underwear underneath my ankle-length skirt and slipped on my shorts. In one decisive move, I undid the knot that held the skirt wrapped around my waist, and let the long, hot fabric drop to the ground. My boyfriend and I had been cycling for nearly a month in Morocco, and despite the ninety-degree temperatures, I usually kept my skin covered out of respect for the Muslim culture.

We had decided to take this detour to Africa halfway through our six-month bicycle trip in Europe. Now I wished we hadn't come here. Bob and I had been dating for five years, and we'd joked that we'd either come back from the trip engaged, or on separate planes. It didn't seem very funny any more.

Wearing just my running shorts and a T-shirt, I felt practically naked. All day, we'd been riding east along the Route des Kasbahs through a broad, flat valley bordered on our left by the Atlas Mountains. As we peddled through miles of empty desert, I thought about just one thing: ice-cold watermelon. It was my birthday, and since we were in the middle of the desert, I knew there would be no fancy dinner and no celebratory alcoholic beverages. But there could be watermelon.

I told Bob my fantasy. As I set up our tent in the garden at the youth hostel in Goulmima, Bob had walked to the market down the street to get a watermelon. A group of men sat in the shade in front of the hostel, talking and drinking sweet mint tea. I had wanted to sit in the garden under the apricot and pomegranate trees, split the watermelon in half, and eat until all that was left was the empty, green bowl of the rind.

Bob had returned, cradling a large watermelon like a baby. In a friendly gesture, he had offered to share the watermelon with the men at the hostel. I, however, wasn't going to budge. As Bob walked back to the men, he promised to bring me a slice of watermelon. I sat in the garden, fuming. Bob didn't come back. Finally, I walked over to the house and saw the men eating watermelon. My watermelon.

"Thanks for bringing me some watermelon," I had snapped at Bob. I was so angry I was shaking. Bob looked at me, startled. This wasn't like me.

I'd been struggling with how to maintain my sense of identity on our trip. The clothing was just the beginning. My relationship with Bob had changed. Public displays of affection — holding hands and kissing, but also the casual touch on the arm — were taboo, and after trying so hard to remember these new rules all day, at night when we were alone in our tent, we forgot to fall back into our old, affectionate habits. But mostly, I hated that we had to call each other husband and wife to appear proper, because I wasn't his wife. And I wanted to be, more than anything.

Suddenly, I felt trapped in the walled compound of the youth hostel. If I couldn't have my watermelon, I was going to give myself something I'd wanted for a long time. And that was when I stripped down to my running shorts.

"I'm going for a run. Alone." I told Bob.

"Be careful!" he called as I turned to leave.

Outside the gate, I looked right, the direction we had come from, and turned left down the dusty street. I'd been a faithful runner for years, but had given it up after a painful marathon. As I started running, it felt like being reacquainted with a lover after a long absence — I remembered how good it used to be, but now it was just awkward. My stride was stiff, and I could feel pebbles through the worn-down soles of my shoes. The wind was blowing dust so thick that I closed my eyes and held my breath as I ran through a tunnel. On the other side, I opened my eyes to see people filling the narrow street.

"Ça va bien?" people called out to me.

Nodding, I replied tersely, "Oui, ça va bien." It's going very well.

It was true. My stride wasn't smooth, and I was breathing hard, but it felt good to run. My feet kicked up puffs of dust as I ran past boys playing soccer and girls filling plastic jugs at a well. Soon, my body took over and I found my rhythm. Running was as easy as breathing when everything's right in the world. As my pace slowed to a walk, I realized it had been a long time since I'd felt at peace with myself.

My anger about the watermelon had been hiding something else: a hurt that sat like a hard lump in my throat. I had thought Bob was waiting for the perfect opportunity to ask me to marry him. But maybe it wasn't about the perfect opportunity. The truth was, I probably wanted more from Bob than he might be able to give me.

I turned around and headed back to the hostel. I wanted to go back and tell Bob about the kasbah I ran past in town. Most evenings we'd sit outside our tent in the dark, drinking tea and talking. But after taking so many turns on my run through town, I wasn't sure how far it was back to the hostel. My mouth was chalky dry, and I regretted leaving my water bottle behind. At the edge of town, when I looked up to see Bob walking towards me, carrying a bottle of water, I almost didn't believe it could be him.

"I'm sorry," he said, and handed me the water. I took a long drink. "Here's your birthday present." He handed me a Picasso postcard from a museum in Madrid we'd been to more than a month ago. On the back of the postcard, he asked me to marry him.

"How did you find me?" I asked.

"I just knew," he said. "I walked out of the hostel and I asked myself which way you would go, and I knew that if I just kept going, I'd find you."

I looked down at the card. Bob always knew when to keep me company and when to let me go on my own, like when he helped me train for the London marathon, and then waited for three months for me to come back from Europe.

"You don't have to answer now, if you don't want," Bob told me.

It was the worst time for a proposal. We'd just had a fight and I was covered in dirt. There was no ring. Instead, he brought me a bottle of water because he knew I'd be thirsty. He followed his heart to find me, and I realized that's all I needed.

"Of course! Of course I'll marry you!" I told him. A group of twelve-year-old girls were watching us nearby, and to their delight, Bob gave me a brief hug. We held hands for a moment, and the girls covered their mouths and giggled as we walk side-by-side back to the hostel.

That night, we sat outside our tent, eating watermelon and spitting seeds into the garden. When you just know, you don't have to wait for the perfect time to ask.

~Jennifer Colvin

36

Who Are You?

You know when you have found your prince
because you not only have a smile on your face
but in your heart as well.
~Author Unknown

I would say, "Yes," if he asked.

I felt sure he would ask, but how long would I have to wait?

Steven was careful in every decision. He researched and planned. What plans was he or wasn't he making?

It wouldn't be the first marriage for either of us. In fact, both of our spouses had died from accidents in our sixteenth year of marriage when they were each thirty-six years old, and we both had two children just entering their teens when we became single parents. We discovered this extraordinary coincidence as we chatted after a concert at our church one Sunday night.

Now, it was a year later. We just left a citywide prayer service asking God to bless us with rain because the drought was becoming severe. Steven had asked me to share the sunset with him at our park.

We sat in the dark a while after the sunset, savoring the cool night air, enjoying the stars and each other.

Steven got up from the lawn chair. I wasn't sure if it was time to go. But then he knelt down on one knee, took out a tiny box, opened it and said, "Sheila Dianne, will you marry me?"

I was totally confused. Of course I wanted to marry him, but he used my middle name. I wanted to respond in the same way he asked me; I want to say Steven (whatever ???). I realized I didn't know his middle name. Why couldn't I remember it? How could I marry a man when I didn't even know the simplest thing about him like his middle name?

"Sheila? Will you marry me?" Now he sounded concerned. I had hesitated too long. It was not the time to admit I didn't know his full name. I would just have to figure it out somehow. I'd look at his driver's license or something.

"Yes, oh, yes. I will marry you Steven."

I threw my arms around him and we kissed. Then he slipped the simple but elegant ring on my finger. I was amazed it fit perfectly.

He told me, "I measured it against a ring I saw at your house. It was a choice between two rings but this one looks more like you—simple and beautiful."

We had just turned the corner to exit the park when I remembered. I did know his middle name. Of course, I knew his middle name! I couldn't suppress a giggle.

He looked over with the one eyebrow raised, "Are you going to share the fun?" he asked.

I was caught.

Now laughing full out I said, "I do know your middle name. I always knew your middle name. It's Steven. It's your first name I couldn't remember! You are Frederic Steven Kale."

"Yeah?"

I explained why I hesitated when he asked me to marry him. We both laughed. Especially as he recounted, "One of the first times I talked with you I asked for your vote on whether I should go by my first name. Remember? I had just moved here. Since I moved to Fredericksburg, I wondered if I should be known as Frederic from Fredericksburg. You and almost everybody else agreed I didn't 'look' like a Frederic."

Steven loves to tease me about how I made him ask me twice.

Recently we laughed again with each other as we shared the story while getting acquainted with a new friend over dinner.

She looked stunned. "Two nights ago I had an awful fight with my fiancé because I thought he didn't care enough to remember my middle name." Looking down at the table, she said, "Maybe it isn't that big a deal. Maybe other things are a lot more important."

~Sheila Sattler Kale

Sweet Surprise

Love must be as much a light, as it is a flame.
~Henry David Thoreau

"**I**'m sorry to leave you with all this, Mom," said my daughter, Jennifer, surveying the kitchen counters laden with cupcake tins, bowls, and ingredients that go with baking.

"That's okay, Honey. Your sister and I can survive without you for awhile."

She grinned and headed out the door.

Heather and I got busy baking six dozen cupcakes for the church youth charity fundraiser. That's seventy-two cupcakes! How did I get myself into these things?

"We're out of icing," Heather suddenly exclaimed, throwing off her apron, "I'll run down to the store for some." She grabbed her wallet and keys as she dashed out the front door.

I was puzzled as I checked the shelves in the pantry. I was sure I bought plenty but she was right. Odd, I thought, and began to clean the kitchen as the cupcakes cooled.

She finally breezed in the door. "I'm back."

I heard a male voice. Who was that? There stood Jennifer's boyfriend, Bob, who was supposed to be 3,000 miles across the country, with a bunch of red roses in one hand and a tuxedo in the other.

My jaw dropped. "What are you doing here?"

He grinned. "I've come to propose to Jennifer."

"Now? You can't," I stammered. "Jennifer isn't here."

"I know. Heather arranged to keep Jen out of the house and then picked me up at the airport in time to set things up here."

"Heather? I thought you went for icing...." My voice faded as I slowly began to put it all together.

"I hid the icing, Mom. It's in the garage—sorry." Heather's dark eyes danced with excitement.

"You flew all the way from Boston tonight?" I asked Bob, bewildered. "Aren't you supposed to be here next weekend?"

"Yes, but it wouldn't be a surprise if I proposed then." He laid his tux on the back of a kitchen chair and propped the roses in the sink between bowls and tins before coming over to give me a hug. "Would it be possible to borrow twelve candles and candle holders? And is there some way to get music to the backyard?"

I nodded mutely and surveyed the kitchen. This is a disaster, I thought, not an elegant and beautiful place for Jennifer's proposal.

We knew this day would be coming since he had asked for our permission to marry her several weeks earlier, but this young Portuguese man was full of surprises.

I sighed and went to find candles while Heather ran upstairs for her boom box. She set it up on the patio table and popped in the CD soundtrack of *When Harry Met Sally*, readying the scene for her sister. Then she turned to me and said, "We have to leave, Mom."

"But... but what about the cupcakes? And where do we go? I'm a mess...." I sputtered.

"We just have to get out of the house for awhile—we'll finish the cupcakes later."

I was banished from my house. My own house!

I should have gone next door and asked to watch the backyard happenings from their glass-enclosed balcony. But I didn't. I must have been in shock. I could think of only one place where I could show up at 10:00 at night and know they'd not be perplexed or annoyed. For the next hour I spent a nervous but excited time drinking tea with my friends, who lived twenty miles away. They were thrilled to be involved in this small way. "We feel like conspirators," they confided with big grins.

Finally the phone rang. It was Heather. "You can come home now, Mom."

I stepped into the house shortly after midnight and was greeted with ecstatic hugs from Jennifer. Then I pulled back and asked, "Well, tell me, did he get down on one knee?"

"Yes," she dragged out the word like it had six syllables.

"And?" I persisted. After all, I'd helped set up the event, now I wanted details.

"Oh, Mom, it was so romantic!" Her eyes sparkled. "The porch light wasn't on when I got home but there was a candle glowing and a red rose lying by it with a piece of paper. I picked it up with the rose and read, 'How do I love thee?'" She took a breath and smiled at her new fiancé, then continued.

"I immediately thought of Bob because that's 'our' sonnet, but I knew he wasn't here, so I figured Heather must be up to something. It was eerie as I cracked open the front door. The house was almost dark but I saw a second candle with another rose and slip of paper. 'Let me count the ways,' it read."

She glanced beyond me, remembering. "I could see candles glowing down the hall and out to the patio. Harry Connick, Jr. was singing "It Had to Be You" from somewhere. I still had no clue what was going on or why. Boy, am I naïve."

She then told me that she stopped at each candle, retrieved the red rose and the next line of the sonnet, and finally made it to the back door. "Then I saw him." Her voice rose in excitement. "He was dressed in a tuxedo and held out another rose." She paused, amused. "You won't believe this but the first thing I thought was that I was wearing about the worst clothes possible: jeans, flip-flops, even a headband. I felt so schleppy."

"Oh, Honey, it doesn't matter what you're wearing, you're always beautiful," I said.

"I need to call Dad," she interjected, flashing her new Marquise-cut diamond ring at me.

I found the out-of-town hotel number where my pilot husband was on a layover and handed it to her. While she dialed, I noticed the frosted cupcakes sat in boxes ready to deliver. I was surprised and grateful.

"Daddy, Bob's here," she squealed. "He proposed to me!"

"You didn't say yes, did you?" he responded.

"Yes, I did," she told him and, with a laugh, added, "quit teasing me."

Their wedding followed the next spring. Everyone received a ribbon-tied scroll with those special calligraphy-penned lines from "Sonnets from the Portuguese."

Now, some fifteen years and two children later, we watch him surprise her with flowers for no reason, sweet notes, and romantic getaways, as we "count the ways" he still shows how he loves her.

~Jean H. Stewart

"Somehow, I think these clues are leading to a happy ending!"

The Counterproposal

A man's wife has more power over him than the state has.
~Ralph Waldo Emerson

I never liked rings. I do not wear a high school ring; I do not wear a college ring, and I did not want to wear a wedding ring. This was not because I did not want people to know that I was married, but because I just did not feel comfortable with a ring on my finger.

After graduating from college I finally was about to "pop the question" to my high school sweetheart, Sharon Gail Weingarton, who was at my side continually after I was almost fatally injured during a robbery.

Sharon was the best—pretty, kind, sweet, and goodhearted. However, what would she say when I proposed and said that I did not want to wear a wedding ring? I practiced what I was going to say to her. I thought long and hard. I finally decided that there was no answer to my dilemma. I would simply tell her, and then wait five minutes for the explosion.

So that night I proposed, and afterwards I told Sharon that I was not going to wear a ring. I simply said: "I just don't like rings. I don't wear a high school ring…." I expected Sharon to become enraged: "WHAT DO YOU MEAN YOU'RE NOT GOING TO WEAR A WEDDING RING?"

However, instead, I merely heard silence. After what in my mind seemed like an eternity, Sharon calmly remarked: "Fine. If you don't want to wear a wedding ring, I won't change my name. I will not call myself Sharon Segal."

On our fifteenth anniversary, I remembered the first lesson of marriage that was taught to me by my wife Sharon Gail Segal as I looked down upon the ring on my ring finger—COMPROMISE.

~Michael Jordan Segal, MSW

My Ninja

Love makes your soul crawl out from its hiding place.
~Zora Neale Hurston

Picture it: Omaha, NE March 21, 2008.

A young girl drives home from a hard day's work. She pulls into the driveway and opens the garage. As the door rises, she sees a blue dress bag hanging. Puzzled, she gets out of the car to further inspect the item. She sees a note taped to the bag. It tells her that she has an hour to get dressed up (in the dress of course), get back in her car, and start driving—she'll know where to go. Surprised and excited, the girl runs inside the house.

The girl goes into the bathroom to get ready. Taped to her mirror is another message telling her to shower in order to get off the "kid-stink" she might be wearing from her day of working with the kiddies. She laughs and jumps in the shower. After getting out, she decides to put on some perfume. On one of her perfume bottles is another message, "Don't forget to wear my favorite perfume." Smiling, she puts on a few extra sprays.

She puts on the dress and is doing her hair and make-up when her phone starts sounding. A text message! It informs her that she has one minute to get to her car. She puts on her heels and runs out the door.

When she arrives at her car, she sees a rose inside. On the rose is a note. The note instructs her to go to a certain Starbucks downtown and to give the rose to a girl named Shay. The young girl is confused. Why would she get so dressed up to go to a coffee shop to give another girl a rose? Enjoying the adventure, she jumps in her car and starts the journey.

Twenty minutes later, the girl pulls into a parking spot in front of the Starbucks. She quickly puts some money in the meter and runs inside. Cautiously, she approaches the counter to find two girls smiling at her. "Does someone named Shay work here?" she meekly asks. "I'm Shay," says a nice girl. "And I have something for you." Shay hands the girl her favorite coffee drink. YUM. But wait! Another note is taped to the cup!

The note tells the girl that the coffee will serve as a pick-me-up from a long day at work. Then it instructs the girl to go check on her car. Excited, yet still confused, the girl tells the nice workers that it appears she must leave again. Before leaving, the girls tell her to come back and let them in on what this scavenger hunt is all about.

When the girl gets back to her car, she finds another rose in the front seat. Knowing she locked her door and was only in Starbucks for a maximum of five minutes, she is sure her beau is near. She stands on the corner and surveys the area... she sees no one. She gets back in her car to read the note.

The note starts to talk about all things French. Toward the end of the note, the writer laments having to be in Omaha instead of France. But then he remembers that Omaha has an arch near the Old Market that resembles the Arc de Triomphe. The note tells her to go there with her next rose.

The girl drives a few blocks and parks. She walks to the arch and stands underneath—ready for something or someone to pop out. Nothing happens. She decides to go look at the water—maybe there's been a glitch, and her beau is running late. She leans against a railing and stares at the water, sincerely wondering where this hunt is going. All of a sudden, she feels compelled to turn around.

The girl turns to find her beau, on bended knee, with a diamond ring. Before he can say anything, the girl embraces and kisses the young man... accepting his proposal immediately. "Yes! Yes! Yes!"

The young man takes her back to the Starbucks, where the girl finds out that everyone was in on the whole thing. Then he tells her he will take her to a romantic dinner for two at a nice restaurant. When the newly engaged couple is led to their table, the young girl is faced with yet another surprise — a room where she finds her mom, dad, grandma, family friends, and future in-laws waiting to congratulate them. The young girl is overjoyed.

How did the young man accomplish such ninja-like feats? He hid in the trunk of her car and allowed the young girl to transport him to every stop.

That young girl is me... and that young man is my fiancé, Brian.

~Jennifer Hofsommer

A Different Calling

The very first moment I beheld him, my heart was irrevocably gone.
~Jane Austen

He was twenty and tall, with blond hair and green eyes. His body was sleek with muscular curves, and his face gave my heart twinges.

I was eleven, short, and wore glasses. I had fuzzy hair and freckles, and the only curves on my body were affectionately referred to as "baby fat."

His name was Ken. He knew my name, but the only attention he really gave me was a sort of pat on the head as he went by. But even then, I loved him, and knew that one day, we'd be together.

I was teased and laughed at by everyone who knew my feelings. They told me to forget it, that he had plenty of women his age. Not a chance, they told me.

I ignored them.

Two years later, I asked Ken to sponsor me for my confirmation ceremony in our church. I was thrilled when he accepted. The year of instruction beforehand would require him to spend more time with me.

Two years after that, I learned that Ken was moving to France to become a monk! I tearfully begged him not to go, but he said it was best. He felt a calling to that life.

The day Ken left I took my dream and, folding it carefully, put it away in a small place in my heart, and tried to forget. But I couldn't.

I knew my feelings for him were real, no matter what others said or thought. I knew in my heart that we were meant for each other.

Years passed slowly, and the letters we exchanged help the pain in my heart. Not much, but enough to get by. We maintained as close a relationship as we could.

Thirteen years after Ken left for France, I received a letter from him telling me that he was moving to the States to help start a priory in Oklahoma. I was delighted on so many levels that I could barely think. He was coming back to this continent. He would be living on the same chunk of land as I was (albeit in a different country). It would cost less to write him. It would take less time for our letters to arrive. And best of all, I could phone him.

I quickly discovered another benefit of his move: he could visit! His few visits home were times of rejoicing for me, even though his behaviour gave me no real hope. He seemed so distant. But I still loved him, and I still believed we were meant to be together.

Shortly after that, I received a very serious letter from him, which scared me even as it made my heart swell with pride for him. He was working with inmates on death row in Oklahoma, and one of them had asked him to be present at his execution. This request lay heavy on his mind, as he did not know what to do. I knew my response would impact him for the rest of his life, and thought very carefully before I sent my letter. In it I told him that, no matter what choice he made, he would wish he had done otherwise. But, as I pointed out, a needy man was asking him to be present at his last hour on earth. Could he really say no?

The next time I heard from Ken, he wrote that he would be present at the execution, and that he might not feel like writing again until it was over. I understood, and made sure he still heard from me regularly. He needed my support.

I called a few days after the execution took place, and sat listening to him cry. We did not use words, but our hearts were talking to each other, and it did not matter much what they were saying. He knew I was there, and that was what counted.

After the execution, I began to notice a change in Ken. It was so gradual that I doubted myself at first, but others in his community were also taking notice. It soon reached a point where he admitted to himself, and to me, that his life seemed stuck in a rut. As monastic life was supposed to be slow, his attitude bothered me a little. My concern grew as his letters showed him getting worse, and I finally decided it was time I went down there to shake him up a bit.

I had intended to travel down to see him after a visit to my uncle in Pennsylvania, but during my stay, I received word that I should forget about my trip to Oklahoma, as Ken was returning to British Columbia to attend his grandmother's funeral.

My family and I attended the funeral. Later that night, Ken and I had some time together. I had something to tell him. Taking him by his hands, I looked into his eyes, and told him that I did not want him to go back to Oklahoma. Then I bowed my head and, with a heavy heart, waited for the polite refusal that I knew was coming.

Instead, he said he didn't want to go back to Oklahoma. Then the dam broke, and it all came out at once. He had always loved me, but felt it truly was best for him to distance himself from me all those years ago because I was so young and there was gossip in our community. So he left and joined a monastery halfway across the world.

But because he still loved me all those years, his superiors would not let him make any final vows. A man cannot swear to a life of celibacy when his heart beats for a woman. So Ken lived with the community, taking part in their life, but remained free to leave at any time. When his grandmother passed away, he decided that, unless something had changed, he would go back to Oklahoma after the funeral, take the vows, and never leave again.

But something had changed. Or rather, something had remained the same. The heart of the eleven-year-old girl who loved him had grown into the heart of a thirty-six-year-old woman who still loved him. We had both been through trials that had left their scars, but the love was still there. So, when he knelt down and asked me to marry him, there was no doubt in either of our minds when I said yes.

~Sharon Graham

Chapter
5

True Love

The Wedding

Now join hands, and with your hands your hearts.

~William Shakespeare

41

Secret Wedding

When love is not madness, it is not love.
~Pedro Calderon de la Barca

We were engaged — complete with a nice-sized ring — and our wedding date was set for October 5th. We wanted to get married ten years to the day from the first time we had verbally expressed our love. We had been high-school sweethearts. Already engaged and planning a wedding a year away, we moved into a place of our own. Then we decided we just needed to be married right away. We made it legal.

It was a small affair with immediate family members and a few friends. Our dearest friends let us get married in their living room. We borrowed some folding chairs from the church and our pastor did a brief ceremony. We exchanged platinum bands, repeated vows, kissed and voilà — we were married. The afternoon was made complete with coffee, two small cakes from the supermarket on the corner, and an arrangement of daisies that cost less than twelve dollars. My best friends wanted to make me a bouquet but I refused. They did, however, convince me to buy a new white blouse to wear with my khaki skirt.

We had the ceremony after church, and then did what we do every other Sunday afternoon — we relaxed with friends. We played spades well into the night and my new husband re-strung his guitar. Peculiar, I know. But in all sincerity we were so ready.

That was my wedding day, well really, my marriage day.

Secret Wedding :The Wedding   161

As I consider all these things, it seems so very un-romantic—all except for the fact that it was a secret wedding, because we were still planning our formal wedding for October 5th, my dream wedding in the rose garden with a white dress, a string quartet, and mini-quiches.

Is it weird that our marriage license has a different date than the day we celebrate our anniversary? That the minister who married us is not the same minister who conducted our wedding? That I still haven't told my grandparents? Are these things that will thoroughly confuse our children one day?

I admit that it sounds weird, but we have a "married" date and a "wedding" date. Even though I don't expect flowers on both occasions, I feel like this simply reaffirms the fact that I am high maintenance. I got two weddings to the same man.

~Stefani Chambers

42

My Purple Wedding

When you love someone, all your saved-up wishes start coming out.
~Elizabeth Bowen

I remember little about the day my husband proposed. Del is a down-to-earth kind of guy, so there were no frills, no fancy romantic dinner or airplane message written in the sky. Just a simple, "Will you marry me?" Caught off guard and uneasy with such a serious moment, I responded, "Sure. If you'll buy me a horse." He said he would.

My dad gave his wholehearted approval when Del asked for my hand. My mother was another story. She withheld her blessing, and as wedding plans moved forward, conflicts arose.

The people Del and I chose to stand up with us did not meet with Mother's approval. The attendants I wanted failed her litmus test. Del's best friend and choice for his best man became a tug of war between me and Mother. He was black and I was informed that if he was in the wedding my dad would not walk me down the aisle. Never having been taught prejudice, I was shocked when it reared its ugly head. Forced to choose between my dad or my convictions of right and wrong, I wrestled with this injustice.

All the while feeling guilty, I chose Dad, whom I adored, and Del agreed to ask someone else. Because his friend knew nothing of Del's original plan, his feelings were spared. Ours were not. Our hearts were broken.

As plans continued it became evident this was not my wedding, but the wedding my mother never had. She chose the people. She chose her favorite colors. Regardless of inflation, the budget for my wedding was not to exceed that of my sister's, who had married nine years earlier. This meant I could have only one attendant, who Mother chose.

As conflicts escalated, Dad offered us money to elope, but we decided to go forward with a formal wedding. Weddings don't always turn out the way we envision them, but healing can come in time.

Our healing came after we had been married twenty-five years. God laid it on my heart to celebrate our anniversary by having the wedding we had always wanted. Giddy as a first time bride, I picked the colors, the people, the cake and even the location for our honeymoon.

When it came time to shop for a dress my goal was to find one in my favorite color—purple. Since shopping is not something I enjoy, Del prayed I would find a dress at the first store. His prayer was answered. From the moment I tried on a beautiful purple princess style, I knew it was my wedding dress, a dress fit for royalty.

We called the friends we originally wanted in our wedding party, including as many as possible. "Oh, Pam," my girlfriend from sixth grade said, "I couldn't believe it when I heard your message on my recorder. I sat down and cried."

We even asked for the marriage counseling, which we never received the first time around.

Del and I were both nervous the night of our celebration. With twenty-five years of marriage behind us, we knew the seriousness of the wedding vows we repeated. At one point in the ceremony, Del was almost overcome with emotion. I saw tears in his eyes, and knew something stirred deep down in his heart. The ceremony ended with a prayer of blessing and two hearts on the pathway to healing.

After wedding pictures, we proceeded to the reception. The original cake topper, with touches of purple now added to the pink, adorned a delicious cake with fruit filling and cream cheese icing. The room, decorated with a white lattice backdrop covered with purple flowers, silver ribbons and greenery, provided a perfect setting for our guests. We mingled with friends from many years and caught up on their lives and shared about ours.

When the evening ended, we loaded gifts into the car and I slipped in beside my beloved husband. With memories of the wedding I always desired tucked away in my mind, I was satisfied for the first time in years.

In those sweet precious moments, I realized not only had my wedding vows been renewed, my heart had been also. Like cream cheese frosting on a hot summer day, all the bitterness, hurt and resentment that had haunted me for all those years melted away. This time, I felt God had been in charge of my wedding. My mother had been a guest. With my heart softened toward her, I looked forward to God's healing and restoration in our relationship.

Del and I spent our honeymoon sightseeing in historical Philadelphia and a romantic getaway in the Poconos. The beautiful scenery and a heart-shaped tub was a perfect new beginning for two romantic hearts joined as one.

~Pamela Humphreys

Decisions

A wedding is a start of togetherness... of walks in the rain,
basking in the sunshine, shared meals, caring for one another
and sensing the love that a marriage carries.
~Author Unknown

The easiest decision my husband and I ever jointly made was to get married in the first place. It was agreeing on all the details of the wedding that almost nullified our union, before we had even properly tied the knot.

To begin with, I had always dreamed of a large and extravagant wedding, with me clad from head to toe in white lace, walking veiled and demure down the aisle on the arm of my proud papa. Nothing, but nothing was going to sway me from that vision, especially not my husband-to-be. Wasn't marriage all about compromise anyway? He on the other hand, a solid pragmatic engineer, had other thoughts on the matter.

"You know how much money we're going to have to plunk down for what is essentially a one-day party? Why not take the money we would have spent, and use it for a down payment on a house? Surely that would be a better use of our money."

The really annoying part was that in a way he was right. He still had student loans, I was paying off my car, and in a short while, we would acquire our first mortgage. Could we really afford this wedding? Still, I wasn't ready to concede defeat yet.

"My parents have volunteered to pay for the wedding, and if they don't mind, why should you? Anyway, I'm the last of their daughters to get married, so they'll be home free after this wedding."

I was to learn that if I could be tenacious, my fiancé could be equally so. "Are you really going to ask your parents to pay for an expensive wedding after they just put the five of you through private colleges?"

Okay, now I was feeling a bit on the guilty side, but not so much that I was willing to relinquish my dreams of a wedding altogether. "What about just a small wedding then with only our families and closest friends?" I sensed my advantage as he hesitated. "No wedding, no marriage," I stated firmly, "and that's my final offer."

"Fine," he conceded, "a small wedding it is then." The smile of triumph he tried unsuccessfully to hide convinced me immediately that a small wedding was what he was after the whole time. Now why oh why couldn't he have just said so in the first place?

The ensuing negotiations to hammer out all the details of the wedding felt a bit like bartering for a used car. Our next big decision was who to invite. Every decision it seemed came with its own set of complicating factors. After we settled on the number of wedding guests, it seemed only reasonable that we each be responsible for half the guest list. The problem was that my family far outnumbered his, and what with all my siblings, aunts, uncles and cousins, I would have a difficult time staying within my limit.

"Even though I have to invite them all, most of the East Coast branch of the family won't be able to attend," I quickly assured him, with much less confidence than I was feeling. As I composed my proposed list of invitees, I carefully penciled in next to their names the likelihood that they would actually attend. "There," I crowed triumphantly, when my list was finally compiled, "I predict with an 85% certainty that a maximum of two-thirds of the guests I invited will actually attend."

"And what if you're wrong," he asked suspiciously, "and we end up with double the number we expected?" No doubt he was having some second thoughts about his decision to marry a mathematician.

"Then we hock the family silver, and use the money to elope," I quickly replied. He had the good grace to laugh.

From the guest list, we proceeded to picking the date, no mean feat as all four of my siblings and my mother were tied to academic calendars, either as grad students or professors. Moreover, half were on the quarter system while the other half were on the semester system, so their vacations didn't exactly match up.

"Let's see," I mused, after making a spreadsheet of all possible wedding dates, it being Thanksgiving Day when we announced our engagement. "It looks like we can go with the last weekend in March of next year, or try to work around everyone's summer vacations." March 28th it was to be then, leaving us a mere four months to deal with selecting the facility, the photographer, the band, the flowers, the attire, the meal, the wedding party, and a whole host of other decisions. There was no shortage of details to work out apparently.

"You know," I remarked casually one day, as I was working out a complex calculation of what was the right proportion of marinated mushrooms to bacon-wrapped scallops on the hors d'oeuvres tray, "maybe we should have just eloped and saved all this trouble. Just kidding," I hastily amended, after seeing the expression on the face of my intended.

Well the big day finally arrived, and the details just kind of sorted themselves out. While there were no major crises to deal with, there were plenty of the smaller run-of-the-mill glitches: the head musician fell sick at the last minute, the top layer of cake that we had carefully set aside for our first anniversary landed icing side down on the floor, at least half a dozen guests who hadn't bothered to RSVP showed up anyway, and a family friend accidentally trod on the train of my wedding gown when we were dancing, dislodging all those tiny silk buttons that held it up so nicely. Somehow we managed to deal with those things, and when all was said and done, our wedding went about as smoothly as we could have hoped for.

The sun broke through the clouds just long enough for the photographer to take the formal pictures of the family outdoors, the food and wine were plentiful, and if I never personally got to taste one of the marinated mushroom hors d'oeuvres that were my special favorite, everyone afterwards assured me they were excellent. One of the highlights of the evening was the rousing hora at the end in which everyone partook, from the youngest five-year-old to my octogenarian aunt.

I'm not sure we fully appreciated what we were getting ourselves into that day, as we solemnly uttered our vows. We were both in our twenties, and life's greatest joys and sorrows were still ahead of us. I am firmly convinced however, that the four months of almost constant give and take as we worked through the details of our wedding was the best preparation possible for our ensuing thirty-seven years of married life. Our next major decision was deciding when to start our family, and how many children we would have, he wanting two, and me leaning towards five, but that's a whole other story!

~Cara Holman

The Seating Plan

I couldn't wait for success... so I went ahead without it.
~Jonathan Winters

One hundred people must sit at twelve round tables. I survey the jumbled pile of hand-written response cards in the red shoebox and grin. Soon Steve and I will hold hands as we zoom away from the quaint chapel and glide through the hills in the back seat of our gleaming limousine. Later, we will emerge from the plush interior, flushed with the glow of becoming Mr. and Mrs. I have planned the perfect wedding. Robin Red Breast will alight on the fronds of the lush palm trees standing sentinel before the stately manor's French doors. The sun will beam. My angelic blond niece in her spotless gown will enter first, scattering pink rose petals along the lace-draped entry hall to herald our arrival.

I take a small stack of cards from the shoebox and lay it out before me like a Texas Hold 'em hand. I look up at the calendar, which displays a respectable distance between today and my blessed event. I had suggested a buffet dinner without assigned tables, but our parents prefer that we create a seating plan.

One hundred people divided among twelve round tables shouldn't be so difficult. One hundred guests divided by twelve tables makes eight or nine guests per table. Why buy software for wedding planning? I grab some paper and begin to sketch. I draw twelve globes orbiting an inner blank space that represents the banquet hall's dance floor. I turn the paper clockwise three times to fit them all into my diagram. The sharp pencil makes a satisfying scratching sound.

Names dance through my mind. The Holland cousins and their siblings will all sit together. They all chat amiably. I pencil a letter "H" on the table farthest from the center of the diagram. I select five cards from the hand laid out in front of me, and fish in the shoebox to withdraw two more. I put all the Holland-related cards face down on the floor next to my desk. I exhale.

I grab another stack of cards. My seven Nugent aunts and uncles dance well, I note, and so I write an "N" on a table near the dance floor. Two seats to fill with them. But with whom? My witty cousin Jenny from Boston? Maybe my former boss Kara and her husband Tim Rudy? I vow to show my admiration for my respected, former supervisor by seating her with impressive people. I pick up another card, this one messily scrawled, "M-Flaherty-2." My Flaherty uncles are quiet. Perhaps I will seat Kara with them and talkative people like my cousin and our friend Dr. Carroll for balance. Wait, darn, cousin Jenny likes to drink, so she can't sit near any of my Flaherty uncles; they're all in recovery. Could Kara sit with Aunt Angela? No, Angela likes to sit near the aisle at weddings so she can take a cake-cutting photo. Sighing, I put the card marked "Mr. and Mrs. Rudy" aside on my left.

Then I snatch up a card that reads "Taranto-4 persons." I pause. Are these the Tarantos from New Jersey? No, wait, the Taranto brother is the groom's cousin who crews for NASCAR. Cool. My eyes dart back to my diagram. I look at Kara and Tim's card. I start to move my pencil downward, listing guests in my mind... Danny Taranto. His step-brother Luke Taranto and his wife from San Francisco... Lilly? Lucy! Lucy Taranto who I know from... from that spinning class last year. Small world. Whoa. That means that she's also the Lucy who went out for late night cocktails with her personal trainer. And my swim coach. And that married lawyer. No way! I won't seat her within a mile of sweet, unsuspecting Tim and Kara.

The phone rings, dragging my thoughts and my fingers away from the insistent reply cards.

"Miss Flaherty? I want you to know we have everything in order for your perfect day," purrs my florist. "I must notify you of one slight impediment, though, regarding your lilies."

Alarm bells clang in my cerebral cortex. "Impediment? Did you say impediment?"

"Yes," soothes her honey-soaked voice. "It's nothing really, only the tiniest of delays regarding the centerpieces, Miss-Mrs. Pagan."

"We'll see if it's tiny!" I interject, breathing hard. "What kind of delay are we talking about?"

"Flower crops can be temperature-dependent," she breezes on. "Thus my supplier informs me that the number of lily stems that you requested, may, and I stress may, not be available by the eighteenth of July."

"Let me get this straight. You can't guarantee that we'll get the lilies we want for the tables?" My manicured fingernails drum on the desk. The calendar glares at me. Throbbing pinkish blotches appear on my neck and quickly spread to my cheeks and forehead.

She pauses. "My supplier can't get enough lilies for all twelve tables in time."

"We paaaaiid," I draw the vowel sounds out, "for lily centerpieces for all twelve tables."

"I am very sorry, Mrs. Pagan, and I am aware of our contractual agreement, but I can not control…"

"As you say, we have a contract. We contracted for lilies on all twelve tables at the manor house on July eighteenth." Then I clang down the receiver into the cradle, relishing my rudeness and the dramatic sound of our landline landing hard.

My eyes turn back to the once-promising shoebox of ivory reply cards. Looking in, my eyes catch sight of the card bearing the names of my wacky Uncle John and new, hippie Step-Aunt Star. I gulp. Where the heck do I seat them? Talk about opening a can of worms! Where would they want to sit? Do I care where they want to sit? Who will talk to them? Who knows? I shove the shoebox away.

I awake my hibernating laptop. I image search "July" and "flowers" and "New York." I half-heartedly inspect the search results. I scan pictures of hydrangeas. I steal guilty glances at the shoebox.

Suddenly, I look up. What the heck are we doing? Forget this! I look at my watch, and then back at the accusatory calendar. I fish a calculator out of the top desk drawer. The second hand on my wrist twitches by. I think long and hard about how many miles stand between us and Las Vegas. I wonder if we have enough gas in the Volkswagen to make it all the way to Reno. Blotches fade down my face towards my neck. My fingers dance over the computer keyboard and my grin returns, broad and free. Maybe we should elope.

That night, my future maid of honor stops by to see how our preparations are going. She knocks zealously. No one answers, and friendly concern gets the better of her. She lets herself in with our obviously placed hide-a-key. My future maid of honor frowns at the unnerving silence. There is no bride in the living room consulting magazines. There is no bride in the kitchen tasting cake samples. There is no bride on the phone scolding the florist. There is no bride in the bathroom on the scale. In the office, my future maid of honor finds a trail of ivory cards littering the floor. Her frown deepens into a fretful mask. Tiny shreds of cardstock dot the floor. Her panicked eyes widen as she spies edges of reply cards falling pell-mell from the gaping mouth of a gleaming, silver shredding machine.

● ● ●

No, we didn't elope but we came close! Three months later, my new husband and I smile broadly as we peruse the sumptuous buffet line at our lively reception. Savory roast beef and spicy eggplant tempt our senses. The bridesmaids stand behind us in line, cradling the adorable daisy bouquets that they have made for themselves. We have ignored our family and friend's well-meaning advice. We have pleased ourselves. We have the perfect wedding.

~P. A. Flaherty

Because of a Fortune Cookie

When you realize you want to spend the rest of your life with somebody,
you want the rest of your life to start as soon as possible.
~Nora Ephron

I ran to the mailbox and opened the lid. There was a letter inside stamped Camp Pendleton, CA and addressed in a familiar scrawling script. I ripped it open and let out a yell.

"Mom, Paul is definitely coming home on leave next week!"

"Well, thank God!" she replied. "You two can work out all the wedding details."

We had been planning a huge wedding through the mail since Paul left for Marine boot camp in January. It was now mid-May and our nuptials were to take place in September. I hadn't seen him since he left; we couldn't talk on the phone, and even writing letters was hard for him. There is a saying in the services, "If the (insert branch of the service) wanted you to have family they would have issued you one." The Marine Corps owned Paul. He confessed that some nights, after writing me a letter by flashlight, he would sneak down the road in his boxers, and deposit it in the base mail slot. We called it "midnight mail." Dangerous at best.

The weekend finally arrived and I was on cloud nine. Paul was taking me to dinner and the theater. I felt like a queen in my new black dress and pearls. He showed up with roses promptly at seven.

"Ready for the time of your life?" he asked after a long kiss hello. I didn't realize how prophetic that phrase was.

"Babe, I've waited for this day forever. Let's go," I replied and with that he whisked me to the car with my parents waving goodbye and smiling at the door.

Paul wouldn't tell me where we were going for dinner but I didn't care; just being with him was enough.

We pulled into the parking lot of General Lee's in Chinatown. Walking up Bamboo Way, I couldn't believe Paul was actually here. As we ate, we kept touching hands across the table reassuring each other that this wasn't a dream.

After the main course the waiter put two fortune cookies down on the table with two orange slices. Paul poured more tea for me while I read my fortune.

"Hmmm… my fortune says 'Don't do anything on the spur of the moment'," I mused. Wonder what that means? "What could we do on the spur of the moment?" I asked.

"We could elope," Paul suggested shyly.

"We can't do that… can we?" My mind raced. "My parents would kill us. My dad has already rented the country club, I have my dress, the bridesmaids have their dresses, the church…"

"You're probably right," Paul interrupted. "Still, it does sound daring."

"Oh, this is crazy," I said. But I knew I loved Paul madly and this was the most thrilling thing I could imagine.

"Where can we elope on a Saturday night?" I asked, still intrigued with this romantic notion of becoming man and wife immediately.

"Well, I read in the paper that if we go to Yuma, you can get a blood test and then slip back into California to a place called Winterhaven. They marry you right away. But you're right, it's a crazy idea," Paul stated.

"Yeah, crazy," I said, sitting there just staring at Paul.

"Can I get married if I'm only nineteen?" I asked, still intrigued.

"Sure, we'll stop by our houses and pick up our birth certificates on the way."

The more we talked the more exciting the idea sounded.

"Well, what are we going to do?" I asked. "Is it the theater or Yuma?"

Paul smiled and whispered, "Yuma."

And with that the idea was set in motion. After paying our tab, we practically ran to Paul's car. We were two love-crazed kids and we were going to be married.

At my house I told my dad I had to have my birth certificate to get into a go-go club and he handed it over, no questions asked. I felt guilty about lying to him, but I was young and in love.

Paul stopped at his apartment and got his certificate, borrowed $50 from his roommate and we hit the road to Yuma. His roommate thought we were doing the most exciting thing in the world and wished us luck.

I was in heaven as we whizzed down the road at speeds approaching eighty. The balmy night air whipped through the open windows as we clung to each other in the front seat. Finally, it dawned on me.

"Paul, I have to let my parents know where I am. When morning comes and I'm not home, they'll be worried sick."

This was before cell phones and e-mail, so we stopped in Indio and sent telegrams to both our parents.

"Have eloped. STOP. Love you both. STOP Sallie and Paul. STOP."

Back on the road, we drove all night except to stop for gas. Paul's Plymouth Fury was guzzling gas like a fiend and our funds were getting low.

We finally pulled into Yuma around six on Sunday morning. We shared a breakfast at a small diner so that we would have enough money left for the blood tests. I was so excited I didn't need much food but my Marine was a hungry guy.

The clinic opened at eight and we were the first in line. We got our results and headed to the Lutes Gretna Wedding Chapel. There before the minister's wife and daughter we said, "I do" with stars in our eyes.

Now I'm not going to lie and say going home to face my parents was easy, but Dad understood, being a romantic at heart himself. He celebrated getting his deposit back from the country club by buying a new Thunderbird. I sold my dress to my best friend, and Paul went back to boot camp a tired, happy, and married Marine. I set up house in a little apartment until we could afford our first home.

It has been forty-five years and guess where we're going to dinner? Here's a clue, it's located on Bamboo Way and serves great fortune cookies.

~Sallie A. Rodman

Ronald

Mirth is God's medicine. Everybody ought to bathe in it.
~Henry Ward Beecher

It was midnight. Richard and I were writing our personal vows for the coming afternoon's wedding ceremony. In addition to the prayers and comments the rabbi would make, my future husband and I wanted to express to one another what we felt and believed about our love and our shared destiny.

June 18th was our wedding day. Richard and I were driven to the synagogue where our ceremony would take place. The setting was breathtaking. The temple was situated on acres of green landscape, and was designed by a Japanese architect. It was starkly elegant and simple, all white inside and outside.

Richard was fifty-one and I was forty-three when we married. It was my first marriage. I chose to walk down the aisle hand in hand with my future husband at my side. That was the way we wanted to start our life together as partners. Literally and symbolically it expressed how we saw ourselves. We were not only lovers but also best friends.

I remember smiling at our guests as we walked toward the rabbi. Everyone there meant so much to us. They smiled back at us, recognizing how special this moment was in our lives. We had waited a long time for this day. It was going to be perfect.

I carried a peach rose, which was the color of the wedding decor and the lettering on our white invitation. Orange had been my favorite color as long as I could remember. The peach roses gave the room a gentle softness that was inviting and delicate. They were breathtaking, their scent exquisite.

Richard allowed me to select our wedding song. I remember the moment I played Barbra Streisand singing "Starting Here, Starting Now" for him. The lyrics expressed what we both were feeling as we were about to begin our life as a married couple. A singer sang that song as we walked down the aisle. In our wedding pictures we were literally glowing.

We had had several discussions with the rabbi about our journey in finding one another. We had likened it to finding a needle in a haystack. The ceremony reflected our appreciation of one another and the future we would now share as husband and wife.

When the ceremony was over, the guests cornered us to extend their congratulations. My sisters somehow broke away from the crowd and walked into the room where tables were set up for our reception.

They gasped at the beauty of more peach-colored roses and the matching tablecloths and napkins. My sister Susan walked over to one of the tables and picked up one of the scripted napkins. She stared at the names and froze.

"Linda, come here," she called out to my sister. "The napkins say Elynne and Ronald."

"Very funny," Linda answered as she walked toward Susan and the napkin. Taking the napkin from Susan's hands, she looked at the names and screamed. "Hurry! Pick up all the napkins on every table!"

While my new husband Richard and I continued greeting our guests in another part of the synagogue, my sisters worked as fast as they could to remove the disaster awaiting us.

They tried their hardest but missed a couple of tables. As fate would have it, this was where Richard's friends sat down to eat. They looked at the napkins in total disbelief. One of his friends told us years later that she thought all the time she had known Richard she must not have known that his real name was Ronald.

Throughout the remainder of our wedding celebration and during our honeymoon I could not resist every now and then calling for Ronald.

~Elynne Chaplik-Aleskow

Carousels

After all there is something about a wedding-gown
prettier than in any other gown in the world.
~Douglas William Jerrold

She seemed to grow taller and more regal as she stood before the three-way mirror.

"That's the one," her twin sister whispered, barely able to breathe.

I nodded as my daughter turned around and slowly smiled. It definitely was THE dress. We found the perfect veil and shoes and left the bridal shop feeling somewhat giddy.

"Okay, what's next?" I asked.

"A dress for you, Mom," was the reply.

We were in the midst of a whirlwind of activity. The bridesmaids' dresses were chosen, so now came decisions about floral bouquets and arrangements, wedding cake, photographer, and music. I hand-addressed the invitations and the reply cards were flooding in.

Then, since I had put it off as long as I could, I began the search for my dress and managed to find a pale pink one that my daughter approved. Her father purchased a new tuxedo. He joked that he felt like a walking ATM machine, only there to write checks or sign credit slips. It was mayhem, yet we were somehow enjoying that special time.

A few weeks before the May wedding, we rushed in from grocery shopping and the bride's sister greeted us with, "Dad, Mom, can we talk to you?"

I glanced at her holding hands with her boyfriend and suddenly knew what they wanted. A half-gallon of milk slipped from my hand, spilled across the wood floors and spread everywhere, even under the refrigerator.

"Oh, no!" I wailed. "I can't believe this."

"Don't worry, Mom, we'll help you," my daughter said as she rushed to grab the carton to stop the rest of the milk from escaping.

We all grabbed paper towels, crawled on our hands and knees, and spent the next hour together cleaning up the mess. Then we sat, the four of us, staring at one another.

He squirmed and fidgeted and finally sputtered out his love and devotion for our daughter.

"We'd like to get married in December," he said, "with your permission."

"Which December?" I asked in disbelief.

"This one," she finally spoke.

"That's only seven months away," I moaned.

Her father and I stole frantic glances at one another. He then queried and pried as he did a year earlier with her sister and her suitor. Finally he smiled and we gave our blessing. They knew we would.

As I sat there watching them, I felt my life spiraling out of control. Panic spread over me like the milk that had earlier spilled across the kitchen floor. I could do nothing to stop it. Two weddings? The thought of another wedding that year was overwhelming. I felt as if I were on a carousel that would never stop.

"Oh, Mom, this is so exciting!" The girls were thrilled that they would stand together at the altar a second time that year in reverse roles.

I couldn't tell them I was considering a nervous breakdown but didn't have time for one. Meanwhile, their father was wondering about bankruptcy.

Sleep was elusive. My dreams were filled with wedding disasters or mixing up the grooms. I'd wake exhausted only to see a white illusion floating before me. Then I'd realize it was the white satin dress on its padded hanger suspended from a ceiling anchor in the corner of our bedroom. The vision of the long sweep of its pearl-studded, lace-embroidered train evoked all kinds of emotions—joy, happiness, worry, nostalgia, and, at times, sheer panic. Especially as I contemplated a second wedding to come.

The days and weeks flew by in a blur of activity and a long white limousine was in front of our house to whisk the bride and maid of honor off to the church before I could catch my breath.

The wedding was perfect, beautiful and sweet, and everything she had dreamed it would be. The next morning I woke to the vision of yet another dress hanging from the corner. Smooth, creamy, pearl-trimmed silk reminded me that I was still on the wedding carousel.

As I pondered the beauty of the dress and what it represented, I came to realize that we go along the road of life and then, every once in awhile, stop and whirl around in the busyness of the place until it's time to step off and continue on down the road.

We took a double ride that year and found the experiences there tender and sweet, funny and poignant, times that will stay in our memories forever.

Life is change. And filled with carousels. I always try to enjoy the ride.

~Jean H. Stewart

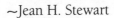

"Two weddings in one year? Why not? I can't think of a happier reason to go into debt!"

The Pearl Necklace

Where there is great love, there are always miracles.
~Willa Cather

It was two days before my wedding. I had promised myself (and my fiancé!) that I wouldn't be one of those brides—the bridezillas who freak out if every detail of the wedding isn't perfect—but I was exhausted from planning, organizing, and coping with too much family and too little sleep.

I decided to try on the pearls my grandmother had given me, but the clasp was stuck. As I tugged, to my horror, the necklace snapped and pearls flew everywhere.

Keeping my cool, I gathered up the errant pearls, consulted a phone book, and began dialing. I received the same reply everywhere: a minimum of two to three weeks to fix. Even when I pleaded that my wedding was in two days, I just received more elaborate excuses: no on-site jeweler, full schedule already, company policy, sorry.

It was the proverbial last straw. I collapsed in tears on the bed, next to my sleeping fiancé. He awoke in confusion, listened to my tale of woe, then suggested, "Borrow my mother's pearls." This set me off into another jag of crying, the only discernible words being, "I want to wear the pearls my grandmother gave me!"

He must have realized I'd passed the threshold of rational thought, so he took charge and did the only thing he could think of under the circumstances: he lied. He phoned a jeweler and told the following story.

"I'm getting married in two days. I was fiddling with my fiancée's grandmother's pearls and broke them. I need them restrung by tomorrow, or else there might not be a wedding."

The necklace was fixed by the next day.

~Sheri Radford

Dancing in the Kitchen

To watch us dance is to hear our hearts speak.
~Hopi Indian Saying

I love my husband. I also love dancing. Over the years we learned from experience, however, beginning with our wedding more than forty years ago, that the two were not compatible. We just didn't dance well together. We seemed to have an abundance of left feet.

So when our son announced that he was getting married, I knew something had to be done. I was not about to let us stumble our way through the official parents' dance. I did what I thought was the easiest and fastest way to come up to dancing speed—I signed us up for dancing classes.

My husband grumbled. He complained that it is impossible to count the beats, do the variations, and feel the music at the same time.

"That's multitasking," I told him.

Women are used to it. Folding the laundry and helping with homework. Cooking dinner and talking on the phone. It comes naturally.

"I'm a focused kind of guy," he said. "I do one thing at a time."

"Good," I said. "Do one thing. Dance."

He was reluctant but, with the wedding approaching in a matter of months, he agreed to go.

Our instructor taught us the basic steps but warned that if we didn't practice, we would forget them by the next class. We knew she was right because by the time we got home that first night we were already struggling to remember everything she showed us.

But where to practice? Our house didn't have an appropriate dance floor. The den was too small, the living room too crowded. We decided to practice in the kitchen. We moved the table and chairs to one side. The room really wasn't big enough for an elegant foxtrot, and it would put a crimp in an enthusiastic swing, but it would do.

It was difficult at first. Our instructor told us that the male and female each have specific parts: he leads, she does the flourishes. Yet between my jittery energy and his resistance, our individual styles, limited as they were, frequently clashed. I would resort to leading when I thought my husband wasn't assertive enough, which irritated us both. With practice, though, we began to sense each other's strengths and respond to each other's timing. Our posture became more confident. We stopped staring at our feet, willing them to go where they were supposed to instead of being surprised by where they ended up.

We noticed that our dancing improved the more we practiced, so we practiced more. We noticed something else, as well. Things seemed to be changing between us—in a good way. We were rediscovering each other. As we accepted our differing approaches to dance, we began to be less critical in other areas. If dinner was a little late, Benny Goodman helped us while away the time. When we held hands as we got ready to dance, the anticipation of our dating days returned. We laughed a lot more when we danced, no longer upset by our mistakes. We started with our instructor's steps and then began making up our own. We were having fun!

We danced at our son's wedding and to our mutual surprise we keep on dancing. Sometimes it is at a party, often just in our kitchen. I can tell when my husband wants to take a swing around the kitchen floor. His eyes light up. I love the grin on his face when we finish a pattern and come out on the right step. I am even more delighted at our laughter when we don't.

Dancing has drawn us closer, renewed our intimacy. There is a lot more hugging, more innuendo, more delight. Maybe it's just our endorphins running wild. Dancing is, after all, an aerobic exercise that releases those wonderful chemicals of euphoria.

The wedding was the excuse to dance but the result was more than a physical exercise. It helped us remember the excitement of who we are together. And as we continue dancing in the kitchen, wrapped in each other's arms and looking into our happy faces, we rekindle our love.

~Ferida Wolff

Chapter
6

True Love

Keeping the Love Alive

*A successful marriage requires falling in love many times,
always with the same person.*

~Germaine Greer

Destiny in the Desert

Everyone says you only fall in love once but that's not true,
every time I hear your voice I fall in love all over again.
~Author Unknown

"We never do anything fun together anymore," I bellyached to my devoted and doting husband Ilan. So Ilan started bombarding me with e-mails and flyers offering "weekend getaways" and other exotic and not-so-exotic "events" all over the country and abroad. "Romantic log cabin with Jacuzzi," screamed one flyer. "Visit Costa Rica," enticed another. But when I noticed a small advertisement for a "midnight walk in the desert," not far from the Dead Sea, I knew I had stumbled on just the right activity which would combine Ilan's affinity for the rugged outdoors with my romantic nature. We bought the tickets online and marked the date in our calendars.

We live in Israel, about 150 miles from the Dead Sea. Because of the narrow, winding, poorly-lit roads as you move farther away from the center of the country, this adds up to a three-hour car ride. Each way. With three young daughters at home, taking a "midnight walk" in the desert required much more logistical planning than a simple stroll in the park.

After dropping our daughters off at the homes of various friends and relatives for the night, we headed south for our rendezvous. We briefly considered detouring into Tel Aviv for a romantic candlelight dinner (which Ilan assured me would be cheaper than paying for the gas we were about to burn), but since we had already purchased our "midnight walk" tickets, we felt that our destiny was sealed in the desert.

We spent the drive listening to music, catching up on the week and enjoying the fact that there was no bickering coming from the backseat to distract us. When we finally arrived at the winding snake path that was meant to guide us to our midnight walk's starting point, we hit a traffic jam resembling that of rush hour in the city. We managed to piece together from other drivers that a semi-trailer had jackknifed somewhere down the road and was blocking the path. I wondered to myself if the semi-trailer driver's wife had also complained that they never did anything fun together anymore and if this was her just reward.

Ilan, who never leaves home without his "coffee kit" (essentially a tool box filled with a small gas burner, six glasses, coffee, tea, sugar and non-perishable milk) decided to make us hot drinks—in the car—while we were waiting. Spicy cinnamon tea never tasted so good. Still, we grew impatient after sitting in the exact same spot for forty-five minutes along with groups of other would-be midnight walkers who were congregating near their cars. So we decided to change the course of our destiny. Ilan knew of a lovely public beach (called, incidentally, Public Beach) where, because we had the forethought to throw our bathing suits in the car "just in case," we could take a swim. The changing rooms were locked so we boldly swapped our hiking clothes for bathing suits right there on the beach! With the moonlight as our guide, we stepped into a warm, comforting, Dead Sea bath. Our midnight walk had turned into a midnight swim.

Holding on to each other as we gently floated in the saltwater under the moonlit sky, we talked about philosophy, astronomy, history, the secrets of a good marriage and changing destinies. We talked about how to get our money back for those unused tickets for a midnight walk in the desert.

And then, at just about midnight, we reluctantly got out of the water, showered ourselves off on the beach, changed clothes, and started the long drive back to the city. Without any effort or preparation, we had spent one of the most pleasant evenings we'd had in a long time. And I realized that my destiny wasn't waiting for me in the desert after all; he's been right beside me for the past twenty years.

~Gayle Danis Rinot

"We never do anything exciting anymore... but at least we aren't doing it together!"

51

The Runner

I'd like to run away from you,
But if you didn't come and find me...
I would die.
~Shirley Bassey

I'm a runner. I'm not a runner in the traditional sense. I run from love. It scares the crap out of me, and I don't know why. There's something about feeling that good which instills fear in me like nothing else. It's impossible to feel that good without knowing you're going to end up getting hurt. It's the way it's always been for me.

It's anyone's guess how I became a runner. Maybe not having a father figure around the house when I grew up had something to do with it. It's possibly nothing more than a simple phobia, induced by something completely untraceable. It could be nothing more than a small part of a much bigger mental illness, which I too would acknowledge, then attempt to do nothing about. Acceptance has never been a problem with me. But taking action, well, that's a whole different story. All this aside, I have this problem—I'm a runner.

We've all been taught to embrace our fears, as do I. I've even been known to search for love, sometimes to even run after it, but the results have always been the same. Find someone, begin a relationship, let love blossom, and when things start getting good, run like a river after spring rains. As I said before, I'm a runner.

Strangely, one of my biggest hopes in life is to settle down with that one special someone. The person who makes you feel like you're home, just because you're with them. The person who can make your heart melt with a simple look. The person who understands I'm a runner, and she waits patiently for me to get tired, and turn to face what she's already faced—that love only gets better with time.

And with the right person, love can blossom into something beyond our wildest dreams.

True love, when allowed to take its course, is grander than the grandest of fairy tales. It is the essence of life, and all which encompasses our existence as humans. Everything else is just life's complements.

Runners never get the opportunity to experience this secure faith in love. It's the initial Wow, and then it's off to the races. There is help for runners, but you would have to want help, more than you want love, because you can't experience one without eliminating the other.

Something happened a few years ago to change my life forever. I met her. The one. The love of my life. For awhile, at least. I mean, I do have some run still left in me.

She seems to recognize this, and from time to time she gives me space. No leash. No restrictions. When I come back around, she takes me in, feeds me, and gives me a heart to lean on. She forgives, but she doesn't forget. For this, I'm grateful. I need the reminder, although she could be a bit more subtle sometimes. Then again, when I step back and look through her eyes, which is easy to do when you're in love, I see the pain I cause her.

This is enough to make me want to run away forever, because the last thing I want to do is cause someone else pain. Especially someone I love as much as I love her. But if I did run away from her with intent not to return, and I tried once, then we both lose.

You see, I learned something about running away from true love. You can't. It follows you wherever you go. True love is inside you. It is a part of you, and it consumes you. It's supposed to. It is, after all, the essence of life.

In a nutshell, true love makes hope look like a distant cousin.

When it comes to things which drive us, and hope, for many, is the grandest of things, love is still the grand master.

As the years have passed, I now run less and less. When I run, I never stray too far from home, because deep down, I know I love her too. She's special. She understands my mental illness like none before. She accepts me as I am, to a point. I'd be disappointed if she didn't want to change me a little. I do have flaws which could use some mending.

Today, we share a unity of life's spirit. I've never felt this before. Hell, I never would have even said anything like that before, but she brings this out in me. Love can be so many things, but in the end, it's what you allow it to be—not what you make it.

I now live to make her happy, as she has done so many times for me. The past is the past, and the future will surely bring many surprises. But for today, I'm happy to be where I'm at in life. I still hope for many things, but none of those hopes compare to the love I feel for this woman.

She fills my heart with joy. She gives me new hope. There's no place to run when you've found where you were going, and that's a good thing. Because, for the record, I'm tired of running.

~Jay Rylant

"In the race of life... true love is the finish line!"

He's a Keeper

Even for two people who are very much in love, learning to live together is
full of challenges. How comforting is it to discover that the conflicts we face
are not unique to our own relationship!
~Marilyn McCoo

The cleaning service had barely backed out of the driveway, our pine floors still damp from the Murphy Oil Soap. Yet, the bathroom mirror displayed smudges along the beveled right edge. Only one other person shared my home with me—my handsome husband of just two months.

"Rob, I want you to come here right now. I have something to show you."

When I was thirty-four, this seemingly perfect man danced into my life. As a health care administrator, I was expected to attend the semi-annual management gatherings at the luxurious Peabody Hotel. That spring night, my suitable escort sat glued to his chair as I stood on the edge of the dance floor, tapping time with open-toed silver slippers. Rob, another manager, motioned me to the dance area and showed me how to rock. Instantly the party livened up as I submitted to the rhythm of the blues, twirling in my handkerchief-hem periwinkle party dress. The night passed quickly as Rob and I danced every number until the band packed up.

"That was fun, thanks," I told Rob, gasping for cool air and appropriate words.

"See you back at the old salt mines," he responded and waved goodbye.

My group of friends and courtesy date waited patiently for me at the hotel exit. No one asked any questions and I offered no explanations. No doubt this had been the best work party ever. I told myself that I might have danced with "the one" that night.

Within a few days, Rob invited me on our official first date—another dance. After almost two years of courtship, I married my own Fred Astaire.

I knew that marriage was not easy, so I had delayed this commitment until my thirties. Friends endearingly chided me, saying "You are too stuck in your ways to marry." As the only daughter in our family, I had grown up with my own room, my own clothes, my own phone, and later my own car, my own apartment, my own everything.

Now married, I had to share everything. The simplest daily happenings that broke with my personal routines caused me frustration at home. However, Rob patiently embraced my idiosyncrasies with gentleness and compassion. He mostly accepted whatever came his way with an easygoing personality. Repeatedly he calmed any stress I created in our new home.

Rob understood that he had married a woman who had been single her entire life. For me, everything stayed in its assigned place, planned for my convenience. Rooms went untouched and my few dishes remained clean and put away in the kitchen cabinet. The cleaning service arrived monthly to deep clean my home, though it was never really dirty.

Now, there were two of us. Admittedly Rob was neat but less obsessed with order. How could marriage change my environment so quickly? Why did I find socks under the sofa and used dishes in the sink? Before marriage, my mirrors stayed clear and shiny. Now I found smudges on the bathroom mirror, only minutes after the cleaning service performed its magic.

"Honey, I have something to show you," I repeated. Rob released the TV changer and ambled into the bathroom. I pushed my chin forward, planting my feet firmly before the bathroom sink.

"Yes?"

"Do you see this mirror?"

"Yes."

"Do you see the fingerprints all over this clean mirror?" Rob came closer to inspect the mirror from several angles.

"Yes."

"Do you know whose fingerprints those are?" Again he leaned over to peer at the smudges.

"Yes."

"Well, whose fingerprints are all over this clean mirror?" I demanded. He paused and looked straight into my soul.

"Honey, those are the fingerprints of the man who loves you."

I stood speechless for a few seconds. All resentment melted as I gazed into his kind brown eyes. This was the man who had chosen to marry a fussy old maid, a spinster, who had trouble coupling. He was the man who loved me.

Rob reached for a towel to clean the mirror, but my hand stopped him. "And what beautiful fingerprints they are," I responded. "I just love those fingerprints—and the man who made them."

Yes, being married meant I had to share; and yes, there would be more to clean. The house would not stay systematized, nor would Rob use my organizing key rack at the back door. But this man loved and accepted me just like I was. Now I had his unique fingerprints on my mirror, a testimony to the fact that I had married "the one" and would not be alone any more. Everyone was right: marriage meant trade-offs, but for me, Rob was a keeper.

~Marylane Wade Koch

"We're a perfect match...
Once you eliminate all
our imperfections!"

Reprinted by permission of
Stephanie Piro © 2008

Little Things Matter

You cannot plough a field by turning it over in your mind.
~Author Unknown

Last year my husband, Bob, and I stopped celebrating many special occasions, including Valentine's Day. We were busy and neither of us felt like going out just to buy cards and chocolate. Usually, I decorate the house with special candles and heart-shaped ornaments that I've had for over twenty years. But I didn't bother. So the day came and went with nothing more than a "Happy Valentine's Day" peck on the cheek.

During a plain omelet supper, I looked over at Bob and said, "I feel badly we didn't do anything special." He did too. It seemed like we were two people who'd been married for many years, and these little things just didn't matter anymore.

But they do.

After supper, we snuggled together, recalling wonderful memories of how we met.

Over thirty years ago, I taught a class called "Life After Divorce." Bob, a handsome blond blue-eyed man, who looks no different to me today, was a student.

Back then, I was crazy-in-love with a fellow I'll call Michael. But I was always unlucky in the love department. That was because I picked guys who were commitment-phobic. I believed I could change them. Finally, I realized I was the one who needed to change.

Michael was "perfect"—funny, handsome, and smart. The problem was that he wasn't in love with me.

The more Michael would get close, then back off, the harder I'd try to win him over. But I failed. With each "failure" I felt more undesirable, which eroded my self-esteem.

While dating Michael, I started hanging out with Bob. But we were just buddies. We had a blast—biking, swimming, hiking. I never worried about what I said or if my apartment was messy. With Michael, I'd berate myself for everything I thought I'd said wrong. I'd usually run words through my "Is this clever and smart?" filter before saying them.

There was no filter with Bob. I never felt self-conscious. We confided our inner secrets and spent most times in joyous laughter. If I dripped mustard on my chin from my hot dog, I didn't care. Had that happened with Michael, I'd have been mortified.

It was such a shame that I wasn't crazy-in-love with Bob.

I can recall a pivotal moment as vividly as an earthquake. I was home, waiting for Bob. I was wearing my baggy shorts and gray T-shirt. It was the only outfit I had put on, which was such a contrast to trying on outfit after outfit before seeing Michael.

Then it hit me. I had a smack-bang revelation. I said out loud, "What are you doing?" It was at this most crucial instant, like Dorothy with her slippers, that I realized that what I had been looking for had been there all along. Someone who loved me as I was, make-up or not, clever repartée or not. In other words, I had found my best friend.

I can still picture looking up at him and taking the first step. I kissed him… and you can probably take it from there.

It was thrilling to change my never-going-anywhere dating path and wise up to what's really important. To me, true love means being each others' best friends.

And now, after so many years of marriage, we still are.

But last month we learned that relationships can't lie still. They need to be nurtured.

After Valentine's Day, I put out our St. Patrick's Day ornaments and candles. Bob came home with a three-dollar heart-shaped cake from the "day old" bin. As he presented it to me, his eyes were brimming with happy tears. He said, "Every day is Valentine's Day with you." I looked up and kissed him… and you can probably take it from there.

And so we vowed we'll never be too busy to make trips for just a card. Little things do matter.

~Saralee Perel

Connecting

The difference between try and triumph is a little umph.
~Author Unknown

Ray and I glide around the ballroom floor to the strains of "The Tennessee Waltz." Ray is handsome in a black silk shirt open at the throat and khaki slacks. He smells of a musky aftershave, and his lead is gentle as he lifts his arm to turn me under. I look into his hazel eyes and my heart skips two beats.

I haven't felt this way in a while. Just this morning I was grousing to Annie, my Golden Retriever, that a second marriage isn't what it's cracked up to be. Too many complications with joint and personal accounts, blended families, and difficult exes. Plus, after ten years of marriage, we seem to be falling into patterns that are more comfortable than romantic.

Ray turns me under his arm again, and once more we lock eyes. My spine actually tingles, sparking memories of younger days and first kisses. As we move with the rhythm of the band, I feel the swell of Ray's bicep under my left hand, and sense the warmth of his body when he pulls me close for a pivot turn.

Driving home, we talk about what a great time we've had. We agree that the eye contact was the thing, even more than dancing, that made us feel truly connected. We vow to look lovingly at each other more often.

How hard can it be?

The next morning, I set the stage. I float two lush, red

rhododendron blooms in a bowl and set it in the middle of the table, then turn on soft jazz. We make a veggie scramble and settle across from each other.

"Nice," Ray says, but he doesn't even glance my way. He reaches for the morning paper just to the left of the flowers.

"Eye contact?"

"Right." He pushes the paper away and looks at me, smiling his fabulous, crooked smile that still stirs me after a decade together. I return the smile and blow him a kiss.

Then we pick up our forks and dig in. The scramble is delicious. I've downed a third of mine when I remember to look at Ray again.

He's reading the sports section.

I sigh and take the front page.

As we rinse the breakfast dishes and load them in the dishwasher, I invite Ray to chat for a few minutes in the family room before we go to our respective home offices. Surely we'll fix our gaze on each other as we talk.

Ray dries the frying pan, puts it away, and settles into an over-stuffed chair, no newspaper in sight.

I head for the couch across from him, thinking I'll tell him how nice the front yard looks since he deadheaded the last of the daffodils and cleared out last year's growth from the ferns. I've taken three steps when Naomi, our little black kitty, crosses my path. With a gravelly meow she reminds me that I've forgotten to give her breakfast. I return to the kitchen and fill her bowl with kibbles. While I'm at it, I fill our dog Annie's bowl with her kibbles, and add a vitamin, a glucosamine chew, and two tiny spoonfuls of a Chinese herb for her arthritis.

As I pass the phone table on my way to the couch, I notice the button on the answering machine blinking red. It will take just a minute to check messages. One is for Ray. I turn to hand him the phone.

He's not there.

A wave of guilt washes over me. I blew it. Did he leave while I fed our pets, or while I picked up the messages? He's probably in his office now, paying bills. I might as well go work on a story.

I'm at my computer, fingers flying, when Ray wanders in. "Sorry I didn't wait," he says sheepishly. "Do you want to talk now?"

"It was my fault. Rain check?" I want that intimate chat, but right this minute I have an idea flooding the page. I know from experience that if I take a break I'll lose it.

And so the day goes. We both down hastily-made sandwiches in our offices. Mid-afternoon we shift gears and go out to the garden, working side by side, weeding and pruning.

When it's time to tie up a bundle of branches spread across a wheelbarrow, I see an opportunity for a romantic interlude.

I gather the branches in my arms and he pulls the twine taut. We're facing each other and I catch his eye. He winks. An electric spark jolts me.

"Hi," I say, considering the idea of abandoning the garden for a more intimate setting.

But Ray turns back to his job, tying a careful knot. I don't even get a sweaty hug.

Maybe if we'd held each other's gaze while we counted to ten.

"Missed my chance in the garden, didn't I?" Ray asks as he seasons chicken breasts to grill and I wash spinach leaves for a salad. "Want to watch a movie after dinner?" At least he's been thinking about all our misses. Watching a movie is sitting side by side, like gardening, except for that moment tying the branches. Still, we'll be together.

"I need ten minutes," I say when we've eaten and cleaned up. "Got a quick read for someone in my critique group."

I disappear into my office and work furiously. One e-mail leads to another. I don't know how long Ray has been standing at my desk when I realize he's there. I check my watch. How can an hour fly by so fast?

"Morgan Freeman, Hillary Swank. That movie you've been telling me about." He shrugs his shoulders. "Never mind. We can watch it another time."

Finishing my work as fast as I can, I go in search of Ray. I find him in the bedroom propped against a mound of pillows reading *A. Lincoln: A Biography*. His evening ritual just before he turns out the light. I've botched it yet again. And I wish Ray had tried harder too. Who would expect connecting to take so much conscious effort?

In the bathroom, I lift my leg to the counter to stretch my hamstring, thinking maybe we'll try again tomorrow. Or next week. Or next year. As I turn on my electric toothbrush, I feel Ray's arms reach around my waist.

There he is, in the mirror.

In the mirror, we lock eyes.

He turns me to face him and I melt into his arms. Yes, this marriage is on a better track.

~Samantha Ducloux Waltz

Sleepless Nights

Hearing is one of the body's five senses, but listening is an art.
~Frank Tyger

No question, when I look back on life with eyes tempered by advancing age and growing wisdom, I readily admit I got married too young. I was barely seventeen when that handsome young fellow (a man nine years my senior) walked into my life.

We met on a warm summer's eve. Our meeting was probably more of an observation event than it was an actual meeting. He and a friend were sitting at a drive-in café laughing at me and my friends trying to ditch a carload of guys we had no interest in meeting. A couple of days later, I met that laughing college boy and by summer's end, the smallest seed of a romance had begun to sprout. But then he returned to his university studies 500 miles away, and I returned to high school.

Time passed. We wrote letters back and forth. He finished up at the university and found a job while I trekked off in the opposite direction to business college in another state. On occasion, we arranged to meet up for a day or two but marriage never seriously entered into our conversations until nearly three years had passed. By then, we had to admit we were in love and perhaps were old enough to settle down. Oh, how little we knew!

I had barely turned twenty and he was twenty-nine when we married. We settled down in a small apartment hours away from either of our families. Perhaps that was a good thing since we had only each other to turn to during the tough times. Being young and in love made us oblivious to the practical things in life—such as living within our means. If social activities were happening around town, that's where we had to be, no matter the cost. Then came baby number one followed by baby number two. That's when the real struggling from paycheck to paycheck began. On top of the money stress, my fastidious nature kept me picking up behind him and the kids, doing laundry in the bathroom sink, wrestling with two busy toddlers, and cooking meals made from meager selections of groceries, while he, tired after a long day's work, simply flopped down in a chair and read the newspaper. Tired and irritated, I took to pouting over the smallest infractions, but he didn't notice—or pretended not to notice, I'm not sure which. A distinct chill factor settled over our apartment.

We decided to fix a bad situation. The solution seemed simple enough. We vowed to never again go to sleep angry at one another. If something bothered us, we would talk it out before going to sleep.

Sounds easy, right? Wrong! Here's why. When a bone-tired person is ready to slip into bed, the last thing that person wants is to get caught up in is a midnight heart-to-heart airing of grievances. Here's how it plays out. First come the tears, then the indignant denials, then more tears, followed by apologies and concessions. Finally, somewhere near dawn, comes remorse and forgiveness followed by the good stuff—cuddling together until sleep comes at 0-dark-thirty in the morning. Exhaustion has a way of making seemingly-huge disagreements seem trivial.

Truth is… the decision to never again go to sleep angry was a good one. We spent a lot of sleepless nights but we never again woke up angry at each other.

This year, we celebrate our forty-seventh year together and still agree that little resolution probably saved our marriage a dozen times over. Back then, it planted itself into our lives as a type of Golden Rule and remains there to this day. By choosing harmony, we allowed a new and deeper type of love to grow. We've seen other love stories fade and slip away because of hurt feelings and unresolved arguments, but we chose to protect our love, even at the cost of surrendering a good night's sleep. Or was it ten or twenty nights, or maybe more? I've lost count. But, no matter, the price was worth it then and it's still worth it today.

~Jean Davidson

56

The Value of a Good Husband

Love doesn't sit there like a stone, it has to be made, like bread;
remade all of the time, made new.
~Ursula K. LeGuin

I'm one of those old-fashioned women who love the idea of a good, strong marriage. My dream of staying home to take care of the house and put dinner on the table has finally come true. Yikes! How did I get to be such a dinosaur?

My blossoming years coincided with those of the feminist movement in the mid-1960s. I'd seen my parents' marriage end badly. So by my freshman year in college I was already part of the bra-burning crowd, telling dates not to open the car door for me and vowing to trample all men on my way up. I promised myself not to get married unless I was a total failure at any desirable career by age thirty, which seemed terrifyingly old at that time.

Unfortunately, that promise lasted about two minutes—I met a guy in college and was swept off my feet. We got engaged when I was nineteen and married two years later. We thought our common interests would enhance the pursuit of our goals. Instead, it created immense competition and jealousy between us. By the mid-1970s, in the throes of "me-ism," we expected way more than any two self-centered people were capable of giving each other. We went our separate ways.

Other guys came along who fit the stereotype of what women were fighting against: irresponsible, wishy-washy, noncommittal and over-the-top macho. They were good for fun and easy to say goodbye to. But casual intimacies left me with an empty yearning. It was like giving a piece of me away that could never be replaced.

I soon began to avoid dating altogether, concentrating on work and taking care of myself. But it eventually began to sink in that I had no one to turn off the lights with at night, or wake up to in the morning, no one with whom to share exciting news and late-night TV. Was I weak? Don't think so. Lonely? Not in a desperate way. There was just an awareness that there might be more in store for me than my ego allowed. I yearned for a touch, a steadiness, an affection that I thought didn't exist in relationships anymore.

Just when it seemed there would never be anyone for me, along came Mr. Beige.

We met at a disco on a night when my girlfriend, Ellie, was shopping for a new boyfriend. When we walked in, we immediately noticed two men in gorgeous suits sitting at the bar. Ellie was attracted to the tall one in the black suit. I thought the shorter one in the beige suit was more handsome, but looked sort of somber.

Since Ellie was too shy to approach them and I didn't care about meeting anyone, I went right up there and asked Mr. Black Suit to dance with her. Their relationship lasted two weeks. I'm still with Mr. Beige after nearly thirty years.

It turned out Mr. Beige—now known as Jerry—had accompanied Mr. Black Suit that night for much the same reason I had accompanied Ellie. But he was determined to counter the culture. He made me enjoy having doors opened. He liked getting dressed up. He was on time, dependable, financially viable, entertaining, resourceful and interested in what I was doing. My growing feelings for him made me want to reciprocate his kindnesses. Besides—he was a great disco dancer.

Both of us were gun-shy from previous marriages, so we initially went the ever-growing route of living together. Six years and one cold feet separation later, he proposed and we walked down the aisle.

Our marriage takes a lot of work, compromise, sacrifice and that new dirty word, "submission" sometimes. Do we butt heads? Sure we do. It's human nature to want our own way. Sometimes I hate the decisions he makes, other times we make them together, and yet other times it's a relief to hand off the responsibility. We've learned that true love goes deeper than seeing flowers and butterflies every time you look at someone, or making the other person ecstatically happy every day. Sometimes we disappoint each other, because nobody's perfect. But our determination to serve one another holds our relationship together during tough times.

I'm happy to mention that allowing God to play a role in our marriage has added to its longevity. It's taken both of us further toward shedding "me"—not losing our identity, but learning to be less self-absorbed and more giving. We have a commitment to be up for the challenge. You have to get brave and take risks to make love last.

~Sheryl Young

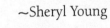

57

Breakfast and a Movie

The secret of love is seeking variety in your life together, and never letting routine chords dull the melody of your romance.
~Source Unknown

Breakfast and a movie. How in the world did it come to this?

It seems that every other issue of every women's magazine on the planet has an article about saving your marriage. And the number one piece of advice in these articles is to make time for you as a couple. But if you have young children, you know as well as I do that "couple time" is pretty much an imaginary concept.

Life wasn't always like this, of course. Back in our childless days, my wife and I would frequently go out. One of our favorite activities was dinner and a movie.

Then baby arrives and things change. No one's got the energy to go out at night. If baby is sleeping, that's a good time for both of you to also catch a few zzz's.

But thanks to all those magazine articles, we worried about our relationship. If there was no "us time," surely our marriage was at risk.

So we occasionally summoned up the courage to have a night out. We'd call up a babysitter and take a stab at that old standby, dinner and a movie.

Big mistake. If we weren't nodding off during dinner, we definitely had a hard time staying awake through the movie. And even if we did manage to remain conscious, the only topic of conversation during our precious couple time was our infant daughter, Sarah, who was at home doing exactly what we should have been doing: sleeping.

We soon realized that dinner and a movie was no longer for us. All it meant was the outlay of extra money for a babysitter, the loss of a good night's sleep, and a disrupted routine.

But we didn't want to give up on this concept of couple time. After all, lots of magazine writers (probably single and childless) were urging us on and we didn't want to disappoint them.

So we came up with a new approach: something we called movie and a dinner. We hired a babysitter for the afternoon and early evening and headed out to a matinee performance followed by the early bird special at a local eatery. This option worked surprisingly well.

Not only did we get to spend time together when we were both conscious and reasonably coherent, we also never had a problem getting a babysitter. After all, we were usually home by 7 P.M., long before the sitter's own social life commenced.

But once our daughter passed the toddler stage, the movie and a dinner option didn't work so well. Sarah had weekend activities and obligations. Or she wanted to have a friend over. Or she just wanted to spend more time with Mommy and Daddy.

As a consequence, we forgot about movie and a dinner. We were too busy with family time and kids' activities. Once again, couple time became the lowest priority.

But we hadn't forgotten our magazine writer friends (probably sadistic and divorced). So we searched for a new option.

Now that Sarah was in school and life was more normal, we thought maybe the old dinner and a movie approach would work. It turns out it didn't.

Although life had returned to something approaching normalcy, it turns out that we had gotten older in the process. The thought of staying up past 10:00 no longer had any appeal.

But surely there had to be some way to find time to spend together. According to our writer friends (probably rich with two nannies), our marriage depended on it. There had to be something we could do on a regular basis. Something that would allow us that precious "us time" without costing a fortune or disrupting our sleep.

Finally, this year we hit on the ultimate couple time solution: breakfast and a movie. With Sarah in school, every so often we take a weekday to ourselves. And what do we do? You guessed it.

We go out for a nice leisurely breakfast where we can listen, communicate and, best of all from my perspective, eat. And then it's off to the local multiplex which just so happens to start showing movies at ten or eleven in the morning.

We pick out a first-run feature we'd like to see, put up our feet and enjoy two hours of uninterrupted movie viewing. Sometimes we even get the entire theater to ourselves.

After the movie is over, we have a whole array of options. We can go out for lunch, go to a coffee shop or browse in a bookstore. We can do a bit of shopping, watch another movie or, my personal favorite, go home and have a nap.

I think this is an option with legs. So long as Sarah is in school, we can continue to do breakfast and a movie. The only potential problem I see is that everyone reading this piece is going to start doing the same thing and the breakfast restaurants will be crowded and the morning shows at the cinemas will be sold out. Oh well, if that happens, there's always takeout breakfast and a rental movie.

~David Martin

Date Night

Reflect upon your current blessings.
~Charles Dickens

"Bye guys," I say, kissing my two girls in the church hallway before heading outside to the car. "Have fun."

It's Wednesday evening—church choir night for my daughters. I have two hours until pick-up time, and like a teenager, I am giddy with anticipation.

"Where do you want to meet?" my husband asked at breakfast. "It's Wednesday, you know."

As I drive to the neighborhood café, I find myself singing along to the radio. Free from my usual dinner-making routine, (thanks to a church choir program that serves my children nuggets and noodles, along with a hefty dose of praise and song) I am carefree. I park the car, then rummage through my purse for some lip gloss. Glancing in the visor mirror, I fluff my hair, tucking a pesky white strand under my (mostly) brown locks. It's silly, I know: primping and fussing for a dinner date with my husband of thirteen years. But, as I walk in the restaurant, I know it's worth it.

"You look nice," my beloved smiles, handing me a dinner menu.

For the next hour, we feast on pizza and salad, swapping family and work stories between bites of pepperoni and cheese. My usual calorie-conscious self, lost to the revelry of the day, eyes a glass case full of cheesecakes and brownies.

"Want to get dessert?" I surprise myself by suggesting such decadence.

My turtle cheesecake, a tower of chocolate and caramel topped with pecans, is sweet and indulgent—just like this evening.

"Can I taste a little of that?" I say, poking my fork deep into my husband's peanut butter pie.

After dinner, we linger over cups of hazelnut coffee. I am full—of good food, companionship, and the comfort in knowing that my spouse is still my very best friend.

I glance at my watch. "We still have a half hour," I say, hopeful to go for a walk or do some window shopping.

Holding hands, we cross the street and enter the public library. I head straight to my favorite section—nonfiction, and give thanks for time to peruse the newest releases without being pulled into the children's room. My husband flops into an armchair and relaxes with a newspaper.

Thirty minutes pass in a flash.

"It's time to go," I reluctantly announce, peering over the top of my spouse's paper. In my arms I hold a stack of books—souvenirs reminding me to return again next week.

"I can pick up the girls if you want," my husband says. "You take your time. We'll meet you at home."

I sigh a bit, sorry to see the evening come to a close. At home, it will be the usual routine: baths and bedtimes, stories to read and lunches to pack. I love motherhood, but I relish this respite.

Despite conflicts and commitments, (I do, after all, have to take a turn as parent helper at children's choir) I will do my best to continue dating my spouse. Although my girls are jealous when they hear tales of cheesecakes and pizzas, deep down I know they benefit. Secure in the knowledge that Mom and Dad love each other, they are free to grow up in confidence, surrounded by the very real possibility that romance can last forever.

Although marriage may be made in heaven, I think its maintenance must be done here on Earth.

Thank goodness for Wednesday choir night: an opportunity to fine-tune the most sacred of bonds.

~Stefanie Wass

Everyday Romance

*Marriage is a book of which the first chapter is written in poetry
and the remaining chapters in prose.*
~Beverly Nichols

"What's the most romantic thing your spouse has ever done?" the MC asked the three couples. My husband Scott and I were attending a wedding for one of our friends where a family rendition of *The Newlywed Game* was taking place.

"I don't know how I would answer that," Scott leaned over and whispered.

"Oh, you're plenty romantic," I whispered back and then promptly forgot about the incident as dinner was served and we talked and laughed with the other guests at the table.

A few days later I noticed that Scott seemed somewhat subdued.

"What are you thinking about?" I asked.

"It still bothers me that I can't think of anything romantic that I have done for you," he replied.

I reminded Scott of several occasions that were romantic, but he didn't feel any better.

As I got into bed that night I began to reflect, "What is romance anyway?" Most people think of weekend getaways or vacations to exotic places. Candlelight dinners and flowers for special occasions might top the list. But those moments, as wonderful as they are, are few and far between the things that take place every day. I thought back to our life together. Maybe true romance is more in the daily happenings of life than in the occasional moments.

Maybe romance is in the way Scott says "Hi Gorgeous" when he greets me, even though after three children, and more than twenty-five years of marriage, I hardly recognize the young bride in our wedding album. Maybe romance is in the daily walks where we talk about the trivial and momentous parts of our day and of our life together. Maybe it's the way we still hold hands and show our displays of affection, ignoring our teenage daughters' cries of "Get a room!"

Maybe romance is the way Scott encouraged me to be a teacher when I shared with him my dreams of teaching children with special needs. We had very little money at the time. And even though it meant Scott had to squeeze childcare duties into an already tight ministry schedule, Scott never complained. In fact, he was my biggest cheerleader.

And he did it all over again when I said I wanted to go back to school for my Master's degree. I thought of how I never tire of spending time with Scott, how even a trip to the grocery store is somehow special, simply because I'm spending time with this man I love so much.

"Maybe," I said to Scott the next evening as we sat down to dinner as a family, "Romance isn't as much about the occasional candlelight dinner or a romantic weekend getaway, as it is about the hundreds of ways you show me you love me every single day."

With that said, I reached over and gave him a big hug and kiss and grinned as a familiar chorus of "Get a room!" reverberated throughout the kitchen.

~Deb Stanley

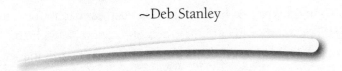

Isn't It Romantic

The essence of pleasure is spontaneity.
~Germaine Greer

"Want to meet me for lunch on the 20th?" Tom asked.

Something about that date bothered me. I glanced at the calendar and dropped the phone. I quickly picked it up; the call was too expensive to waste minutes. I put the receiver to my ear and managed to get out, "Huh?"

"I said meet me for lunch on the 20th."

"But… but that's the day you are returning from Japan!"

"I know," he laughed. "Get a sitter for the weekend and meet me for lunch in San Francisco. I've already booked your flight."

Now I held the phone in a death grip. A romantic weekend away! In California! He didn't have to ask again. Our first vacation alone without the boys in five years.

After we hung up, I felt like I was walking on clouds. He'd been gone for almost two weeks, and I'd been feeling lonely and overburdened. The house was in total disarray, the kitchen without a floor, the refrigerator in the living room, and the powder room toilet in the foyer. I'd been so upset when he had to take this business trip in the middle of renovations, it just added to the stress of married life with children and responsibilities. But now we were meeting in San Francisco for an entire weekend, just the two of us, with no kids, no household disasters to fix, no worries at all except maybe where to eat dinner.

Then I heard the school bus pull up in front of the house and I realized that I was going to have to do one of the world's biggest juggling acts. I spent hours that night on the phone calling everyone several times until all the schedules lined up. My younger son, who was still in preschool, was going over my girlfriend's house for Thursday and Friday nights. My older son, who was in elementary school, needed to spend Thursday night with my parents who lived two blocks away so he could catch the school bus. Friday afternoon my sister was going to pick him up after school and keep him Friday and Saturday nights. In the meantime, my parents were meeting my friend at the mall to pick up my younger son Saturday afternoon. Then both boys were to get home Sunday to spend the rest of the day with a babysitter. I was exhausted just making those plans and then I realized it was Tuesday and I was leaving in two days. I rushed around buying some new clothes and getting one of the worst haircuts I'd ever had.

Friday morning, I got up at 5:00 A.M. and drove to the airport for a 7:30 flight to independence, freedom and, of course, romance. I never got to fly by myself and I was nervous and a little scared, but when I arrived in California, my heart started racing and I was so excited about seeing my husband that I bought him a bouquet of flowers from an airport vendor.

I only had to wait twenty minutes and then we were together hugging and kissing and after ten days apart, it felt so good to be back in his arms. We never got that lunch I'd flown out there for. Instead, we went to our hotel on the Wharf, watched the seals barking and sunning from our balcony and relaxed for a few hours. Tom must have been so happy to see me that he didn't even mention my haircut for hours. We were both exhausted, me from rushing everywhere making sure the kids had everything they needed, and Tom from traveling halfway across the world.

But we didn't give in to our tiredness because we only had a weekend to enjoy San Francisco. We did all the tourist things—a tour of the city, a stroll in the Japanese Garden, walking up and down those famous steep streets, dinners at Fisherman's Wharf, a boat tour of the bay and Golden Gate Bridge and shopping for souvenirs for the kids.

It was wonderful, rejuvenating, and romantic. That is until we got to the airport. Tom's ticket was first class, and alas, mine wasn't. We had hoped to upgrade my ticket, a prospect I was looking forward to, but the flight was overbooked. The best we could do was move my seat all the way up front, right behind the first class section.

I blinked back tears. I didn't want Tom to see how disappointed I was. What a way to end our weekend getaway, in separate sections of the plane.

After everyone boarded, Tom approached the man sitting next to me and asked, "Would you mind trading seats with me so I can sit with my wife?"

The guy looked at the first class seat Tom had just abandoned and agreed in a heartbeat. Only a fool would have said no!

The flight attendants couldn't believe it. Tom had traded down so he could sit with me. They kept coming up to us and saying, "I can't believe you gave up first class to be with your wife. It's just so romantic!"

In fact, they thought it was so great they catered to us the entire flight. They gave us the movie headsets for free, gave us each a glass of wine, and even served us the first class dessert.

Before the plane landed, the three flight attendants, a man and two women, came up to us and asked us how long we'd been married. I said twelve years. After we landed they stood together and handed me two pink carnations and Tom a bottle of champagne. "Wow, even after twelve years," one of them sighed. "This is because you are a really romantic couple," they gushed.

On the drive home from the airport I held my flowers, smiled and said, "Those flight attendants didn't understand how right they really are. I know you sat with me because I am your wife. After all, you have to live with me for the rest of your life."

Tom laughed and didn't deny it, but I know he really sat with me because he wanted us to be together. Whatever the reason, it was a romantic weekend and a flight that I still remember fondly even after another twelve years together.

~Dina A. Leacock

61

Three Little Words

To the world you might be one person,
but to one person you might be the world.
~Author Unknown

It was on an ordinary wintry evening after many years of marriage that I realized how much I meant to my husband. On that particular evening he said three little words that sent me into a euphoric spin and made my heart swell with the beat-skipping, pitter-pat feeling usually reserved for puppy love or a new romance.

Oh, he told me often that he loved me, never forgot our wedding anniversary or my birthday, and was a considerate mate in every way. We had settled comfortably into an uneventful, unexciting, drama-free existence, which was fine with me.

He had worked late, as he often did, and his dinner waited for him in the oven as our three boys, who had been fed and bathed, were sprawled in their usual places between the fireplace and the television set with our two dogs and two cats.

I was in the basement, transferring clothes from washer to dryer, when I heard the front door open and close. When I was almost to the top of the stairs, he hung up his raincoat, and surveyed the wall-to-wall array of little boys and pets before him. Then I heard him say three little words, "Where is everybody?"

~Jackie Fleming

Chapter 7

True Love

Lessons in True Love

Remember, there are no mistakes, only lessons.
Love yourself, trust your choices, and everything is possible.

~Cherie Carter-Scott

62

Dancing Lessons

Dance is the hidden language of the soul.
~Martha Graham

I learned about true love when I was very little. Every night after I was tucked into bed and kissed goodnight by my mom I knew that something magical would happen very soon. I found it easy to believe in true love when I witnessed it night after night with my very own eyes.

The sound of my mom in the shower would always awaken me shortly after I drifted off to sleep. Through the thin walls of our home, I could hear the shower running. I would hear the water turn off, and after a few minutes I would hear the hairdryer come on. The smell of my mother's perfumed face powder would come through the walls, filling my room with its scent. I could picture my mom putting her make-up on in the mirror: putting on eye shadow, lining her eyes to perfection, curling and darkening her lashes. Not that my mom needed all that—she was a natural beauty who became movie-star beautiful every night after we went to bed.

Just as my mother was done in the bathroom, I would hear the door open and my father would walk in. The smell of the oil on his clothes would overpower my mom's delicate perfume. He would walk in and they would meet in the hallway, repeating the same ritual every night. Out my mom would step from the bathroom, wearing a beautiful dress, hair falling softly around her face, her heels sparkling from the light cast by the living room. My father would take her hands in his and twirl her around. They'd smile at each other and then he would go into the bathroom. Once again the shower would come on, and the strong smell of the soap he used would fill our room. I could hear my mom putting a record on in the living room. The soft music would fill the air as my father finished getting ready in the bathroom.

My father would step out of the bathroom, dressed in his best slacks and a crisp shirt. Gone were the oil and grime that covered his hands, face, and clothes from a long day of working at the oil rigs. He looked so handsome and strong. Old Spice would tickle my nose as I looked on. My mom would meet him in the hallway. She would come to him and they would stand for a few moments, looking at each other. Then he would softly kiss her. My mom would always smile and laugh after the kiss, and take my father by the hand as she led him to the living room.

Once in the living room, the music would be raised a little—although not much, so as not to disturb us children. From my angle in the bedroom I could not see them as they danced, but when they neared the hallway, I could see their shadows dancing on the walls. Slowly they danced, on and on, sometimes silently, sometimes whispering and laughing. Every night I would fall asleep to this beautiful sight. I never had to wonder if true love existed. I saw it every night dancing upon our walls.

~Cynthia Bilyk

Brown and White Butterflies

True Love comes from God, and love is demonstrated through character.
~Philemon Laida

What do you do when the fire that once blazed with romance in your marriage dwindles to embers? Deep within the sweltering jungle of Costa Rica, my marriage hung by a thread. My husband and I served as missionaries in a small, isolated village on the Pacific coast. Time, responsibilities, kids, pregnancy, disappointment, and fatigue had taken their toll on our hearts and relationship.

As the host for short-term mission trips, I led the devotions for the teams that came down to help with our building project. We always tried to create an environment that would allow each person to see God in a new way.

One particular week, I decided to write a series of devotions called "Whispers of Love." Despite the ever-deepening hole in my marriage, I wanted this group to know how madly and perfectly God loved them. I led this group, which ended up being comprised of mostly men, on a journey into God's passionate pursuit of his beloved.

We talked about the love notes God sends us each and every day just as a reminder that he is deeply and totally crazy about us. So, we looked, and we listened. Some found him in the vastness of the cloudless sky. Others were blown away by the brilliance of a star-lit night. Still others were brought to their knees by the power of the surging sea. The circumstances could not have been more perfect for this study. I told them to look at the majesty of the sun as it disappears behind the sapphire sea. I encouraged them to sit on a mountain and watch the trees dance upon the melody of the wind. They were challenged to observe the intricate fabrication of a spider's delicate domain. For behind each of these wonders, someone is whispering words of undying faithfulness.

Each day, the group would expound on the majesty of nature and the unfathomable greatness of God's love. These tough men were truly being swept off their feet. I couldn't help but wonder if God had forgotten that women are the ones who like to be romanced. The time came for the God-walk, a chance for each person to go into the jungle alone with God. Almost everyone went away with grand hopes of a love letter in the form of a ferocious jaguar or a howling monkey.

I set out for my own time alone with the Creator of all this splendor and lover of my soul. I, however, didn't feel very loved. While everyone else had been swept off their feet, I felt that God was distant and unaware of my feeble existence. I prayed, "Lord, show me something big. Please, just take my breath away. I need to know that you care about me too." I sat down on a hilltop overlooking the turquoise ocean and began to wait. Nothing happened. After a few minutes, a small, brown and white butterfly floated down to a nearby piece of grass.

I have to admit that I was thoroughly disappointed. "Come on, God," I thought. "You can do better than this. I mean, this is the rainforest. Haven't you heard all the great things I've been telling these guys, and all I get is this ugly little moth? At least send something with some color." Meanwhile, this moth-like butterfly fluttered around me, pausing every so often, for what purpose I did not know. Then, suddenly, as if it was being called by someone, it lifted up and floated away. I was left with a gnawing emptiness in my heart that I had just missed something big. In my certainty that God was going to blow me away with the expression of his love, I had missed what he was trying to say.

I used this experience for another team later on to remind them that God's love letters may not come wrapped in exquisite envelopes. After this group's God-walk, one lady came running out of the jungle up to me. Breathless, she told me of her time with God, and how he had sent her a brown and white butterfly as well. Because of my story, she went over to it to take a closer look. When it paused on a branch, it stretched out its brown, boring wings. But what she saw then, I will never forget. For on those ugly brown wings lay the intricate design of two, perfectly shaped, white hearts. The message shouted to me that sometimes love doesn't show itself in the big things, but it's there even in the little, boring parts of everyday life.

I still often think about that butterfly. In my mind, it is the most beautiful of all the butterflies I saw while in Costa Rica. Even today, I think about it as a parallel to my marriage. I find myself sometimes complaining to my husband, asking him why he isn't romantic any-more. Why doesn't he sweep me off my feet like he used to? But what I find is that the deepest expression of love isn't found in long-stemmed roses, a candle-lit dinner, or elaborate surprises. It's in the strength of arms that hold me every night. It's in a hammock under-neath the stars on a fall night. It's in a midnight trip to Taco Bell to satisfy a pregnant craving. It's in a heart that stays faithful to me even when I'm not exactly pleasant to be around. These are the brown and white butterflies, the fullest expression of the deepest love.

My marriage survived the jungle. It survived because I realized that it is more than romance, even though that is certainly impor-tant. It survived because I started looking IN the little things rather than FOR the big things. And guess what? Our love was indeed rekindled!

~Melissa Harding

Snitterfield

The more you invest in a marriage, the more valuable it becomes.
~Amy Grant

In July of 1994 my husband Bill and I were enjoying a vacation in England. While driving north along the east coast we saw several road signs pointing to the nearby town of Snitterfield. We chuckled at the name and at one point I said, "Perhaps that is where I ought to send you whenever you get into a snit." To this day we use the word Snitterfield as a synonym for being in a grouchy mood.

In December of 2006, Bill had several major "snits" within a short period of time. I was feeling very uncomfortable about his frequent outbursts, which were often misdirected toward me. Early one morning I woke up crying and when Bill asked me what was wrong I told him how uneasy I was feeling, not knowing when or where he was going to have another "snit." I asked him to think seriously about what he could do to change that behavior.

Suddenly Bill bolted out of bed saying, "I'll be back shortly!" He disappeared into his study and an hour later he emerged with a freshly printed document which he posted on the refrigerator. He announced to me that he had created a Snitterfield Scorecard.

"A what?" I asked, half asleep.

Bill explained that he wanted me to help him monitor his moods by giving him some daily feedback about his behavior.

"And how can I do that?"

"Put a mark on my calendar at the end of each day. You're a teacher. You can figure out a good system."

"Are you serious?"

"Yes, very!"

So I came up with the following symbols:

+   no snits
?   a few grumbles
-   serious grouchiness
!   run for your life

For the first week of our plan, every day was marked with a +. In twenty-three years of marriage I had never known Bill to be so even-tempered and patient with himself and with me. As he gained more self-control, I relaxed more. I could hardly believe the changes we were experiencing.

Once in a while Bill would revert to his old ways. When I put a "?" on his calendar, he expressed genuine regret that he had spoiled his record and he often apologized.

At the end of January I let him know how much I appreciated the effort he was making and told him I thought we could now let go of the scorecard idea.

"Marti, you have no idea how important it is for me to look at that calendar every day. Please continue to help me make progress."

I thought to myself, "Small price to pay for such a big payoff!" And so we continued using the scorecard through February, through March, through April. We talked about changes in his temperament and about how much happier we were in our relationship and daily life together.

Once in a while I would sense that an outburst was pending. When I started singing softly, "Do you know the way to Snitterfield…?" Bill would laugh and his energy would change immediately. At the end of April I sent Bill an e-mail with "prospective tourists" as the subject:

"The mayor of Snitterfield wishes to inform all prospective tourists that the residents of Snitterfield have recently voted to change the name of their town to Summerfield. So if you are planning a trip to Snitterfield, please note that it is no longer on the map."

Bill laughed out loud when he read the e-mail. Then I told him that after four months I had decided to resign from my position as his scorekeeper since my job was no longer relevant.

And that's the end of the story. We had found a seemingly silly way to address a serious long-term problem and it worked! Now, two years later, we continue to lead an (almost!) snit-free life together, full and love and laughter.

By the way, next time we go to England we are planning to visit the real village of Snitterfield, which is, in fact, a lovely rural village of 1,400 people in the West Midlands. There is a church there dating from the thirteenth century. Snitterfield was the home of Shakespeare's father. The name Snitterfield was originally Snytenfeld which meant a "meadow for birds."

~Martha Belknap

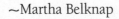

Aged to Perfection

If you live to be a hundred, I want to live to be a hundred minus one day,
so I never have to love without you.
~Winnie the Pooh

Looking through my old yearbook I came across a comment by one of my girlfriends. She wrote, "May you find your prince charming, tall, handsome and rich." We used to talk about our "perfect" loves at high school slumber parties in between painting our toes and dancing the twist. In college I added intelligence, compassion, and a sense of humor to the list of attributes that included broad shoulders, narrow waist, thick head of hair and, of course, treating me like I was the most beautiful creature walking the planet.

Now, as a member of AARP, I get magazines with updates on who is keeping it together and still glamorous at age sixty (most likely with a few nips and tucks) and I find it takes a lot longer to lose the pounds that I used to shed by just thinking about it. And what ever happened to the "perfect love" of my youthful dreams?

In the chair next to mine lies the object of my thoughts. Mouth open, he snores to his own private chorale, his abundant belly rising and falling in time with the cadence. Sigh. Where did I go wrong? I glanced at the thinning hair and lines around the eyes of the man I have been with for almost twenty years. Where did the narrow waist go and what happened to the glorious thick, golden hair and… I stop myself. "Go back to your list, Linda, and take another look." There were other attributes just under all those meaty physical ones. I went over them one by one.

1. Sense of humor: Oh yes, he is always ready to laugh at my jokes (even when he has heard them before) and especially at himself. That's where those cute little wrinkles around his blue eyes came from.

2. Compassionate: The man will cry at a sad movie, sharing tissues with me. He would give his heart to anyone in pain, especially any of our kids. Together we held our old tabby cat and sobbed when we had to put him down.

3. Intelligence: Yes, he is definitely an intelligent man. He built his own business from nothing and earned the respect of his employees and his clients. And he can fix things—saving us a considerable amount of money on minor home repairs. That man knows a thousand ways to use a wire coat hanger to create some widget to repair some thingamajig.

4. He treats me like I'm beautiful: Okay, so now I am blushing, and not a little humbled. He still tells me I look great and is not shy about telling others how beautiful or how funny he thinks I am. He rarely walks by me without touching me. He always kisses me before going out. As my waistline expands and contracts in true menopausal form, he has never once complained, especially about my mood swings. He listens and he holds me when I need to be held. And, hey, his shoulders are still broad enough for me to cry on or rest my head. He tells me he loves me.

5. He cooks: If I buy the food and plan the meal, he will cook it better than I could. He actually likes cooking and has a family recipe for homemade lasagna that makes me salivate just thinking about it. It is a two-day process. When we had a little competition over who could make the best chicken soup he won, hands down. He has this knack for combining just the right spices.

Oh my. A small lump forms in my throat. Humility is hard to swallow sometimes. My list could go on and on, with nary a slender waist or full head of hair in the lot. So what if he is barely an inch taller than me? He loves it when I wear heels that take me to a lofty 5' 10". I look over at my man again.

He wakes himself up with a particularly loud snort to find me staring at him. I must have this stupid grin on my face because he says, "Okay, what's going on? What did I do? Was it something embarrassing?" I smile at him. "You know, I was thinking." He gives me a wary look that means, "Uh oh, she's been thinking again; this can't be good."

I lean over and whisper, "How about I take you out to dinner, my treat?" His eyes narrow. "Uh, okay, but what is it going to cost me?"

Hmmm. Have I been that shallow? I lean in closer. "Nope. Let's just call it an appreciation dinner—long overdue." At that he grins hugely and says he will take a quick shower and change.

As he gets up, he brushes by me patting my backside in that sweet, absent-minded way he always does. I grab his arm. "Don't ever stop doing that." He stops and looks at me. "Stop doing what?" I feel my face turning red and it is not a hot flash. "You know, the way you always grab my, um, well, you know." He looks more closely at me smiling from ear to ear. "Why, I do believe you are blushing. Woman, you still surprise me. And, as far as that other 'you know' thing, you can count on it."

I giggle, little bubbles of laughter that make me feel almost adolescent. Yep, things are definitely as they should be. Now, where did I put that cologne he likes?

~Linda Leary

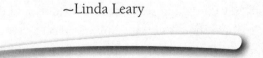

A Lesson in Commitment

Who would give a law to lovers? Love is unto itself a higher law.
~Boethius

After living more than a half century in New Jersey, opportunities for "firsts" are few and far between. But in 2007 I experienced a new "first"—I attended the civil union ceremony of a co-worker and her partner of twenty-plus years.

My colleague handed me a homemade, rainbow-colored flyer on a Thursday, inviting me to their commitment ceremony scheduled to take place the very next day. My initial thought was that my invitation must be an afterthought, so I mumbled something about having other plans and that I doubted I'd be able to make it. While driving home that evening, I realized the governor had signed a law that had taken effect just that Monday establishing civil unions for same-sex couples. I couldn't help thinking about what this new law might have meant to my co-worker and her partner, knowing that their twenty-year relationship was finally being validated. Surely they would feel relief that they could take advantage of important benefits of the new law that enabled them to provide financial security for each other and their children. And honor for a commitment that they certainly didn't need a piece of paper to affirm. Although in reality, they clearly had a right to that piece of paper.

My co-worker and her partner needed to accomplish many tasks during the seventy-two hour waiting period following their application for the license. They had to scout for an appropriate (and willing) house of worship for the ceremony, find a venue for the celebration, print the invitations, order food and a cake, decide what they would wear… I still couldn't understand the hurry. Were they afraid the law would be rescinded? Why was it so important to be among the first?

I was able to change my plans and I'm so glad I did. For all intents and purposes it was a wedding, minus a few very important legal rights. It was definitely a step in the right direction, a step toward a future without government or social interference in our right to choose a life-partner. The smiles on the couple's faces were brighter than the candle the minister lit to symbolize their union. Family and friends in attendance surrounded them with a blanket of love and acceptance. They were euphoric in their joy and pride. I chuckled when I noticed the cake during their simple post-ceremony reception. It was missing that little figurine of a bride and groom, a key element of a traditional wedding.

My feelings about marriage are conflicted, cynical at best, having been married and divorced. I suppose it's a "been there, done that" attitude, that marriage as an institution is easier to get into than out of. Since my divorce, I've met and have enjoyed a solid relationship with a wonderful man. He proposed more than nine years ago and I've given him one excuse after another as to why I don't have time to plan our wedding. It's not that I don't love him… I know I do. I couldn't have put a finger on the reason for my resistance, until I thought about my colleague's and her partner's civil union. Witnessing their non-traditional union enabled me to draw obvious comparisons to my own non-traditional relationship, so similar, yet vastly different. What's the difference? My fiancé is black and I am white. I asked myself, would I have procrastinated so long if we were both the same race? I am ashamed to admit the answer—probably not.

The Monday following the civil union ceremony, I stopped by my co-worker's office to drop off a gift that I hadn't had time to buy prior to the ceremony. I wanted to thank her for giving me the opportunity to share in her joyful event. As she expressed some of her thoughts about her relationship, I remarked that I thought she and her partner were extremely brave. I told her about the shame I felt by not having been courageous enough to marry the man I love. Prior to that conversation, she hadn't known much about my personal life, but she immediately empathized with my position. I told her that when I compared my relationship to hers, I realized I'd taken my right to marry for granted, a right that was mine simply because, unlike her, I'd fallen in love with someone of the opposite gender. Was I resisting a second marriage out of fear, because I was avoiding the public display of a relationship that doesn't match the little figurine that sits atop a traditional wedding cake? I realized that my resistance denied my fiancé and me the pleasures that were blatantly evident at their civil union ceremony.

I learned so many lessons during those two weeks. I realized that my fiancé deserves no less than my total commitment. A colleague became a dear friend. By inviting me to share in their civil union, she gave me a tremendous gift of clarity, to see what I was missing while I still have time to fix it. And I learned that if she and her partner could plan a civil union in seventy-two hours, I should be able to plan a wedding in a reasonable period of time. My new friend and her partner will be the first names on our invitation list… and, our cake, like theirs, will be minus that little figurine at the top.

~Ann M. Sheridan

67

More than Red Roses

Love is the condition in which the happiness of another person
is essential to your own.
~Robert Heinlein

How does a man show a woman he loves her? I used to think he bought her a dozen red roses and dinner at a cozy restaurant along the Willamette River. I've seriously revised my thinking.

My husband shows love, or at least a great deal of tolerance, by sharing our white-carpeted home with a large dog that gravitates toward mud puddles whenever outside, and sharing our bed with a cat that likes to hog all the covers. He gardens alone when I go to the barn to see my lovely Arabian mare.

I, in turn, show my love by partnering in household tasks, helping him manage his commercial properties, and opening my heart to his adult children and their families.

Generally our routines work well, and we've been moving quite happily toward our tenth anniversary. But there are times when he is convinced that I love Naomi the cat, Annie the dog, or Vida the horse more than I love him. Naomi, Annie, and Vida are getting older, right along with Ray and me. If Naomi, an eight-pound black kitty, starts losing too much weight, I obsess about every kibble she eats. If Annie, an eighty-pound Golden Retriever, starts limping too much from the arthritis in her right shoulder, I rush her to the vet. If Vida, my Arabian mare, flattens her ears when I put her into a trot,

I postpone all household tasks and spend extra hours at the barn massaging knotted muscles. At those times my relationship with Ray gets a bit ragged.

I'd been in an obsessing-about-kitty phase, and Ray was already feeling unloved and unappreciated, when my horse suddenly got so ill I thought I might lose her. She spiked a fever, dropped liquid stools, and her heartbeat nearly double-timed with a worrisome "whoosh" added to the beat. She grew so weak within a matter of a few days that when the vet came out Vida literally fell over twice as he examined her.

I sobbed my worries to Ray while I waited for the results of the blood work. Ray isn't fond of horses. In seventh grade he rode a horse called Little Buck at a friend's birthday party. Though the horse never even crow-hopped, Ray expected with every lurching step that it would live up to its name, and the fear settled deep in his cells. He would rather eat glass than go to the barn with me. But he did care that I was upset, and listened to me babble about Vida for hours.

I could think of nothing else. Talk of nothing else. Vida is my dream come true. Growing up, I saved every dime I could find to ride the electric horse at the grocery store, and read every book about horses in the library. I handled turning forty by buying my own horse, and turning fifty by riding her on the beach. I couldn't lose her.

Blood work confirmed that Vida had a serious infection, probably staph. A daily intravenous injection of antibiotics seemed our best hope of saving her.

I considered giving Vida the shots myself to reduce vet bills, and set up a training session with the vet to learn to give them. My face must have been as white as Vida's blaze when he showed me a syringe as long as my forearm and explained the things to avoid so I didn't endanger my horse's life.

I went home to Ray, terrified and babbling even more.

He put his book and glass of wine aside, listened as I told him what I was feeling, then said, matter-of-factly, "I'll help you."

I dropped into a chair, speechless. When I found my voice I said, "We're talking every day. You'll help me?"

"I can do it."

"We're talking the barn a half hour away. A thousand-pound horse. Foot-long shots into a vein near her heart."

"I'll do it. I used to give myself shots every day."

Shots every day? He'd never told me that. I eyed him dubiously. Ray panicked when he had to wash gravel out of my shoulder after a cycling accident. "Why did you give yourself shots?" I asked.

"For my allergies."

He did have allergies, so I supposed he might actually have given himself shots. If so, maybe he could help me with Vida. I drew my chair closer to his. "How old were you?"

"Twelve."

A smile broke through my worry. He'd given himself shots more than fifty years before. He sounded supremely confident, and terribly earnest. "Let me make sure I have this right," I said. "You gave yourself shots every day."

"Well, my mother did it most of the time."

My chest hurt from holding in a burst of laughter. "You gave yourself shots every day except that your mother did it most of the time? How many shots do you think you actually gave yourself?"

"I don't know. At least one. They hurt."

Now I had to hold my sides not to double up. "How long did this shots thing go on?"

"A couple of weeks. They didn't work that well."

I got up from my chair, climbed into his lap, and gave him a huge hug. "You would have really done it for me, scary horses, scary needles and all, wouldn't you."

"I would have."

He wrapped his arms around me and I rested my head against his chest. Our conversation had helped me relax enough to see what I needed to do for myself and for Vida. Tough as it was for me to pull out my plastic, the vet accepted credit cards. I'd still need to go to the barn every day, but I'd worry about Vida a lot less and so be able to talk with Ray about something else, at least for a while.

Now I know how a man shows a woman he loves her. It's far

more than red roses and dinners alongside the river. He surrenders his personal interests, packs up his courage, and goes wherever she needs him. That's true love.

~Samantha Ducloux Waltz

68

Stronger Together

Snowflakes are one of nature's most fragile things,
but just look at what they can do when they stick together.
~Fay Seevers

"I promise to love and cherish you in sickness and in health, for better or worse, as long as we both shall live." Like most couples, Nolan and I spoke these vows in 1972 never realizing what the future would hold for us as a married couple.

"Your baby has cystic fibrosis and probably will die before the age of thirteen. But don't get your hopes up because most kids with CF do not even live that long," cautions the young intern. He promptly walks out of the dismal hospital room. The news is incomprehensible. Our precious baby is only three months old… how can a doctor talk about her death? Nolan and I caress our infant and wonder what the future will hold for our little girl. How long will Rebekah live? Tears are uncontrollable.

The next day a counselor advises that our attitude toward this devastating disease will determine how Rebekah deals with cystic fibrosis. Also she warns, "The majority of couples who have a child with an incurable disease get a divorce. The financial burden and emotional stress is just too great." Nolan and I assure the counselor that our marriage will last. The counselor says, "I hope you are right and that your marriage will not be another divorce statistic."

Distraught over the counselor's information, we talk about the importance of communication to keep our marriage alive. Daily,

Nolan and I discuss situations and make each decision together. Together, our determination and commitment will help fight this deadly disease. We know we are stronger together than apart. The wedding vows we made to each other five years earlier were for better or for worse. This event certainly is "the worse" in our marriage. We are determined to survive this disease as a family committed to loving one another. We have a powerful weapon… prayer and faith in our mighty God.

During the hospitalization, we learn the effects of this progressive disease. We must administer breathing treatments to our baby to prevent lung congestion. Doctors, nurses and counselors are available at the hospital to answer questions and help us learn more about the deadly disease. But we wonder, "What will happen once we take our little girl home?"

Finally, the day arrives and we leave the hospital. A breathing machine and numerous medications are necessities we take with us. We are determined to enjoy our beautiful daughter for as long as she lives. Nolan and I believe that we can handle the daily stress associated with CF because we have each other's love and strength.

Our family settles into a routine. We want to keep things as normal as possible for our daughter and two-year-old son, Bryant. But each time Rebekah coughs repeatedly, fear engulfs us. The responsibility for her health is overwhelming.

Constant hospitalizations do put a strain on our relationship. Sometimes, we are on an emotional roller coaster. We are more determined than ever to make every moment count. Rebekah's health is always a great concern. We know that our marriage must remain strong. So, we decide to consciously make a time for each other every evening to talk. As soon as the children go to bed, we turn off the television and share the events of the day. We discuss and solve problems one at a time. Our home is a place of calmness and loving acceptance.

Years pass quickly. Rebekah enters a private school where teachers commit to understand CF. It is extremely difficult for a parent to leave a child with a critical illness anywhere, especially for long periods. I seek an activity to keep me busy while Rebekah is at school. My husband suggests enrolling in college. So, I do. While my children are in school, I attend classes to pursue my lifelong dream of teaching. Often I say to Nolan, "I don't think I can handle college and house chores in addition to all of Rebekah's special needs." My husband is adamant and encourages me. Nolan helps both children with homework and administers Rebekah's breathing treatments. After the children are in bed, he helps me with my homework until after midnight.

Our hard work pays off! Finally, my dream comes true. I am a college graduate at age forty. I apply to teach at the Christian school my children attend and they hire me to teach second grade. So, I am fulfilling my lifelong ambition to teach.

At times, our life seems almost normal. Rebekah amazes us with her determination to succeed. She participates in sports, drill team and cheerleading. But, she battles constant fatigue and chronic lung infections. But even with all of my daughter's accomplishments, often I am frightened that the doctor's predictions will come true. Will Rebekah die soon?

To our amazement, Rebekah lives past the age of thirteen. Our daughter has a dream of teaching and wants to attend college after high school. But to our distress, she develops diabetes, a frequent complication for adults with cystic fibrosis. Now, in addition to CF and two to three hours of daily breathing treatments, Rebekah must control blood sugar levels by exercise and insulin. The disappointment is great! Nolan and I struggle to deal with an additional disease. But our amazing daughter says, "This is no big deal! What's another disease! I have learned from the two of you that our family can handle anything together. We love each other and we are a team! You and Dad have taught me that!"

Our team seems to be challenged often. The death of my beloved dad is overwhelming. Nolan helps me through the grieving process. We take walks and I pour out my emotions. We visit the gravesite together and remember my dad and his influence on my life. Nolan and I face another challenge together… two teenagers. We experience the joy of success with good grades, awards, and winning teams. Rebekah participates in dance recitals, volleyball teams, and an award-winning cheerleading squad. She receives a national cheerleading award. Bryant pursues soccer, baseball, and varsity football. We also encounter the frustration of two teen drivers with speeding tickets and car wrecks. But we survive the teen years. Our marriage is strong because we are committed to tackling each problem together with love.

Our son has even noticed a difference in our marriage. Bryant says, "Lots of my friends' parents divorced, thinking that would solve all of their problems. I know it took extra efforts for you two to stay together. I don't know how a separated family could handle problems like CF. I appreciate how our family focuses on God and has always worked together as a team."

Our daughter graduates from high school and takes college courses with a fierce determination to succeed. Hospitalizations occur every six months. Rebekah is finally a college senior but the last semester is physically demanding and her body is ravaged by pneumonia. At age twenty-three, she is sicker than she has ever been. The fear of losing our beloved daughter is ever constant. The counselor was right. The stress is great with a chronically-sick child. However, when Nolan and I pray together, God enables us to overcome the fear.

After ten days of hospitalization, Rebekah's physical strength returns and her lungs are clear. She gets to go home in time for Christmas. Amazingly, she continues college. A miracle happens! Rebekah graduates from UNT with a degree in education. On that day, tears flow freely as Nolan and I marvel at the accomplishments of our daughter. Rebekah hugs us and says, "Thanks so much for supporting and believing that I could achieve my goal of a college degree."

Our theory of stronger together is proven true year after year! We praise God for the power to conquer the daily effects of our daughter's disease. Stress, fear, financial obligations, and even dealing with medical insurance frustrations… we can handle together. Now, the average life span for an adult with CF is the mid-thirties. But, we've met adults with CF who are fifty and researchers claim a cure for CF in the future is realistic. We believe that our daughter will continue to accomplish her dreams.

Our marriage is stronger now than when we first made the wedding vows. The reason is simple: we love each other, pray constantly, communicate daily, and have faith in God. What a team! And after thirty-seven years of marriage, "I promise to love and cherish you in sickness and in health, for better or worse, as long as we both shall live" is a vow that still endures. We can definitely say, "Our marriage will last for better or worse as long as we both shall live because of faith in our mighty God."

~Marilyn Phillips

69

Anything for a Buck

It's so easy to fall in love but hard to find someone who will catch you.
~Author Unknown

If "Living without a Primary Source of Income" were a place, I would be the Queen of the Land. I don't accept this title willingly, but I have repeatedly been given the opportunity to learn how to manage our household on an irregular, minimal budget. In the ten short years that I've been married to my King, he has been out of work four times. Three times were for a period of almost a year. When he lost his job this time, the first words out of my mouth were "You'll get a new job immediately! You'll be back to work in a month!" I half-heartedly believed my words, uttered through a pasted-on smile, over a year ago.

This time we were victims of the economy, like so many others. My husband was replaced by a young chickadee taking home a paycheck half the size of his. However, knowing that fact didn't make it any easier to digest that all of our financial dreams were going to be put aside. We were going to slip out of thriving mode into surviving mode—again.

The next few days were a blur. Not just because I had difficulty seeing through my tears, but I was blinded with anger. I couldn't make eye contact with him, let alone body contact. I was physically unable to provide what my hurting man needed the most: an ego-building, estrogen-driven boost of confidence from his loving wife. How could he allow himself to be in a position that could jeopardize his loving family—again? Would he ever be a consistent provider? When would I have the security that I longed for? And the hardest question of all: Did I marry a loser?

I knew my most important wifely priority was to be my husband's number-one cheerleader in order to prevent him from becoming engulfed in both depression and our deep, comfy couch. Some couples quote their timelines by new babies or houses. Our timeline is based on "Oh, yeah, that was after you were laid off from the ice cream manufacturer but before you sold nuts and bolts." At least we had a freezer full of Ben and Jerry's to get us over that hump.

Terry has never simply been fired, or at least never fired simply. When I get into the details of his employment history, I begin to doubt the truth myself, and I was there. If another man's wife told me this dramatic tale, I know I wouldn't believe her. How can one man have such a long string of unfair treatment? I began to convince myself that not only had he deserved it, but he brought it on himself. But then I stepped back and took a look at the big picture. I realized that was logically impossible. If it wasn't Terry's fault, maybe it was God's. If even God wasn't going to help Terry with his career, who would be willing to hire a man who has never held a job for more than a few years? On top of my fear that I had possibly chosen the wrong man to marry, I had begun to develop a mistrust of employers. Any company that would hire him wouldn't be worth working for, and any job he was offered wouldn't be worth accepting.

Wow—some cheerleader I was turning out to be. But, I have to admit I was both surprised and proud at how Terry reacted to the situation. He got himself back into his job-hunting groups, signed up at the workforce center, and wasted no time in updating his résumé. He got a haircut, sent his suits to the cleaners, and registered for unemployment. He knew the drill, the steps that had to be followed, and he did them. He even skipped some of his usual self-deprecating detours like anti-depressants and getting sucked into watching infomercials in the wee hours of the morning. If he could deal with this like a mature adult, why couldn't I?

As word began to spread of Terry's new employment status, calls of condolence and curiosity began to come in from across the country. Most were kind and supportive. Some just dripped with pity. But one anger-driven, venomous call came from a relative who loves me dearly. She spewed indictments and grilled me with accusatory questions. How dare she label my husband as selfish, accusing him of not making his family the top priority? It was okay for me to think it, but for her to say it out loud? The nerve. In hindsight, I am grateful for her inappropriate behavior because it provoked me to fight back. It was in the act of defending my husband that I began to see the return of the respect I once had for him.

Each time a new call came in, it became easier to brag about the positive steps that Terry was taking to move forward. Each time I hung up the phone, I found it a little easier to feel the respect for him that he deserved. Eventually, I became the cheerleader that he longed for and requires for success. I support and encourage him in all his job-hunting efforts from application to interview. Participating every step of the way has made it "our" job search, "our" career goal.

If our past year were a game show, I imagine it would go something like this: "I'm Bob Womack, your host of *Anything For A Buck!* The game show that challenges your humility by asking 'Just what will YOU do for a buck?' Our first contestant is a happily-married father of two from Colorful Colorado! Welcome Terry!"

"Thanks Bob, glad to be here."

"As you know, Terry, our game is all about just how you are willing to humble yourself to earn money. So, contestant number one, just what will you do for a buck?"

"Anything, Bob. I am willing to do anything to care for my family. I will get up hours before the sun in the dead of winter and drive to the state line to set up cardboard cutouts of the Seinfeld cast on a college campus in order to put food on the table. I will carry two cases of beer, three dozen licorice ropes and a duffle bag filled with peanuts up and down the steep steps of a football arena, a baseball stadium, the rodeo show grounds, and two concert pavilions if it means I can pay the mortgage. I will do market research studies on consumer products and political opinions. I will mystery-shop hamburger chains and barbershops. Bob, I will even dress up as a six-foot gecko, ride around a racecar track in a golf cart and shoot T-shirts into the screaming crowd to keep the lights turned on. I will do anything for a buck!"

The real winner of this show is me. I won the grand prize: a husband I am proud of. One who is willing to do anything not just for a buck, but for our love and for our family. How could I not respect that?

~Karen O'Keeffe

70

Twice in a Lifetime

The past is behind us, love is in front and all around us.
~Emme Woodhull-Bäche

"All our efforts to save him failed." A faceless doctor's words echoed in my head, as I sank to the emergency room floor in total disbelief. My fifty-six-year-old husband, Sid—my soulmate for almost thirty-eight years, was dead from a sudden heart attack.

After the shock of his death wore off, I struggled with the many stages of grief, including depression, anger and confusion. Grief counseling helped tremendously, particularly with issues that were so unexpected, like happiness guilt.

When I then met and fell in love with Tom, I was elated and confused at the same time. How could I love someone other than Sid? I felt like a cheating wife. My head told me that Sid would want me to be happy again, but getting my heart to accept that fact took a lot of time and work on my part.

One of the things that helped me deal with those guilty feelings was the realization that I was really a lucky woman. Many people never find true love once in a lifetime, yet I loved and was loved by two wonderful, very different men. Sid was perfect for the young, naïve, teenage bride, and Tom was right for the sixty-year-old more confident, independent woman I had become since my husband's untimely death.

Almost two years after Sid died, Tom and I visited his grave. I was in the arms of one man I loved, sobbing over another man I also loved. But oddly enough, it did not feel strange. And as we sat there, total peace began to surround me. I was comforted by Tom's loving embrace, but it was more than that.

That chilly November day, the wind was as cold as the large concrete bench that stately guarded the family plot. Suddenly a gentle warm breeze kissed my face and caressed my hair. I knew it was Sid telling me he was happy for me, and that he was with me—just a smile away. My heart would always hold those wonderful memories of love from the past. But also I had enough love in my heart to give to someone new. I felt the last remnants of happiness guilt float away, and I imagined those feelings assimilating into the fluffy clouds above us.

I sighed and rested my head on Tom's shoulder. "How blessed I am," I said. "I found true love twice in a lifetime."

~Melinda Richarz Lyons

What You Don't Know

Love one another and you will be happy. It's as simple and as difficult as that.
~Michael Leunig

When you are young and uneducated in the game of life and picking a spouse — particularly if you are a young, stupid Christian and trying to obey God — your reasons for getting married probably don't go much further than the fact that you are "In Love" and your hormones are raging. A year seems like a long time to have been together, thirteen years is rather obscure, and a lifetime is unfathomable.

You don't know that thirteen years will pass in the blink of an eye.

When you put on the white dress and vow "for better or for worse," you don't know how bad the worse can really be. You don't know how hard it is to suffer three years of infertility, defend your decision to adopt to people who think you should put your resources into fertility treatments, or how another three years of postpartum depression when you do have a baby can tear you apart. You don't know when you vow "for richer or poorer" how poor that really means. You don't know that the $100 a month you lived on in college will look like a windfall after thirteen months of no income with small children.

When you pack up your things and move into your new home together, you don't realize that that pair of pants that he wads up on the floor will always be there, and the dishes she leaves in the sink will, too. Even though you didn't intend to marry your father or mother, you don't know that you will pull them into an argument in order to make your point that dishes shouldn't be left in the sink and pants don't belong on the floor if you intended to wear them again.

You don't know that those deals you made in the first week, on the honeymoon, won't be kept and that no matter how much you hate it, no matter how many times you remind them, the dirty dishes will still be out and the toilet will still have a ring (until the mother-in-law comes to visit).

You have no idea that he will still want you with baby flab and saggy breasts. You don't know how special it will be to look into little blue eyes and see your spouse. You don't know that when you look into the brown face of your son, you will also see your husband because nurture makes a fool of nature. You don't know that when you do finally get pregnant after adopting that your husband will tell you that when a white baby comes out, he'll know you've cheated because his babies are brown.

You don't know that when you get a wild idea to become a writer or start your own company that your spouse will be your biggest cheerleader. You don't know that when even your family thinks your spouse is crazy, you'll cling even tighter to him. You don't know the good that will come.

Face it, when you're young and stupid, you don't know what you are getting into.

You don't.

But I'm glad I got into it.

~Jamie Driggers

He Turned Me into a Queen

Love is not love which alters when it alteration finds.
~William Shakespeare

Gene, my fiancé, held me close as we exited the doctor's office. "Nothing will happen to your eyes." He lifted my chin with his fingertips and wiped a tear from my cheek. "We have a wedding to plan."

I relished his tenderness, but my thoughts still echoed the doctor's words just minutes prior. He had shined a bright light into my dilated pupils. "Hmm...your retina is deteriorating."

My hands got moist and my heart drummed.

"You need to prepare," he said. "No one knows how long you'll have your sight."

I leaned on Gene, his body strong and loving as I dismissed the bleak prognosis. Besides, for the moment, my eyesight was fine, I was in love, and my dream wedding was about to come true.

Months passed, and my wedding day finally arrived! Dressed in pure white, I prepared to walk down the aisle and meet my prince.

"Are you ready?" Dad whispered.

I nodded and put my trembling arm through his. Our steps were slow as we made our way down the aisle to the sound of royal and elegant trumpets. The colorful arrangements of fresh flowers along the sides made an invisible canopy of soft fragrances. The sun beaming through the huge stained-glass windows painted reflections of a variety of hues on the marble floor, adding to the magic of our day.

"For better or for worse…"

Those words referred to a distant concept back then, and my heart lit up with dreams of the "better." But nine years later, my world darkened with the reality of the "worse" as the words from the ophthalmologist way back then echoed with a sobering truth. My peripheral vision had begun to close in, and it was closing in way too quickly. I sat beside Gene on the couch. "I need to tell you something."

He pressed the remote, silenced the TV, and turned to me. "What's the matter?"

"I don't think I can drive anymore. Something's wrong with my eyes."

The explanation for my frequent bumping into the children and open cabinet doors, and even missing steps, didn't surprise him. He knew and so did I. But talking about made it painfully real.

With each month that passed, my field vision decreased. Desperate searches for treatments, and visits to specialists increased, but all of the answers gave us no hope. Our anguish intensified.

A few short months swept by. All I saw was what one sees through a keyhole. Then the day came—I woke up and my narrow field vision had closed in completely. Bitterness and anger filled my days. And the unfair misfortune touched us both. What we dreaded became an unwelcomed intruder into our marriage.

Each of us faced it differently. He withdrew, and I fought my own desperation at losing my ability to be a wife, a mom, and the woman Gene married. I felt worthless, unlovable, and ugly. But our three small sons gave me a reason to keep on trying, keep on adjusting, and continue to live a normal life in spite of my blindness.

Gene and I began to pray together—an uncomfortable thing for us—but we persisted anyway. "We'll be okay," he assured me.

The household tasks I performed easily before now took twice as long. But the outcome revealed Gene's patience. Separating the laundry—white from color—was an impossibility for me. One day, in a hurry, I emptied the clothes hamper into the washing machine. That's when Gene's understanding radiated as he softly suggested a bit of bleach was needed for his pink T-shirts.

The dishes I prepared didn't follow written recipes. Instead, I added ingredients according to my tastes. To my delight, the results pleased Gene and our small sons.

Years swept by, turning the pages of our lives together. Some of the pages were stained with the pain of losing our youngest son, while others wrinkled with adjustments to unexpected financial setbacks. But each page was carefully taped together, framed with the commitment reflecting God's power in the midst of adversity.

Although unable to see my own reflection in the mirror, I saw God's image in the mirror of our marriage. The faint, but sweet aroma of Gene's cologne surrounded me with reassurance as he held my hand and prayed for my day before leaving for work.

When I commented, "It sure is chilly in this restaurant, isn't it?" moments later, I felt a light sweater around me. Gene had quickly slipped away and retrieved it from the car. He draped it around me and deposited a kiss on my cheek. "Can I fix you another plate from the salad bar?" he asked at the precise moment I finished what he'd brought me the first time. Far from an isolated incidence, this thoughtfulness continues to this day.

My thoughts often wander. How I wish I could return what he has given me—his unconditional love. How I long to have one opportunity to say, "Don't worry, honey, stay home and rest. I'll take care of those errands." Or maybe, "How about if I read something to you for a change." But these thoughts never come to fruition.

On one occasion, he paused after reading a book to me for a long while. I asked, "Do you sometimes wish you were married to someone who could see?" I'd never asked this before, but I continued, "Then you wouldn't need to do so much. Tell me the truth." I held my breath waiting for his answer.

After a few moments of silence, I heard him place his eyeglasses on the table. "The truth is, you probably do much more for me than I ever do for you. We make a good team just the way we are, and we'll make it to the end."

Lying next to my sleeping husband, I stretch my hand to find his strong arm. In the stillness of the night, my thoughts race. Tears stream down my cheeks as the well of gratitude within me overflows. Listening to the sound of Gene's rhythmic breathing, I sigh with admiration for the man who saw beyond the ugliness of my blindness. With his love and understanding, he turned me into a queen.

~Janet Perez Eckles

Shaken and Stirred

Love is like an earthquake—unpredictable, a little scary, but when the hard part is over you realize how lucky you truly are.

~Source Unknown

My husband and I needed this vacation on the Big Island of Hawaii. Work back home in Southern California had been hectic for both of us and the hours we'd been putting in meant we had no time for each other. Dinners were fast and on the go, weekends we caught up on paperwork or yard work, and forget about sleeping in late or just cuddling. I couldn't remember the last time we actually held each other longer than a quick kiss on the cheek.

The second morning we were there, we were finally getting into the groove of being on vacation. We looked forward to a drive around the island, stopping at little stores along the way and having lunch at a local restaurant.

"I'm going to shave, then you can have the bathroom," Roger said.

I stood near the floor-to-ceiling windows at the front of our fifth-floor room. "Okay," I replied.

Suddenly, the room started to shake. The windows rattled, the mirror above the dresser banged against its mount, the floor quivered.

"Earthquake!" Roger yelled.

"Oh, my God!" I shouted.

"Come over here, quick."

I ran into his arms and he held me close. So close I almost couldn't breathe. The hotel shook so hard there was no way to get out; the floor and the walls were moving so much we couldn't have walked anywhere. I kept repeating the same thing over and over, "Oh, my God," and surprised myself with how many times I said it. It seemed to go on forever. I was terrified that something would fall on top of us, or the floor would split or the walls would crack. The whole building shook so violently that I thought it would crumble into pieces.

My husband used one arm to hold me tightly to him and the other to shelter my head. I was petrified, but his strength felt comforting. Finally, the violent shaking stopped.

"That was a big one," Roger said. "Let's get outside—there might be aftershocks."

We threw on some shoes, I grabbed my purse, and Roger took the car keys. We ran down the stairs and were barely twenty-five feet from the building when everything started shaking again. We ran as fast as we could to the parking lot.

"What happened?" a woman from Minnesota said.

"An earthquake," a man replied. "The first one was probably more than a 6. The second was an aftershock."

"We're on an island; won't the water rise and drown us?" said another.

"Yeah, what about a tsunami?"

Panic rippled through the crowd. The hotel manager gathered everyone. "We're glad you are all out and safe. Stay here until the hotel is checked for structural damage. We'll let you know when you can go back inside."

Roger and I went to our car and turned on the radio. The news announcer said it was a 6.5 earthquake and a 2.9 aftershock. The epicenter was just six miles away.

"No wonder it was so bad," Roger said. "We were almost on top of it."

The news also said we were not in danger of a tsunami, but that didn't quell the panic rising in the people around us.

"You guys are from California, right?" a man asked with his wife and two children at his side. "We're from Boston. Was this a bad one, or what?"

"Yeah, it was pretty bad. The worst we've ever been in," we replied.

"Would you leave? Will you get out of here?"

"No, we'll stay. If they say it's safe, we'll stay."

We waited in the parking lot, and turned our car on periodically to get updates. Airports were closed and power was out. Two hours later, a ripple of terror filled the air. People started running away from the hotel, up toward the hillside. "Tsunami warning! Get to higher ground!"

We hadn't heard any news of danger, but still it made me nervous. "Should we go higher?" I asked Roger.

"They said no danger of a tsunami." He grabbed my hand and held it tight. "We'll be fine," he reassured me.

Later, they allowed us all back inside. A young girl, walking just behind her parents, commented. "My mom thought we were all going to die." I put my arm around her. She cried quietly.

That afternoon the sun came out. The trade winds caused the palm trees to sway. The hotel put out a free barbecue for all the guests. We sat outside with others, grateful that we had escaped an act of nature that often included a high toll in deaths.

"I'm so glad to be alive," I said.

"Me, too," Roger said. "Do you want to leave when we can get off the island?"

"I don't think so, do you?"

"We have these at home sometimes too, except we're not usually right on top of them. I'm okay here if you're okay."

"As long as we're together, I'm fine."

He reached out his hand for mine and pulled me out of my lounge chair. "Come here," he said. I sat beside him and he put his arms around me.

"I love you," I told him.

"I love you, too."

We stayed, even after the airports re-opened and flights resumed. Many places were boarded up and closed for good, but the only thing that happened to us personally from the shaking was a stirring in our souls. Life is sometimes short. An earthquake can open your eyes to that fact. We came home from our trip with a renewed sense of what is really important in life, and it isn't long hours on the job, though we have to work to pay bills. What's important is taking time out for each other. Now we spend more time hugging, cuddling, and enjoying the quiet, still moments. I wouldn't wish for another earth-shaking experience, but that one did stir a little passion in our souls and re-ignited our love for each other.

~B.J. Taylor

On the Way to Forever

Soulmates are people who bring out the best in you.
They are not perfect but are always perfect for you.
~Author Unknown

I once thought that love meant flowers and chocolates from a handsome man in a dashing tuxedo, singing love songs. I was sure that love meant being swept off my feet by someone who thought that I was the most beautiful girl in the world. I was blessed to find exactly that.

My wonderful soulmate appeared in my life when I was not sure what to do with him. I could feel that something was missing—something that school, work, and friends were not providing. When God sent Layne into my life, as clichéd as it sounds, something clicked and I felt whole.

Our courtship was short, but sweet. He took me to fancy restaurants and on carriage rides around the city. He made me lasagna and played "Moonlight Sonata" on the piano. We talked for hours about everything and nothing. I was excited to hear his voice on the phone and counted the hours until I could see him again.

We were married on a cold day in February, surrounded by family and friends. The idea of forever didn't seem like long enough to spend with someone I loved so much, and I can honestly say that on that day, I loved Layne with my whole heart and soul. I couldn't imagine loving him more.

Our first two years of marriage were fun. Sure, we had the usual adjustments, but our lives fit together very well and the time passed quickly. Soon, however, the two of us felt like something was missing.

That something turned out to be three beautiful children who came over the next five years. Our lives had been fun without them, but now they were hectic and crazy, and rich and full at the same time.

Gradually, I began to see how very little I really had loved him on that cold day in February. Granted, I had loved Layne with my whole heart, but something happened on the way to forever—my heart grew by leaps and bounds.

You see, we've experienced our share of trials. We've seen deaths in our families, children in hospitals, and financial struggles. We've faced the everyday battles of too much to do in too little time. Life has happened to us, just as it happens to every family.

Each and every challenge we've overcome—every sickness, every mistake and every tragedy—broke my heart. The funny thing about broken hearts though, is that when they are mended by love, the process of repairing makes them larger.

Love looks different to me now. Instead of flowers and chocolates, I am swept off my feet when my wonderful husband offers to clean up vomit. I am flattered (and grateful) when he tells me that I'm beautiful even though I'm wearing my cut-off sweats with my hair in a crooked ponytail. And, I've found that he's even more handsome singing lullabies to our babies in his bathrobe than when he used to wear tuxedos and sing love songs to me.

Just like on our wedding day, I can't imagine loving him more than I do today. However, I am wiser now, and I know that growing old together will give me countless opportunities to increase my capacity to love him. I look forward to all of the blessings and even the sorrows inherent in intertwining my life so completely with that of another person.

Suddenly, forever seems like the perfect amount of time to spend with someone I couldn't imagine living without.

~Kimberlee B. Garrett

Chapter
8

True Love

Happily Ever Laughter

Laughter is the shortest distance between two people.

~Victor Borge

Husband Instruction Manual

Why does a woman work ten years to change a man's habits and then complain that he's not the man she married?
~Barbra Streisand

Congratulations on the acquisition of your brand new 2010 husband. You have chosen the best that modern biology has to offer in the way of life partners. While your 2010 husband is built to last a lifetime, these care and handling instructions will help you get the most out of your man.

Laundry instructions: Although we have implemented many improvements in this year's model (e.g.—automatic toilet seat replacement, limited childcare abilities, expectoration and flatulence control), we have not yet perfected an automatic self-laundering option. Thus, you must repeatedly remind your husband to pick up his dirty clothes, sort his laundry by color, and wash appropriate-sized loads. Some owners have found it easier to simply perform these functions themselves.

Dressing instructions: Most husbands come with only two wardrobe options—work and casual. Therefore please ensure that you assist your husband in any clothing purchases in order to avoid nasty fashion surprises. As in past years, the 2010 husband has pre-set fashion preferences which may clash with your taste. To date, we have yet to perfect an acceptable "color sense" module although the deluxe accessory package does include a formalwear option for occasional use. WARNING: Constant wardrobe monitoring is strongly recommended especially on weekends. Repeated exposure to baggy sweatpants and hole-filled T-shirts may void the warranty.

Cooking instructions: If you chose the deluxe accessory package, you can count on your husband to successfully cook meals on his own for many years to come. The standard model, on the other hand, has few kitchen skills and a limited cuisine. Unless you're willing to invest the time necessary to train your husband in the culinary arts, don't expect much beyond making toast and boiling water. However, all models do come equipped with the outdoor barbecue function.

Listening instructions: Despite years of research, we have not yet been able to produce a husband who really listens. Wives are free to urge their spouses to listen and "express their feelings" but we can offer no guarantees that you will achieve any meaningful results. Through persistent effort, some customers have trained their husbands to adopt a semi-satisfying simulated listening posture.

Fitness instructions: Your 2010 husband is properly proportioned and in good shape. However, in order to retain that shape and those proportions, you must insist on a strict regimen of daily exercise and a healthy diet. Failure to keep your husband active and eating properly will often result in a sluggish spouse with a widening waistline and a sagging seat. WARNING: Do not rely on in-home exercise equipment and always ration beer, pizza, and chips carefully.

Romance instructions: Although the listening capabilities of the 2010 husband are limited, he does possess excellent eyesight. Thus, in order to activate the romance function, emphasize visual stimuli. Sophisticated conversational and emotional skills are still not available on the 2010 husband although our genetic engineers hope to have an improved product ready by the next millennium.

LIMITED WARRANTY: Our 2010 husband is guaranteed against defects in workmanship for ninety (90) days. If, for any reason, you wish to return your husband during the warranty period, we will issue a full refund but only if he is returned in his original packaging. After that, you're on your own.

~David Martin

"The finer points of the new model husband. He may not be perfect but he's all mine!"

76

Married to a Metrosexual

We cannot really love anybody with whom we never laugh.
~Agnes Repplier

I still remember vividly my first date with my husband. He showed up on my doorstep wearing a black silk suit with elegant lace-up shoes and took me to see a jazz pianist. Before that, I'd mostly dated sloppy, preppy types clad in faded Izod shirts, whose musical tastes ran to Dire Straits and Warren Zevon. So it was a bit of an adjustment to be seen with a man who openly sported a thumb ring and was known to purchase the odd facial product.

Over time, however (fifteen years to be precise), I've come to terms with the fact that I'm married to a metrosexual. But it hasn't been easy.

Take a recent incident in a sporting goods store. We were on a trip back to New Jersey from our current home in London when my husband decided to buy himself a new outfit for power yoga.

"What do you think?" he asked the proprietor, emerging from the dressing room in a pair of form-fitting yoga pants.

The small, muscular man looked away awkwardly. "I... um... I think those are meant for... the, uh... ladies."

Even my otherwise soigné husband felt sufficiently chagrined that he opted for the less well-fitting Men's Medium over said

Women's Large. But not without second-guessing himself the entire next week.

"They did fit better," he kept insisting.

"Was it the panty-liner that got you?" I wanted to ask.

According to Wikipedia, "metrosexual" is "…a neologism generally applied to heterosexual men with a strong concern for their appearance, or whose lifestyle displays attributes stereotypically seen among gay men." In the self-editing spirit of Wikipedia, allow me to offer some empirical data to flesh this definition out.

First: "a strong concern for their appearance." Absolutely. At one point, back when we lived in Chicago, my husband even had a personal shopper. This man—I think his name was Oscar—would leave messages for my husband inviting him to "Men's Night" at the local Marshall Field's. He'd invariably come home with all these tight-fitting ribbed sweaters à la Will of *Will and Grace* (prompting me to question whether Oscar's interest in my husband's look was entirely commercial). And, yes, in case you're wondering, my husband has experimented with cologne (he didn't inhale).

The second defining element of the metrosexual is a taste for the finer things in life. The first time they met, my husband described the wine as "grassy" to my father (who grew up in Newark and was thus more familiar with Pabst than Pinot Noir). More recently, when we were trying to remember the name of a certain *chocolatier* in Paris, my husband told me to go into his Outlook folder and search for the "Dark Chocolate" entry. It goes without saying that we only drink espresso in our home. Indeed, we've been together so long that it didn't strike me as odd when he recently e-mailed me a video about the optimal way to froth milk. And did I mention the yoga?

Finally, the metrosexual has an avowed fondness for gadgets. The $1,200 espresso machine and matching grinder are perhaps the most visible expression of this trait in our home. But my husband is forever reading catalogs from places like Levenger's, rendering us the proud owners of (to list a few): that magical thing that holds your bagel in place while you slice it in half… that essential stand that props your newspaper up so you can read one column at a time…

and that miniature razor blade that cuts newspaper clippings without having to use scissors. While emptying our suitcases after our recent forage through Target, I was not at all surprised to discover a device that doubled as an avocado scooper and slicer. Because you never know when you'll need one of those….

To be sure, there are some advantages to having a husband who isn't—in the vernacular of my adopted country—terribly "bloke-ish." For starters, I have my very own live-in fashion consultant. My husband's well-honed Euro-sensibilities mean that whatever I'm wearing is also subject to his critical eye: "You really shouldn't do high-waisted," he'll observe as I come downstairs in a pair of shorts that extends a centimeter above my navel. Or "Oh no! Eggplant is definitely not your color." And though I'm often loathe to admit it, he's invariably right. I think I'm the only woman I know who's shopped for bras with her husband. (The owner of the bra shop thought he was a pervert, but no matter….)

Second, I've also picked up some really useful skills along the way. Formerly a Mr. Coffee kind of gal, I can now tamp an espresso with the best of them. In a city like London, where a cappuccino can easily set you back five bucks, it's highly cost-effective to be able to rival the best brews on High Street. And how many people do you know who can scoop and slice an avocado in one seamless gesture?

Finally, what other guy would be willing to watch all those Merchant and Ivory films with me?

Mostly, however, I revel in the nuances that my husband's unabashed metrosexuality affords. Jung famously suggested that all men harbor an inner feminine figure in their unconscious. I like to think that my children benefit from having a dad who's more in touch than the average Joe with his inner Josephine. My son, in particular, knows that it's okay to play the violin and enjoy museums, and that you don't have to give up those interests just because you also like soccer. And in a world where we make all sorts of gender-based stereotypes—some with profound consequences for public policy—I'm proud to have a husband who defies easy labeling. Finally, how cool is it that more than a decade into our marriage—yoga pants notwithstanding—I still find myself agreeing with the gay office intern who once confided to me that my husband was "hot"?

Would you care for an espresso?

~Delia Lloyd

"They may be meant for the ladies, but I think I'm man enough to carry them off!"

77

Dolores and the Eggs

You know what they say: "My son's my son until he gets him a wife,
but my daughter's my daughter all of her life."
~Stanley Banks in Father of the Bride

olores was alone in the kitchen making breakfast when I walked in and sat down at the table. We exchanged a polite, but guarded "Good morning," and I watched her as she huddled over the stove. She was frying the eggs, so I concluded the tears I saw suddenly welling in her eyes were not from chopping onions for an omelet.

My future mother-in-law had met me for the first time the night before. I had recently arrived back in the States following two and a half years vagabonding throughout Europe after graduating college in 1971. It was the thing to do back then, and I arrived at her home sporting the typical regalia of those wandering times: shoulder-length hair, a full beard and absolutely no prospects for the future, other than a decision to marry Dolores' only daughter Denise, whom I had met while traveling. That news had preceded my arrival, and I could immediately discern that my overall appearance had done nothing to soften the cold shock of that original announcement.

I watched her focusing in on that frying pan like it was an air traffic controller's screen. She was attempting to conceal her tears, but wasn't doing a very good job of it.

"Are those tears about me?" I asked. She nodded affirmatively.

"Is it because I'm marrying your daughter?" Her affirmation was again quickly forthcoming.

"And you're afraid I won't be committed to the marriage?" Her less-than-reluctant nod confirmed I was three-for-three. I admired her honesty, and I'd like to think she admired me for diving right into those eggs of hers without having her daughter taste them first.

Over the years my commitment to my marriage took on less significance in my mother-in-law's eyes than some of my decision-making within its confines. Like the time I had quit my first job as a bank teller, without another job waiting in the wings. That my decision had been driven by a third armed robbery in less than a year at the bank seemed little justification compared to suddenly exposing her daughter to a husband without means. Or my hesitancy over having children. Or the time I had decided to buy our first house in a section of South Philadelphia that had not as yet shown any signs of "coming back" demographically speaking. Or the time I decided to take a job in far upstate New York, thus banishing her only daughter and now beloved twin grandchildren to the American Siberia. By then I am sure my continued commitment to the marriage had become a lot less important from her perspective. That the house I bought there was "old, run down and ugly" according to my father-in-law probably was more than enough to convince Dolores that I would provide only the bad things enumerated in the marriage vows (i.e., poorer, sickness, death).

But while Dolores could not hide her feelings about me (there was a certain wordless gaze she could cast my way as if she were looking toward a distant hill, one containing perhaps a silhouette of a hanging tree) she always kept her own counsel. In every way, she comported herself as the ideal mother-in-law, never meddling or intruding in her daughter's marriage—except perhaps the occasional early nudge about children, which I ultimately and manfully assisted in providing. After becoming a parent to adult daughters myself, I could look back and understand better the train wreck she thought I'd turn out to be. I have the highest admiration for her. And she was the absolute best grandmother you could ever hope to have for your children.

Some years later, I accepted a transfer to more hospitable climes in Atlanta. On what turned out to be our last destination Dolores would be alive to see, she visited us in our new home. It was a bright, modern colonial with aluminum siding and a patio deck that looked out to a private golf course. South Philly and northern New York State it was not. I admitted to Dolores one afternoon that I had finally bought a house her daughter considered a dream home. Dolores fixed what had become that recognizable gaze of judgment and execution, but this time that familiar gaze came with words.

"And it's about time!" she exclaimed with a special emphasis that seemed to echo back through all the previous years to that initial meeting in her kitchen.

Dolores passed away in that dream home of her daughter's during one of those Atlanta visits. Maybe she felt her work of protectress had been completed at long last, and she could trust me to do the right thing from there on in. From many perspectives, Dolores had died too soon, but from the point of view of trusting me to do the right thing, it may have been the most untimely of those perspectives. There followed two questionable and unfulfilling moves out to the Midwest, before the sensible one of returning her daughter to the Philadelphia area finally took place. But even with that, there was one more twist of fate that I'm certain would have made her rue her decision not to put something in those eggs back when she had had the chance.

A friend once described my decision to leave the relative security of the corporate world to become a fulltime writer as "courageous and foolish." The decision still bounces back and forth between those two poles. After ten years, there are still many afternoons when I am pacing the floors of my home, anxiously awaiting the arrival of a freelance check in the day's mail needed to pay bills that are due. I swear at those times I can sense a stirring in my mother-in-law's grave. It makes me think she is somehow maintaining a presence that prevents even more foolish decisions.

As a precaution, though, I insist on making my own eggs to this day. For there are times when Dolores's daughter, who over the years has transformed her mother's distant gaze into something that can only be described as The Look, suggests that it is probably a wise course of action to take.

~Reid Champagne

78

More than Words

Are we not like two volumes of one book?
~Marceline Desbordes-Valmore

Last week, my husband Bob and I celebrated our twenty-fifth wedding anniversary. I think one of the reasons our marriage works is because we speak so well in silence.

Recently we were at a brunch where an obnoxious fellow was spouting about politics. Bob and I sat across the table from each other. With just a glance, we communicated, "Yuck, yuck and… did I say yuck?" We continued this conversation, neither of us saying one word out loud.

"Can we go now?" Bob asked with a look I know so well.

I poured him some wine. "Not yet," that signaled.

"Get us out of here," he pleaded with his eyes.

I sat next to him. "I'm thinking! I'm thinking!" I said silently.

He coughed. I took his hand, which meant, "Don't do the flu thing. Everybody always knows you're faking."

He squeezed my hand. "Say you have a female problem. No one will ask you about it," I could tell he was saying.

I squeezed back. "I had that last month. If I say it again, people will begin to think I'm icky."

He touched his upper lip, which told me, "There's a white glop of clam dip stuck to your face." I wiped it off and nodded silently, "Thanks."

I get nervous at parties. Okay, I get nervous everywhere. But at one holiday gathering of writers, I forced myself to talk to a woman who intimidated me. Fortunately Bob was behind me. And our silent communication really mattered. "I loved your story," I said to her. From behind, Bob could see that I had my velvet blouse tucked — not into my velvet slacks — but into the panty hose which were much higher on my waist than the slacks. It wasn't pretty.

He sidled up next to me and made darting motions with his eyes, in the direction of my panty hose. "Not here," I said without words. "Are you perverted or what?"

He put his arm around me, looked down at my questioning face and quickly untucked my blouse from my hose. I smiled gratefully up at him. "Could you check my hair for toilet paper?" he heard me think. "Last year there was that piece on my head. I still can't figure out how it got there."

He looked down at me. "You are so unsophisticated. I love that part of you," he was thinking.

"I am sophisticated," I wordlessly replied while spreading a chunk of Brie on a cracker with my fingers.

And so, for our twenty-fifth anniversary, I had a pal from Indiana overnight a dozen Krispy Kreme donuts for Bob. They're not for sale where we live.

That floored him. But get this. He handmade a sampler for me. On it, he embroidered the words to our favorite song, "I'll be loving you… always." It's the most beautiful cross-stitch sampler you could imagine.

But I'll tell you. If the sampler had no words on it, I would have known what he meant to say. And when it comes to what makes a relationship work, I think that's it. A compassionate awareness of how the other feels. Bob's warm touch when I'm scared, for seemingly no reason, in the night. A leap into his arms when a story I've written gets accepted by a publication. A "keep trying" hug when my next ten stories get rejected. An "it doesn't matter" shrug when I am terribly embarrassed because of something I should or shouldn't have said at a party.

Silent communication. I bet we all do this a dozen times a day.

But with someone we love, I think that moments like these are what matter the most. Because they mean more than words can ever say.

~Saralee Perel

"Sometimes we don't need words to get our point across... because love is the perfect communicator!"

79

Chicken Soup for the Soul

One of Those Mornings

Flowers grow out of dark moments.
~Corita Kent

The irritating buzz of the alarm dragged me from my dreams. I stretched my arm from beneath the covers to silence it. My fumbling fingers found the snooze button, pressed and then recoiled in shock at the feel of the frigid plastic. "Oh no," I groaned, "not again!"

Rolling on to my side I hauled the covers higher on my shoulder, pressed up against my wife, Carol, and kissed her awake. The radio clicked on and the local station's morning man confirmed my fear. Overnight, the temperature in Orillia had plummeted to a record thirty degrees below zero. This would be, "one of those mornings."

As newlyweds, Carol and I had overcome many challenges, not the least of them learning to work together to cope with rural life in Canada's mid-north. One of the toughest tests of our love was surviving our first winter in the wilds. It was mid-February 1970 and I was teaching in a nearby town. Although we were eager to move to the heart of Ontario's "cottage country," like most young couples Carol and I were long on ambition and short on cash. However, we had managed to scrape together a down payment and over Christmas break we abandoned our comfortable city apartment and took up residence in a very old cottage on the shore of Lake Couchiching.

Although idyllic in the summer, our new home was isolated and ill-suited to winter occupancy. We had managed to install an indoor toilet and a bathtub, but the conditions were still spartan. A tiny acorn fireplace and temperamental old oil stove were our only sources of heat and there was no insulation, so frozen pipes and drains were a common and frustrating occurrence in our frigid abode. We prided ourselves on our ability to cope. Outfitted in arctic boots and one-piece snowsuits, we spent that first winter shoveling tons of snow, splitting forests of wood, and on really cold mornings using a hair dryer to thaw our frozen plumbing. Our love was tested and grew stronger as we battled the elements together, coming to grips daily with the rigors of rural living. However, it seemed that this morning would provide us with our toughest test yet.

We had awakened in a freezer! The minus-thirty degree temperature had jellied the stove oil, cutting the flow of fuel to the space heater, and I knew our water lines would be frozen. It would have been a perfect day to stay in bed; however, as a probationary teacher, I just had to get to school.

I tested the temperature with a puff of breath over the edge of the bedspread, and watched in horror as a vapourous cloud rose toward the ceiling. Bracing myself, I flipped the covers off and leaped to the floor. The icy cold of the linoleum seared my naked feet as, like a novice firewalker, I danced my way down the hallway to the oil heater. I opened the reserve tank, struck a match and thankfully the flame caught.

Fortunately the pipes in the bathroom had not split and after some carefully applied heat from the blow dryer, hot water steamed from the bathtub spout. As I settled thankfully into the wonderful warmth of the water, I heard some thumping from the front room. Carol must have risen to begin her chores. After thawing the kitchen taps, she would leave them running to flush the system and she would use her trusty hatchet to split kindling for the fireplace.

"What a team!" I thought, as I lay in the bath, unaware of the drama unfolding in the kitchen.

Although the kitchen taps had thawed, the sink's drain was still frozen. The water running in was not running out. The sink soon overflowed and water began splashing onto the super-cooled surface of the linoleum floor. Distracted, Carol turned her attention away from her task, just as the hatchet was descending. Her shriek of pain split the arctic air.

Galvanized, I leaped from the tub, water streaming from my body as I rushed to her rescue. When I reached the front room, I was confronted by a grisly scene.

My mate was seated in front of the fireplace, left hand clutched in her right, blood seeping from between her fingers and dripping on to the hearth.

She was crying, "I cut my finger off! I cut my finger off!"

With my attention focused on Carol, I failed to spot the danger awaiting me and stepped, naked and unprepared, firmly onto the slick icy floor of the kitchen. My feet flew out from underneath me; I crashed down butt first in the slush, slid wildly across the room, and slammed into the wall. By the time my head cleared, Carol was alternating between sobbing in pain and laughing at me.

Still, it was obvious that swift medical attention was needed. Carol was already dressed, so I wrapped her hand in a makeshift tea-towel bandage and hastily donned my own snowsuit for the trip to town. Thankfully, the block heater had kept our faithful Chevy warm enough to start. However the rest of the vehicle, including the heater, was frozen solid. No problem! With me driving and Carol wielding a window scraper in her uninjured hand, we pounded on flat-spotted tires along miles of rural road to the town hospital.

The nurse in Emergency escorted Carol directly in for treatment, leaving me to handle the paperwork. Needing my wallet, I reached up and grabbed the zipper on my one-piece snowsuit and pulled, opening it to my navel. "Oops!" I was nude underneath.

While the receptionist and I turned matching shades of red, I hastily re-zipped and provided from memory what information I could.

A nurse appeared and invited me into the treatment room. Carol had been very lucky! The doctor explained that although she would suffer a permanent loss of feeling in the tip of her finger, the bone was undamaged. Her nail and much of the severed flesh would grow back! After some stitches, a bandage and sling, and a call to my very understanding school principal, we headed home.

Once there I carefully rekindled the fireplace and made coffee. As Carol and I sat quietly in the glow of the fire, looking at each other over the rims of our steaming mugs, subtle smiles spread slowly across our faces. Although bruised and bloodied; we toasted each other and sipped, silently congratulating ourselves on surviving another trial.

Our young love would face more challenges before we reached our first anniversary and overcome many others as the years passed. But early adversity builds strong relationships and now forty years later, when winter's winds wail and the temperature plummets in Ontario, we toast each other over our morning coffee in Arizona, thankful that we no longer have to face "one of those mornings."

~John Forrest

One Damaged Headlight

Laughter is the sun that drives winter from the human face.
~Victor Hugo

Three years into my marriage, I was diagnosed with Advanced Stage III breast cancer. From the beginning, my husband was there for me. He called for referrals, scheduled my appointments, and gave me extra tender, loving care. His gentle, quiet force wasn't just a nice guy act. He was my unsung hero, and I loved him deeply.

He drove me from one doctor's visit to another without complaining. He laughed and cried with me and was more faithful than Lassie. I don't know what I would have done without him.

After my second chemotherapy treatment, tiny little hairs began shedding all over, so he offered to shave my head. He buzzed the sides, and then stopped long enough to take a picture of my Mohawk before finishing the task.

He handed me a mirror and said, "Smile, Mr. T."

"Very funny."

Our song when we first started dating was Randy Travis's "Forever and Ever." The words couldn't have been more fitting: He sings about how he is not in love with her hair and if it fell out he'd love her anyway. And he did.

After six months of chemotherapy to shrink the tumor, the

surgeon performed a partial mastectomy. Due to the huge bandage, I had no idea what my incision looked like.

On the way to the doctor to have the sutures removed, my husband read the troubled expression in my eyes. He'd assured me from the beginning that all that mattered was that I win the battle against cancer so we could grow old together. But now would he still feel the same way?

"Honey, don't worry," he said. "It's going to be fine."

When my name was called, he offered to go in with me. Not sure of my own reaction, I promised I'd be okay. The doctor unwound the last of the gauze, and I was shocked to see the damage to my breast.

But he seemed pleased with his handiwork and said, "It looks great."

Easy for him to say.

My husband jumped up when I walked in the waiting room and asked "Is everything alright?"

I nodded, but deep down, I worried about how he'd feel when he saw my body. We tried conversation, but silence worked best.

Back home, I ran for the privacy of our bedroom and took a good long look in the mirror. Quietly, my husband joined me and gave me a gentle hug. But when he looked down and started laughing, I was not amused.

"Honey, you remind me of my '55 Chevy."

"What's that supposed to mean?" I asked.

"You've got one headlight pointing in the wrong direction."

Glancing down, I discovered he was right. Removing over a fourth of my breast had the effect of an upward lift—one was pointing due north, and thanks to gravity, the other was headed south. His belly laugh filled the room. He explained that he and his brother had taken their old wrecked jalopy raccoon hunting. The damaged headlight shined up into the trees and assured a successful hunt.

He tried to keep a straight face, but a huge grin spread to the corners of his mouth. When I broke out in fits of giggles, he supported me in his arms and we laughed till it hurt.

When we finally stopped cackling, he said, "The hides are probably worth a lot more today."

Without skipping a beat, I said, "When are we going hunting?"

I was ready to move on with my life with my partner at my side.

~Alice E. Muschany

81

Laurel Rosenberg Schwartz Rosenberg Schwartz Rosenberg

What's in a name? That which we call a rose by any other name
would smell as sweet.
~William Shakespeare

For the moment, I am Laurel Rosenberg. I used to be Laurel Schwartz. Before that, I was Laurel Rosenberg, and would you believe before that, Laurel Schwartz… and before that my birth or commonly called "maiden" name Laurel Rosenberg. Each change distinguished by a different husband. Perhaps you could say I have gone full circle or certainly squared.

When I was a young girl, listening to Johnny Mathis, I dreamt of finding Prince Charming and marrying him. Names like Frankie Avalon, Ricky Nelson, Steve McQueen, Bobby Darin, Neil Diamond, Paul McCartney and even Elvis Presley danced through my imagination. I would write my name… Mrs. "Any of the above" on tablets of drawing paper and decorate the edges with hearts and butterflies. It was all very romantic. Never in any of my fantasies did I imagine my future to be an extended hyphenation.

I truly believe a "love chip" must have been implanted in me before birth… a magnet programmed to attract Rosenbergs and

Schwartzes. It must be in the back of my neck because I never see them coming... until they capture my heart and I marry them.

And lo and behold I sail away on a sea of matrimonial bliss without concern, over and over and over again. It's good I don't get seasick.

Some women would rather have their husband's last name because they don't like their own. Not me. For me it's all the same, except there is no DNA or family relationship tie. However there is an inherent confusion cast upon me and many who cross my path.

Let's start with my legal identity. Do you have any idea how many documents there are to fill out when you change your name? Lord knows how many times I have had to call, write, and further communicate to make changes. I am careful to speak clearly. It's like playing "Who's on First." The conversations go like this: "What is your maiden name? Then what is your married name? No, you said that's your maiden name," and the more times I repeat the correct name, the more it goes on and on and on till I am not sure who I am. I have had forms returned because "they" think I have made an error with my own name. Across desks and counters, I have received stares of disbelief, and everything from winks and grins to robust laughter. Beginning with my social security, driver's license, credit cards of which I have many, passport, insurance and real estate licenses, forms, forms, and more forms. Then there's my vehicle registration, and the post office, bank, the IRS... and my utility bills and my house, etc. So all in all, approximately fifty documents changed four times equal at least 200 documents over my lifetime... and it's not over yet.... I have the intention to marry again "someday."

And with that, I raise the issue of the monograms on my towels and linens. The luxuriously soft Egyptian cotton bath wraps, and the slinky silver satin and the white lace elegantly stitched sheets. If I had any idea of what was in store, I would have kept them to match the appropriate last name. My sterling silver, Old Maryland Engraved, has remained with me longer than any relationship. Luckily it was never engraved or the handles would have worn away.

Regarding personalized jewelry, I am careful when I wear it and pay close attention to my rings. Although on one occasion, an elegant dinner party, that current spouse brought to my attention the fact that I was not wearing "our" wedding ring. I quickly asked for another glass of champagne.

Mail creates another problem. Even with alerting the post office of my name change, some acquaintances, friends, and business associates cannot always keep up, while some mail carriers have given up even trying to figure it out. They get rewarded at Christmas.

Not to mention my embarrassment when, on any given day, I answer to either Rosenberg or Schwartz only to realize I am currently the other. In this day and age, it is common for a lady to be confused and forget her age, but her name? People get worried.

Since there are new options for changing last names, and I have already hyphenated mine, I understand that it is acceptable to combine both last names. Please, Schwartzberg-Rosewartz, or a variation thereof?

Now, let's talk about the in-between times during my states of single status which is called "Divorced," yet another label or name. So besides that stigma and not to confuse you further, please consider my confusion as to what last name to use.

Not wishing to date myself, but do you remember at baggage claim when they still verified your identity? I was stopped at the airport and created quite a scene, with some fellow passengers snarling at the delay while others were giggling at the reason. Somehow the claim ticket had been pulled off my luggage during transit and the leather nametag, on my suitcase was Schwartz, while the name on my ticket was guess who? Rosenberg! So I had to show my identification and explain my "legacy" once again, very slowly and to several attendants.

I am not a gambler by nature. The odds of mating with someone of the same last name are high… marrying them very high… my odds are off the chart. Want to place a bet?

Since my last marriage there have been four more Schwartzes, a Schwartzstein and a Rosenberg who gallantly attempted to win my affection. Oh and there was another gentleman from Rosenberg, Texas.

Even with the help of professionals, my "love chip" seems impenetrable, so I fervently request all Smith, Jones, Kennedy, etc… PLEASE line up and step to the FRONT!!!!

Or perhaps husband # 4 will take my last name.

In the meantime, "Let the Rosenberg-Schwartz be with you," It's already been with me!

~Laurel Rosenberg

82

Domestic Romance

Only two things are necessary to keep one's wife happy.
One is to let her think she is having her own way, the other, to let her have it.
~Lyndon B. Johnson

In my ongoing attempts to bridge the linguistic chasm between the sexes, I thought I had the meaning of one word down pat: "romantic." After all, how hard is it to define that word?

"Romantic" is a moonlit walk hand-in-hand along the beach. Or a quiet candlelit dinner for two at a quaint out-of-the-way country inn. Or a late night torch-lit champagne dip in a backyard whirlpool.

Whatever "romantic" meant, I knew it had to be at night, involve my wife and include a word ending with the suffix "lit." Even a flashlight-lit night camping in a tent should qualify by my reckoning.

But apparently "romantic" has a far more flexible and mysterious meaning if my wife's lexicon is any indication.

On more than one occasion, Cheryl has suggested some work-related endeavor that the two of us could pursue together. Something like digging up the garden or assembling a piece of IKEA furniture. When proposing such a project, she invariably closes by saying, "It would be romantic."

At first, I always thought she was kidding. After all, sweating, grunting, and groaning while holding a hammer, saw, or shovel does not seem romantic to me in the least unless, of course, it involves some slightly kinky sexual role-playing.

But I'm now convinced that my wife really means it when she says that performing household chores together will be romantic.

Recently Cheryl mentioned that the apple tree in our backyard desperately needed some major trimming. Notwithstanding it was the first day of my holidays, I foolishly suggested we rent a chainsaw and cut the offending branches. "Yes," said Cheryl, jumping at my offer. "That would be romantic."

So we headed off to the hardware store where we picked up a chainsaw and some chainsaw oil. Since the rental was for four hours, the only thing I had in mind was getting home and getting the job done as quickly as possible. Cheryl, on the other hand, seemed to be enjoying the romance of the moment.

For our romantic encounter, I donned work boots, old pants, a red flannel work shirt, and a pair of work gloves. In my mind, this was undoubtedly the least sexy outfit I had ever worn, except perhaps for my gardening ensemble which features rubber boots and a silly hat. But for Cheryl, it was apparently akin to a knight in shining armor.

Four hours later, we had removed and trimmed two large branches from our apple tree and a couple of smaller ones from the neighboring birch. Tied-up bundles of branches and two bags of leaves, twigs and apples ended up at the curb for pickup and some prime firewood was delivered to a neighbor for his fireplace.

At the end of our afternoon of torture, I found myself sweaty and exhausted. Years ago, I might have considered that an apt description of a romantic encounter. But since this one involved a chainsaw and a ladder, it was hard for me to find the romance in the now-completed task.

Yet Cheryl persisted in her belief that our afternoon chore had been romantic. Since it took place before sunset and there was no extra light involved (apart from the sunlight reflecting off my sweat-soaked brow), I failed to see how it qualified. To me, the only common denominators seemed to be that I had to wear protection and I needed to take a shower after it was over. But I sure didn't have that satisfied feeling I usually associate with romance.

After our latest romantic afternoon, however, I think I have a better handle on the meaning of the word "romantic." It doesn't necessarily have to occur at night with soft lighting. Apparently it can happen any time so long as it involves the two of us and some measure of extended physical exertion.

As I now see it, romance simply involves togetherness. So to husbands everywhere, the next time you want to sweep your wife off her feet, forget about candies, flowers, dining and dancing. All you have to do is say: "Honey, let's clean out the septic tank." It may sound like work to you, but trust me, it will be sweet music to her ears.

~David Martin

83

The Detective

Anyone can be passionate, but it takes real lovers to be silly.
~Rose Franken

There really is truth to the statement that those who are in love literally know each other's thoughts and can see into one another's... uh... ice cream bowl. This truth became extraordinarily real to me just days before our twenty-second wedding anniversary.

At about 11:00 A.M., the phone rang at our home. It was my husband Gary—just calling to see what was up:

"Hello," I answered.

"Hi. What are you up to today?"

"Oh nothing," I said, "just having a little early lunch while I work on the computer."

"So... how's the coffee ice cream I bought?" he asked. I could almost "hear" him smiling.

"What?" I asked innocently.

"I asked how you like the ice cream you are eating."

I was stunned—absolutely stunned. I swung my head around and looked behind me at the window to see if somehow he could see me. The shade was down. How in the world did he know I was eating ice cream?? I NEVER get into the ice cream... especially in the morning. Plus, he knows that I had been trying to diet... again.

Nonetheless, I could barely hide the laughter in my voice as I calmly asked, "Why would you think I'm eating coffee ice cream?"

Gary chuckled. "Uh… several things. One being the fact that you said, 'Just having a little early lunch' in a guilty, high-pitched voice." He then imitated it before going on. "Two… your tongue must be a little frozen because your words were a bit sluggish." (I'm laughing out loud now.)

Spurred on by my laughter, he kept going… "The other thing is, I figured that when I cracked the seal on that carton of coffee ice cream last night and you didn't eat any, that it was sort of like leaving a line of cocaine on the counter for an addict to find."

We laughed long and hard together before he asked me, "What happened?"

"What do you mean?" I said, still laughing.

"Something must have happened to make you eat ice cream before lunch," he answered sympathetically.

Suddenly, I felt a rush of love for the man on the other end of the line. He knew me well—cared enough to find out what was bothering me, and trusted me enough to help me laugh at myself. What a satisfying and beautiful testament to twenty-two years.

I was reminded at that very moment, that whether I was blessed with one more year, or fifty more years, I would always and forever love my husband.

~Elizabeth Schmeidler

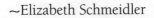

Chapter 9

True Love

Gifts from the Heart

*May no gift be too small to give, nor too simple to receive,
which is wrapped in thoughtfulness and tied with love.*

~L.O. Baird

84

22 and Counting

At the touch of love, everyone becomes a poet.
~Plato

For my 22nd wedding anniversary, I got a wild idea. I decided that I would write my wife Sheila twenty-two poems to describe my love to her. Not being a poet, I had no idea what I was about to embark on. I also decided that I would have a surprise party to catch her off guard; after all, who has ever heard of a surprise 22nd wedding anniversary party?

I started out months in advance, writing poems and coordinating with a couple of my wife's friends. One of them ran a small printing business and another does crafts and drawings. So, I enlisted their help in making custom cards for each of the twenty-two poems.

Had I known how much effort it was going to be to make twenty-two custom cards for twenty-two poems about my love for my wife, I might have come up with a different idea. However, by the time I was beginning to run out of ideas for poems, I was within reach, so I kept on task.

I also decided that I was going to have twenty-one of her friends at the party to each give her a card and a rose. Then, I would recite the twenty-second poem from heart in front of her friends.

Some good friends volunteered to host the party at their house. The question then was how to get my wife to the party without raising her suspicions. I told my wife that for our anniversary I would make reservations at a suitably nice restaurant, so she didn't have to plan anything.

There was one other crucial decision: Which poem would I recite to my wife in front of all of her friends? Being a guy, one of the shorter ones seemed like the logical choice, but in the end my heart was drawn to a particular poem that describes how we met. I've always believed that there was divine intervention at work to bring us together, and I had written a poem about that. I couldn't shake the thought that this was the poem I needed to memorize. The problem was that this particular poem had nineteen verses. I had to get busy memorizing—and fast!

Finally, on the day of the party, I had pre-arranged with the party host to call me at home early in the afternoon to set the trap. He called right on cue to say that he really needed to get back a book that I had borrowed. In my wife's presence, I told him that we were heading out to dinner and could drop the book off on our way. Now, we could drive right to the party house without arousing suspicion.

When we pulled up to the house, I suggested that perhaps Sheila should accompany me to the door and say a quick hello—we wouldn't want to be rude to our friends.

We made our way up the steps and inside the house where the surprise was sprung. We had a terrific dinner surrounded by friends. One at a time, twenty-one of Sheila's friends presented her with a card and a rose. Then, I got up and recited all nineteen verses of a poem titled "Pure Luck." I wanted desperately to get it right—and I did!

That was five years ago, and I can still recite all nineteen verses by heart.

~Dan DeVries

85

A Dying Gift

There is a land of the living and a land of the dead, and the bridge is love.
~Thornton Wilder

Out of the blue he said, "I think it's time we get that puppy you've been wanting for so long." He was wrapped in a furry lap robe, sitting in the glider I had moved into the kitchen so he could be near me while I prepared meals. His black hair had turned to silver, his voice had lost its clarity, and the sparkle had faded from the dark brown eyes that had shown his love for me through forty-eight years. I knew that he knew it wouldn't be many more months before the cancer won and the chemo treatments would become ineffective.

For several years I had been begging to have a puppy, but his response had always been, "Not until you retire, because I don't want to be the one getting up in the night with a whining pup!" Now I had given up my job, not because I was of retirement age, but because I needed to be home to care for him while he battled the monster lurking in his bone marrow.

We went the next day to West Rock Kennels and picked out an adorable Shih-Tzu puppy, the healthiest-looking one of the litter. For several days I concentrated on choosing the perfect name for this adorable little distraction. Precious? Fritz? Piddles? At the suggestion of my sister, I finally settled on Skoshi, the Japanese word for small. While part of me wasted away along with my dying husband, Skoshi provided a silly kernel of delight that kept me going.

The diagnosis had come as a complete shock in the summer of 2002. During a routine checkup at our local clinic, his primary physician noted an unusual spike in a blood protein and referred us to a specialist for further follow-up, never mentioning the dreaded "C" word. As we drove up to the professional building in Robbinsdale, Minnesota, our hearts skipped a beat as we read the words "Humphrey Cancer Center" in bold design above the door. After further tests and consultation with an oncologist, it was confirmed. He had multiple myeloma, the technical term for bone marrow cancer, considered to be one of the more difficult cancers to treat.

As the months went by, we had many conversations about his impending departure, and he made lists of the important things I should know how to do when he was no longer around. To put his mind at ease, I assured him that I would be fine and that he needn't worry about me.

One day, in October 2005, a clinic appointment for a blood draw indicated that his chest cavity was filling up with fluid, and he had to be hospitalized. The doctors planned to remove the fluid the following morning and advised me to go home and get some rest. Sleep did not come. I prayed and committed the man who had been my best friend and lover for so many years to the Lord's care, asking that he be spared further suffering.

The next morning I rushed back to the hospital and found him somewhat confused. I reminded him who his visitors had been the previous day—grandson William, son Bruce, daughter-in-law Jeri, Pastor Tim. Then a strange look came across his face, as he said, "Oh, Marg, I feel so dizzy, so dizzy!" He lost consciousness, as I frantically ran into the hallway, calling for the nurse. Within minutes the once vibrant man I had loved since our teenage years lay still and silent, as I lay my head upon his chest and wept. The inevitable day had arrived.

I was strong and resolute throughout the week of making plans for his memorial service. Our grown children came to be with me. Together we chose music that he had loved, flowers to grace his casket, and special friends to take part. The last time I looked on his dear, familiar face, I wanted to climb into his burial bed and go to eternal rest along with him. But I greeted friends and relatives with a smile. I watched proudly as his children eulogized him, his granddaughters read his favorite Scriptures, and his seven grandsons carried him to the family plot to take his place alongside his mother, father, and grandparents, where one day I will finally lie beside him again.

Kicking aside the dead oak leaves as I walked the circle of my driveway in the late afternoons, I called out to the sky, "Where are you? Do you see me? Do you know my heart is broken?" My husband was finally free from the cancer's pain and suffering, but I never dreamed being left behind would hurt so much. As I walked, Skoshi faithfully watched and waited from the kitchen window. Day after day, spent from crying, I went inside to the joyful, wiggling, tail-wagging welcome from Skoshi, who needed my attention.

Friends called me from time to time to ask how I was doing. I always replied with a lie, "Oh, I'm fine. It's hard, but I'm doing fine." Funny how we want everyone to think we can handle situations that have rendered us immobile, unable to cope. I continued attending church, my one refuge, but as I sang the beautiful praise songs, the tears would not be denied and would soon stream down my cheeks. I felt a compulsion to destroy things that once held meaning to me, but no longer did. I stood in my living area and contemplated ripping all the books off the shelves and slamming them around the room. When I went to my closet to dress in the morning, I wanted to pull the clothes off the hangers and stomp on them.

I could sense that my children were becoming concerned, especially my daughter who began calling every night just to chat and make suggestions.

"Mom, maybe you should make an appointment with your physician and ask about taking an anti-depressant?"

"Mom, I'm worried about you."

"Mom, have you thought about seeing a counselor? Take down this number; he's a good one."

Most days I wanted to stay in bed, turn my face to the wall and never get up. As I lay there on a dark December day in 2005, Skoshi, curled in sleep behind my back, began to stir. He stretched, stood up and found his way to my pillow. As he licked my chin, I finally realized I needed help. I gathered that precious little dog into my arms, the last gift of love my life partner had given me, and murmured, "Thank you, my beloved Gordon," into Skoshi's furry little body. Once again, even in death, he had come through for me. Skoshi smiled at me, as Shih Tzu are known to do. Then with all the courage I could muster, I picked up the phone and dialed.

~Margaret M. Marty

86

Best Friends

A friend loves at all times…
~Proverbs 17:17

I'm a hopeless romantic. But my husband, Mike, is probably the most unromantic guy I know. When I was growing up I pictured myself being married to someone who would take my hand when we went for walks, shower me with affection, and enjoy long, heartfelt conversations about special feelings and philosophies.

I think Mike reached for my hand once since we've been married. He was lying in a hospital bed waiting for surgery and fearing he might die. That doesn't count!

Hugs I get—when he wants a new car, a $300 Precision Graphite Classic OS tennis racquet, or a golf trip with his buddies.

As for philosophical talks, forget it. I don't even try.

And when it comes to romantic lingo—after I say "I love you" Mike's typical response is, "Right back at ya, kid," or "Me, too, you, Babe." Hardly heartwarming.

I think Mike was the inspiration for the story about the woman who said to her husband on their anniversary: "Honey, we've been married forty years and since our wedding you have never said I love you." The husband replied, "I said it once and if anything changes I'll let you know."

But there is chemistry between us and a joyful oneness of spirit—like when he says or does goofy things to make me laugh so hard my sides ache and I can't catch my breath and I have to beg him to stop; or when something happens that reminds us of the past and we say the same thing at the same time and others haven't a clue what we're talking about; or when he looks at me during a concert of beautiful music with tears in his eyes and wipes my wet cheek knowing our hearts are one at that moment.

Mike says I am his best friend. I guess that's more important than a lot of romantic jargon, public display of affection, and all those other fantasies of mine.

And I do know that he loves me. After back surgery, the doctor said I shouldn't use a vacuum cleaner for at least a year. Now, twenty-nine years later, Mike still does all of the vacuuming. "It might hurt your back," he says. He has never voiced a complaint or even accused me of bribing the doctor. Now if that's not love, I don't know what is!

~Kay Conner Pliszka

87

A Bottle of Cologne

Grow old with me! The best is yet to be.
~Robert Browning

The bottle sits on my bathroom counter next to my comb and brush. It is three-quarters empty now. "Casaque by Jean d'Albret" proclaims the label, its blue color faded over forty years.

I use my special cologne sparingly now and only on very important occasions, because there will be none to replace it when these last few precious drops are gone.

It is the second bottle of this particular scent that I have owned. Jack gave me the first bottle... a very small one... on our first anniversary.

I'd heard the sound of the noisy muffler on our old maroon Ford and the crunch of its worn tires on the gravel of our driveway. He'd come home from his medical school classes early that Wednesday afternoon many years ago. After pausing for a moment to sniff his appreciation for the pie I had cooling on the kitchen windowsill, he handed me a small paper sack.

"Happy anniversary, honey! I brought you something special."

"Special and expensive, I think! The bag says Suzanne's. You know we can't afford anything from there."

"I can't afford NOT to give something special to the world's most beautiful bride. Especially for one who baked such a wonderful-smelling dessert for our anniversary dinner."

His arms circled my waist and he untied the strings on my apron.

"Now come in here and sit down and open my present."

He led me into the only other room in our tiny apartment and sat beside me on the worn old sofa.

My hands trembled as I took a small package from the bag. I hesitated to disturb the artistry of the elegant gold foil wrapping paper and black velvet ribbon.

"Open it, honey. Open it."

"But I thought we agreed to save the money for your tuition and not get each other anything," I protested somewhat half-heartedly.

"Open it, honey," Jack persisted.

The lovely wrappings fell away to reveal a bottle of French cologne. I knew it must be very expensive. I held it to my nose and smelled the most delicate odor I could ever imagine.

"Oh, Jack! It's heavenly! I'll never wear any other cologne as long as I live."

Looking down at my faded blue jeans and ugly, ragged tennis shoes, I wondered if I would ever be worthy of this marvelous scent. I would certainly try.

I used my precious Casaque carefully and sparingly over those early years of our marriage. Even after Jack's medical school and postgraduate training were completed and our life was easier financially, still, I was frugal. Even when we had a new sofa in a big, new house and five children to fill that house, I continued to jealously guard my fragrant treasure, a symbol of the foolishly extravagant love of a young husband.

And then one day three-year-old Jim drank my precious Casaque!

The day had been depressing because of the gloom and the rain. The new puppy had kept me awake half the night with his whining and barking. And I had just looked in the refrigerator to find we were out of milk. I went into my bedroom to get my purse and car keys only to discover that Jim had drunk my Casaque! The evidence was clear. He was sitting on the floor holding the empty bottle, his lips were wet, and he was making an awful face.

"Jack, come quick," I wailed. "Can cologne hurt the baby? Jim just drank the rest of the bottle of my Casaque!"

"It's mostly just alcohol, honey," Jack reassured me. "But we'll take him to the ER just to be sure."

Little Jim was fine, and my concern for my child assuaged, I now mourned my empty cologne bottle.

"Don't worry, hon. We can afford another bottle."

A few weeks later Jack came home, again with an elegantly wrapped package… this time a much larger bottle of my beloved scent.

"Sorry it took me a while to replace it. The lady at Suzanne's had to order it from Kansas City. They don't sell a whole lot of it anymore."

Though life was good and worries about tuition payments and cars with noisy mufflers were long past, I prized my new bottle of Casaque as much as I had the earlier one and used it with care bordering on parsimony. Still, one day it reached the half-empty mark, and I thought it best to get another bottle. It might have gotten even harder to obtain than it had been years ago.

The young lady at the counter at Suzanne's smiled what I'm sure she considered a charitable smile as she said, "Casaque? We haven't had any of that for years now. In fact, I don't think there is even a Jean d'Albret maker any more. We have some other lovely scents for a woman of your age, though."

"Is Miss Suzanne here? Maybe she knows how to order it. She got some for me a few years ago… from Kansas City, I think."

"It must have been quite a few years ago. Miss Suzanne has been dead for five years. The shop is now owned by her son George."

Time goes so quickly. One day I look at the cologne bottle and there isn't much left. I've been so careful of it over the years. Jim and his four siblings are all grown now. He is a successful lawyer and doesn't drink cologne anymore. He has moved on to more sophisticated drinks. Jack's hair has grown gray. He goes fishing and spends time surfing the Internet and would still buy large bottles of Casaque for me if Jean d'Albret still existed. I think he is perhaps even foolish enough to think I'm still a beautiful bride.

My bottle of Casaque is not three-quarters empty. It is still one-quarter full. Perhaps at over seventy years of age… if I'm very careful… I can count on using it for the rest of my life.

~Toni Somers

Nutty as a Fruitcake

...love knows not its own depth until the hour of separation.
~Kahlil Gibran

The marriage of my maternal grandparents was pretty out of the ordinary for an older couple. They often yelled at each other or snapped an insult over simple everyday tasks. I remember as a child wondering why they were even a couple. At times they were like oil and water, not a retired couple enjoying their golden years.

It seemed as though they had to have each other though. She didn't drive and he couldn't cook. He ran errands daily for her. She always sent him looking for just the perfect pepper or a certain cut of steak. If he came in with anything slightly different than she had requested, he was on the receiving end of a tongue lashing. She could cook anything. The minute you walked in the house, you smelled something cooking. She made fresh biscuits and gravy, mashed potatoes from scratch, and any kind of cake or pie you could ask for. You had to eat something at each visit. People came by daily for leftovers and conversation.

He was happy to be the chauffeur and gofer. He went out four or five times per day. He said he enjoyed the peace and quiet.

They worked together at Christmas to make her signature cakes as gifts. Each year everyone had an orange slice cake, a spice cake, and a fruitcake from my grandparents. The fruitcakes were fodder for many arguments and insults during the baking. They spit insults at each other during the entire process. Of course, they were funny to everyone.

"Are you blind? This is NOT the brand of cinnamon that I sent for!"

"Of course I'm blind—I married you!"

Several days and many arguments later, many cakes were delivered. I don't really remember eating the fruitcakes, but they were my grandfather's favorite. They made several extra and he ate them long after Christmas was over. It was his afternoon snack with his coffee or late night treat with a glass of milk. She would tell him he was going to have indigestion for eating so late and he would eat another slice.

My grandmother passed away in the spring of their fifty-third year together. My grandfather was completely lost without her. Everything he saw or heard reminded him of her. Nothing he ate tasted like her cooking and he was unable to eat much at all. Her birthday came soon after, the family reunion, Mother's Day... all days that she loved. Getting through each of the firsts was almost unbearable for him.

As Christmas approached my cousin and I dreaded the thought of him alone in the house, knowing it was time to make their special cakes. We decided to bring a new tradition to him. We would bake cakes and have him help decorate and deliver them. He finally acquiesced but really wasn't in the mood. The house was certainly lacking her presence and it was evident that he was missing her.

Even though he and my grandmother really did nothing special on Christmas morning, I couldn't stand the thought of him being alone. I made it a point to be there as early as I could. As I came in the back door to the kitchen, I saw him eating a slice of fruitcake for breakfast. I asked him where he got that one, secretly hoping he wouldn't offer me any.

He looked at me with a tear in his eyes and said, "This is the last fruitcake that your grandmother made. She put it in the freezer last year and I never did eat it. I'm so glad I didn't because now I can still have her with me at Christmas."

The years that my grandfather lived after that opened my eyes to the love that they really shared. He was dedicated to her memory and then I saw that their marriage was more than a dependence on each other. They were together because they wanted to be. They were in love.

~Dena May

My Special Angel

Perhaps they are not the stars, but rather openings in heaven where
the love of our lost ones pours through and shines down upon us
to let us know they are happy.
~Inspired by an Eskimo Legend

The day I married my childhood sweetheart was the happiest day of my life. We had been friends since the third grade and had always assumed that one day we would marry and raise a family. Our dreams had come true.

Over the course of the next three years, we lived in a dream world. We loved one another from the very depths of our souls and treated each other with respect, kindness, and compassion. We never thought of ourselves and always put the other first. There was nothing we would not do for each other.

We were seldom apart. We had common interests that ensured that we enjoyed each other's company. We would walk to the store together, holding hands, just to buy a loaf of bread. As well as being husband and wife, we were lovers and best friends.

After three years of marriage, I discovered I was pregnant. We were both delighted. We spent hours in the stores, picking out clothes, furniture, and accessories for the newest addition to our family.

Our daughter was born on a bright, sunny day in February. Our area had been hit by a heavy snowfall the week before and the world was white and beautiful. It seemed that this was an omen. Our family would have a bright future.

For the next ten months we nourished our daughter, watched her grow, learn to walk, and say her first words. My husband's heart soared the first time she looked at him with her big brown eyes and uttered the word, "Daddy." The world had never been so perfect.

Christmas was a great joy. We dressed Michelle in a red Santa suit and hat, played Santa and watched with joy as her eyes lit up at the sight of her first Christmas tree. We lay together later that night and reminisced about the joys of the day. We were ecstatic and talked of Christmases to come.

In the wee hours of New Year's Eve, my world came crashing down. I awoke to find my husband sitting on the edge of the bed, clutching his chest and crying out in pain. Before I could throw back the covers and get to him, he began screaming. He stood, pushed me to one side and staggered into the living room. I followed, fear gripping me as I asked over and over what was wrong. He never answered. His screams rebounded off the walls of the small room and almost deafened me. Suddenly, he fell face first onto the hardwood floor. Then… silence.

The deadly sound of silence seemed to fill the room even more than the screams of a moment before. I scrambled for the telephone and called an ambulance. It seemed an eternity before it arrived. I later learned it was actually a little over four minutes.

After I made the call, I dropped to my knees beside my husband. I shook his shoulder, rolled him onto his back and called out his name as tears ran down my face and fell onto his. There was no response. As the ambulance pulled into the driveway, siren wailing, I already knew that he was dead.

The next few days were a nightmare. I picked out his casket, made funeral arrangements, and stood by his coffin shaking hands and accepting the sympathy of family and friends. I felt no emotion whatsoever at this time. It was as if I had turned to stone.

At the cemetery, my father stood beside me, his hand on my shoulder in a gesture of comfort. I knew his heart ached. He and my husband had gotten along splendidly. I couldn't bring myself to comfort him. When they began to lower my husband's casket into the ground, I began to sob, deep wracking sobs that seemed to tear away my soul. As far as I was concerned, my life was over. Not only had I lost a husband, but also my lover and best friend. It had all happened in the blink of an eye. I leaned against my father's chest while he smoothed my hair with his work-worn hand and crooned words of comfort. I remember wondering at the time how the world could be so cruel.

Over the next few weeks, I went through the normal grieving process. I was angry with my husband for leaving me, angry with God for taking him, and angry at the world in general. I didn't have the opportunity to go through the denial process. My husband had died right before my eyes and the reality of it was not to be denied.

For three weeks, I barely slept a wink. Each time I drifted off, my husband's screams revisited. Then, I would awaken, hoping it was all a bad dream and trembling uncontrollably. I couldn't eat, lost weight and wished that I had died with him.

During this period, I stayed at my parents' house, refusing to set foot in my own home. I couldn't bear the thought of entering the living room where my husband had died, and was afraid the bedroom would echo his screams of pain. I ignored my infant daughter, locked myself in the bedroom of my childhood where I remained for hours, and turned a deaf ear to my mother's pleas to come out and join the family. Though I continued to wish I had died with my husband on that fateful night, I never once contemplated suicide. I didn't realize it at the time, but this was a good indication that I was going to make it.

After a month, my father told me that I either had to go back to the house to live or give the landlord notice that I was moving. I understood the logic of this but wanted nothing more to do with that house. I wrote a notice to terminate my tenancy, asked Dad to deliver it and begged him to sell everything in the house with the exception of our personal belongings and a few mementos. At first Dad protested but finally he relented. He thought I should face my fears—my ghosts—so there'd be closure. Again, I refused.

Dad made arrangements to meet a used furniture dealer at the house and one day, just after my daughter's first birthday, went to take care of things. It seemed like he was gone for hours and my imagination ran wild. Had something happened to him? In my sorry state of mind, I felt the house was cursed.

When I heard Dad's truck pull into the driveway, I breathed a sigh of relief. All of the reminders of that terrible night would now be gone. I would never have to step into that house again.

Dad entered the house looking haggard and drawn. He took off his coat and hat, hung them up, took a small package out of his pocket and handed it to me. He told me he had found it in the mailbox at the house.

The return address on the envelope was that of the jewelry store where my husband and I had purchased our wedding bands. I tore it open, curious to see what was inside. When I dumped the contents, I found an angel pendant about a half-inch high on the finest gold chain I had ever seen. Embedded in one of the angel's wings were three birthstones. An amethyst represented my daughter, a blue sapphire for me, and an emerald for my husband. I looked at Dad. He shrugged. Apparently he knew nothing about it.

It was then that I realized there was something left in the envelope. The letter inside was addressed to my late husband. It was a letter of apology, indicating that though they had promised Christmas delivery, there had been a delay and they were giving him a partial refund. A check was enclosed along with a handwritten note from my husband. The note read: "When you wear this beautiful angel, always know that I am near."

As I read, I could feel my husband's presence and almost see the smile on his face. I fastened the chain around my neck, knowing that he would be beside me always to guide me through the trials and tribulations of being a single parent. Peace enveloped me and in that moment, I knew that for his sake and that of my infant daughter, I must get on with my life.

Luckily for me, Dad had ignored all of my requests. The furniture was still in the small house where my husband and I had lived, loved, and laughed since the day we were married. The notice that I had told Dad to give to the landlord was still in his pocket. Michelle and I were going home.

The very next day, I bundled Michelle into her snowsuit and took her back to that house. I made a decision to pursue my lifelong dream of being a published writer. That fall, I enrolled in a writing class. Over the course of many years, my writing began to sell. How proud my late husband would have been.

The grief didn't leave overnight. Sometimes, I would awaken in a cold sweat, frightened and lonely. When this happened, I would hold my special angel between my fingers and rub her gently. Always, peace would envelop me and I would fall into a relaxed sleep.

I lost my special angel some years ago. At first, I was heartbroken. Then, I realized that I no longer needed to depend on her for peace and comfort. My only hope is that she brings peace and comfort into the life of the person who found her. She will always be my special angel and I will never forget the gift that my first husband sent me from beyond the grave. It truly was a gift of love.

~Mary M. Alward

The Last Valentine

The love game is never called off on account of darkness.
~Tom Masson

The day before Valentine's Day that year, I stared out at the bleak hospital parking lot from a small window for the hundredth time, wishing I could see something new, some sign of hope beckoning from an invisible horizon. Instead, all I could see was fading light over cars and concrete. It seemed to be fading inside too, temporarily softening the usually sterile setting in which my father now slept.

I turned toward his bed. Daddy breathed quietly, as though trying not to disturb anyone, maintaining a gentle dignity befitting his solitary nature. I was relieved that he appeared comfortable. This illness, stealthy and slow, had gone on so long that people no longer sent flowers or cards. They no longer knew what to say and, like the light in that room, simply faded away.

I was still young, and unused to the waiting times so familiar to those who helplessly stand watch over a terminally ill loved one. My mind retreated to happier times and I reviewed images from memories of my father. In each picture he was with my mother; adoring her. He would give her flowers and she would clap her hands together and purr with her sweet southern voice, "Oh Dave! These are the loveliest ever!" Then a soft kiss on his cheek and he would blush with pleasure. She tucked his cards away in an old wooden box which after so many years became so filled to the brim that it would no longer shut properly.

And now, my mother, who had never left his side before, was at home, getting a few hours of desperately needed sleep. Without her the silence in this room felt threatening and ominous. The inevitability of death and impending grief hovered unseen, waiting. Prayers of petition for his recovery seemed useless and unwise. Why would I want my father to linger in pain? I closed my eyes and silently implored, "Father... Father..." speaking to both of them.

A nurse walked briskly into the room, stirring up the silence with her purposeful efficiency. Then, with customary, but oddly out-of-place cheeriness, she sang out, "How is our patient?"

I turned from the window and smiled but didn't reply to the obvious. As she held my father's limp wrist and listened for his faint pulse she chattered on. Only half listening I slid down into a chair in the corner of the room and looked up at the window. Dark now. Nothing to see.

A moment later snippets of her words nudged me out of my numbing thoughts. "Tomorrow... Valentine's Day... Have you bought your Valentine's cards yet?" The gift shop was open for another hour if I wanted to run down and get some and she would be happy to sit with my father until I came back. For the first time I looked at her, saw her soft pink sweater, her younger hands holding my father's old hands. I nodded gratefully and hurried to the elevator.

In the gift shop I looked at the rows of cards. I picked up the ones that said "For my Father" and then unexpected tears slipped down my face. Why should I buy him a valentine when he might not live long enough to see it? Why would he care about Valentine's Day?

I was returning them to the rack when I realized I had picked up one that said, "To my wife on Valentine's Day." I remembered the cards in my mother's old box, representing almost forty years of marriage and then, without thinking about the impossibility of what I was preparing to do, bought the card and hurried back to my father's room.

After the nurse had left, I leaned over the bed, listened to his faint breathing, and whispered "Daddy, you have to do one more thing. Please Daddy. Just one more thing." There was no response.

I slipped a pen into his hand and laid the open card on his chest. He didn't move. "Please, Daddy. This is for Mom. A valentine. You've never forgotten." He seemed beyond my sense of urgency, beyond such a childish request and didn't move.

I stepped away from the bed, feeling a sense of shame that I had asked of him what he could no longer do and whispered a prayer of apology to God for being foolish. Time crawled slowly forward. Many more hours until sunrise. I pulled the chair closer to the bed, lowering myself slowly into it and closed my eyes. And I slept.

Hours later I awoke with a start, disoriented and alarmed that sleep had taken me away from my father's bedside. I rose from the chair and reached out to take the pen from his hand. The valentine had slipped to one side and as I reached for it, I saw my father's lips move. I leaned forward but I couldn't hear him. There was the tiniest trace of a smile on his face. The hand that had held the pen moved slightly. I picked up the card and looked inside. There, in shaky letters he had written, "Love, Dave."

"Thank you, Daddy." I whispered. "Mom will love this." He raised his fingers in a kind of benediction and I hugged his frail body one more time before releasing him to what had to be.

He died three hours later, as dawn was gathering light for this part of a waiting world. And when my mother entered the room, resting by the pillow was his last valentine for her, miraculously signed by him because love will always have the last word.

~Caroline S. McKinney

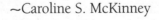

91

The Perfect Gift

If I know what love is, it is because of you.
~Hermann Hesse

Ten years ago in a fit of rage and intentional cruelty, my ex-husband David destroyed my family roots when he lit a match to my heirloom quilts that had been passed down to me from my grandmother. I stood by helplessly as her tangible legacy of love, courage, faith in God and hard work went up in flames.

Whenever I felt depressed, I had pulled out those quilts, carefully stored in her cedar chest, and wrapped myself up in them for comfort. They always gave me the courage to face my fears and future with hope. The quilts triggered fond memories because they were made from scraps of my hand-me-down school clothes. They transported me back in time to simple pleasures of snuggling beneath those "comforters" as Grandma tucked me into her four-poster bed and read me a bedtime story in her farmhouse. I always felt that I was covered by the Almighty because she told me there was a prayer in every stitch that God would bless me and keep me safe and secure as my guardian angels watched over me.

David even burned Grandma's quilting frames that I had planned on using to make legacy quilts for my two own daughters and future grandchildren.

I told my boyfriend Todd of David's numerous cruel acts and couldn't stop weeping when I lamented about my irreplaceable quilts. Over the past seven years that we've been dating, Todd has proposed to me many times and I've continually turned him down—the Queen of Excuses. In a heated argument, Todd asked me why I kept rejecting his proposals. Finally, I confessed that after my first experience, I didn't think I could ever get married. How could I possibly risk being hurt again? How could I learn to trust anyone again with my heart and what precious belongings I still had?

Then, one December day, Todd called, saying he was coming over to give me my birthday and Christmas present early. Little did I know that he had discovered the "perfect gift" that would melt the ice in my heart and set me free.

Todd shooed me out of my bedroom while he carefully arranged his gifts for maximum impact. Then he gently took my hands and whispered, "Before I let you see your presents, I want you to know that these are not intended to replace what you've lost. But if you can bring yourself to trust me, I hope they'll adequately express that I would give the world to make your life whole again."

Todd opened the door and I burst into tears of joy and screamed at the sight of three quilts of exquisite beauty spread out on my bed. I was amazed that Todd could be so caring, patient and compassionate in giving of himself to ease my pain. I didn't realize how angry and bitter I had become until his gift of love broke down the protective barriers I'd erected around my soul. Those quilts and his tender-hearted kindness and sensitivity toward me have restored my faith in people and given me the courage to love again.

~Judy Fox as told to Judy Howard

Timeless Love

Love is not only some-thing you feel. It is something you do.
~David Wilkerson

y son-in-law, Chris, fiddled with his watch and tapped his finger on its glass until he had my daughter's attention. He had come to pick her up after a long day of work that had followed the short-sleep night of new parents and he was tired.

Hilary looked up from buckling their baby girl into her car seat and smiled at him.

Chris yawned and stretched his neck. He picked up Emily's car seat and waited for Hilary to make her rounds of hugs and thank yous to all the loved ones who had come to celebrate their baby and shower her with gifts. Chris and Hilary had been married just over a year and in that time he had mastered the fine art of waiting and waiting and waiting and waiting....

But, after waiting for years to fall in love and start his family, this former confirmed bachelor counted these minutes of waiting among his blessings before finally waving goodbye and taking his wife and baby home.

I was happy for my daughter. Hilary had been through so much. Her first marriage had been painful and short, the happiness beginning to change just twenty minutes after leaving their large and elaborate wedding.

Hilary had worked hard to regain her confidence and equilibrium and then Chris came into her life and his love helped complete her healing.

My aunt and I were picking up after the shower when she said, "Cindy, I really like Chris, but I'm a little worried now."

That puzzled me. "What do you mean?"

"Didn't you see what he did when he got here? He no sooner came in the door then he was hurrying Hilary, pointing to his watch and tapping on it!"

"Yes, he does that a lot." I answered. "Isn't it sweet?"

That puzzled her until I explained.

Chris and Hilary were married in a small ceremony, with only their parents in attendance. After we had briefly rejoiced with them, Chris had scooped up his new bride and carried her off to his car. As they pulled out of the church parking lot and headed to his house to start their life together, he could feel Hilary tensing up. As they got farther from the church and closer to what would now be their home, her apprehension grew.

Chris reached over and took her hand. They drove like that for a few more minutes until his watch's alarm started beeping.

He dropped her hand and tapped on his watch. "Well, Hilary," he said, "we've been married twenty minutes and I still love you."

He smiled at her. Hilary slowly returned his smile and then teared up in her relief. Chris had given her the best wedding day gift of all, the reassurance of his kindness and love.

And these five years later, he continues to reassure her in their day to day life, through his love and care of their daughter and two-year-old son.

And when the words can not be spoken or the depth of his feelings can not be expressed, he gently taps on his watch, an intimate and personal reminder to Hilary of his timeless love.

~Cynthia Hamond

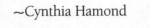

Gold Stars

Of all the shooting stars I knew, I never fell for anyone but you.
~Ozma

On August 7, 1999, I was on vacation in Red Lodge, Montana sitting on a bench watching a parade when my life changed forever.

It was a sunny, warm beautiful day and very possibly the entire population of 2,400 and all the tourists were crammed on the sidewalks. The town was full of excitement. But I saw nothing of it. My eyes were focused on something else. Behind my sunglasses, no one could see where I was really looking, especially the person I was watching.

Amidst all the people meandering about, I couldn't help but notice this one man who had walked back and forth in front of me at least four times. To be honest, I had noticed him a few days earlier. I was walking down the street. He was sitting outside a coffee shop surrounded by people chatting. He was just about to take a sip of coffee when we made eye contact. I smiled; he immediately lowered the cup and with a smile said, "Hello."

Now here he was again. I'm sure I wasn't the only woman watching this tall, handsome man. What aroused my interest the most was his sense of being very comfortable in his own skin. He was intriguing to say the least.

When the parade was over, almost instantly, the people disappeared, including the lady sitting beside me. I thought I should go, too, but because I had nowhere to go I stayed put. There he was standing in front of me. He said, "Is this your own personal bench or can anyone sit here?" I said, "It's not mine. Have a seat."

From the moment he sat down, we were both very at ease. It was like talking with a dear friend you hadn't seen in a long time. They say it happens when you're not looking. I wasn't and it did.

We talked for hours, each telling our life stories. Ed was fifty-three and I was forty-nine, so we had plenty to tell.

We were both honest right from the beginning. We spoke of our finest hours and confessed to our worst. There were no judgments. Neither of us was perfect and we were never going to be; we accepted each other just as we were.

On one occasion, I told him of a situation I encountered with a man from my past. I was explaining that what I wanted from a relationship was simply to be appreciated. The response I heard was, "Tena, I'm fresh out of gold stars." Several days after I told Ed this incident he asked me to get something out of the trunk of his car. To my surprise I found a card and just as I opened it a breeze rolled in and gold stars were flying everywhere. He wrote in the card, "You will never have to worry about being appreciated and I will never run out of gold stars." My heart leaped and tears of joy ran down my face.

We spent a glorious six weeks together until my vacation was over. In order to spend a little more time together, he offered to drive me home, as opposed to flying home alone. When I got in the car, he told me to look in the back. I couldn't believe my eyes. He had bought me the bench where we met. It sits in my backyard and is my most valuable possession.

That was ten years ago. Whether this relationship lasts until the day we die or ends tomorrow, I'll never forget him. No one has touched my life so profoundly.

He's taught me so many things. I can be in a relationship and still be myself—an individual on my own. Who knew? Not me.

He believes in me and has no doubts I can do anything I put my mind to. He's given me the joy of living with my best friend. I can tell him anything, no matter how stupid or profound. There is no need to keep my insecurities and fears to myself, or my triumphs.

We have fun together whether we are golfing, having a night out, or just hanging around at home. In addition, I've had great adventures with him, such as whitewater rafting, something I would never have considered before — way too scary.

He loves me without controlling or suffocating me. I wouldn't have missed sharing my life with him for anything in the world. I believe the greatest gift he's given me is to experience the depth and intensity of love I can feel for another person, while always aspiring to give more than I receive.

~Tena Beth Thompson

Secret Soup

Love is the poetry of the senses.
~Honoré de Balzac

My husband Matt and I have a secret nighttime ritual. It's one that even our closest friends and relatives don't know about. To the rest of the world we probably seem just like any other average middle-class, mid-life couple. Our philosophy is that whatever happens between two consenting adults is okay, as long as no one is harmed. We have decided to come out from behind closed doors and share this glimpse into our private life. Our secret... Matt reads stories to me from the *Chicken Soup for the Soul* series.

To me, the most beautiful sound in the world is Matt's voice. It has a rich masculine resonant quality. Whenever he sings in church, his powerful baritone voice can be distinctly heard above the rest of the congregation. After the service is over, the ladies in our church often compliment him on his singing. I believe it is the combination of his robust voice and boyish enthusiasm that captures their attention.

While we were dating, Matt and I would meet each other for coffee after I finished work at the hospital. We sat for hours in our favorite booth holding hands, sharing our dreams, and planning our future. Afterwards, he waited patiently for my call to let him know that I had arrived home safely. We then spent several more hours talking on the telephone. Matt's voice was the last sound that I heard before drifting off to sleep. It is amazing how little rest you need when you are falling in love. He still teases me, "I married you so that I could get some sleep at night."

Matt learned the art of reading aloud from his mother, as she read to each of her nine children. He continued the tradition with our own children. Danielle and Michael always enjoyed it when he read stories to them. His characters leapt off the page, as he brought them to life by varying the pitch and tempo of his voice. I loved listening as he read, treasuring this time together as a family. Gradually, as the nest emptied… I began to miss hearing Matt's stories.

Over the years Matt and I have shared the joys and challenges of life together. One of our most devastating setbacks was immediately following my back injury. A back injury is disastrous to the career of a bedside nurse. Along with severe pain, emotional and economic loss, there has been an extensive rehabilitation period with many relapses. Matt has been loving, supportive, and patient throughout my recovery.

One of the most troubling symptoms that I experienced during this stressful time was insomnia. I tried every known remedy including: establishing a regular bedtime, eliminating caffeine, drinking warm milk with nutmeg, lavender aromatherapy, and relaxing music. For a brief period, I resorted to taking sleeping pills. I hated the drowsy feeling the next morning and feared becoming dependent on them.

One particularly difficult night Matt suggested that I try reading a book. I was too tired to read and too restless to sleep. He offered to read to me. A natural choice seemed to be *Chicken Soup for the Nurse's Soul*. The book is a collection of encouraging uplifting stories about how nurses make a difference in the lives of their patients. This simple gesture combined the happy memories of hearing his voice over the telephone and listening to him read stories to our children. As he read, I began to feel more relaxed and after a few stories I was able to drift peacefully off to sleep. Thus began our nightly ritual of Matt reading stories to me from the *Chicken Soup for the Soul* series.

An added benefit has been the inspiration that we have both received from the stories themselves. As soon as we finish one book, we start another. Many of the volumes have been re-read several times. Others have been passed on to friends or family members. We select titles related to whatever is going on in our life. From time to time, the power of a story will cause Matt's voice to crack with emotion or a tear to roll down his cheek.

"That was a good one."

"You know… one of these days, one of my stories will be in *Chicken Soup for the Soul*."

"Yes, Laura, it will and I will read it to you."

~Laura Wisniewski

Chapter
10

True L♥ve

Love Everlasting

We loved with a love that was more than love.

~Edgar Allan Poe

Night Visit

Where love reigns the impossible may be attained.
~Indian Proverb

I woke up from a deep sleep.

I was enfolded in warmth. Howard's warmth. I could feel him, solid against my back. My head was pillowed on his left arm. His other arm was over me, his huge, rawboned hand holding mine against my breast.

"H-Howard? I thought you were dead," I said.

"Nah. I'm here. Go back to sleep," he whispered.

He hugged me closer and I went back to sleep, no questions, accepting.

But I remembered, in the morning.

I remembered the warmth, the love, even though the sheets behind me were cold.

~Evelyn L. Stringham

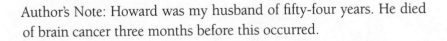

Author's Note: Howard was my husband of fifty-four years. He died of brain cancer three months before this occurred.

The Girl Next Door

Love is a symbol of eternity. It wipes out all sense of time,
destroying all memory of a beginning and all fear of an end.
~Author Unknown

My father had always been healthy until he was stricken with Parkinson's Disease. He was slowly losing his motor skills and memory. He started telling me about a girl who lived next door who he really liked.

Week after week, he would tell me how much he liked this girl and how much he wanted to marry her. This went on for months. Each time I would see him, he told me that he loved her and was going to ask her to marry him.

He sometimes would not remember who I was, or he would confuse me with my sister. He would often tell me he saw people who were not in the room or he would ask me who that was with me even though there was no one there.

I did not know how to break the news to my mother that after all these years of marriage my father was in love with another woman. I hoped he was imagining it until one day my mother told me (as she was laughing) that Dad asked her to marry him today.

All of a sudden it made sense. My mother lived next door to my dad when they met in 1945. He wasn't imagining it at all. He was reliving it. Dad taught me that true love is never ending. Thanks, Dad.

~Jean Hale

Special Friends, Special Love

We are each of us angels with only one wing,
and we can fly only by embracing each other.
~Luciano de Crescendo

The story of Louis and Deb began thirty-five years ago on the yellow minibus that drove them to and from the special school for the developmentally-disabled. Deb was a beauty, with a porcelain complexion and soft, brown hair. Her countenance was serene, a contrast to my brother's lively, never-ending encyclopedia of facial expressions. Deb was, for the most part, nonverbal. When Louis spoke, it was in halting phrases punctuated with his own brand of hand signals. Somehow, though, they understood each other.

After several years of sharing bus rides, their routine was predictable. Louis would exit the bus, call out, "Goodbye, Deb," from the curb, and watch his friend wave from her window seat as the bus rounded the corner. As the teen years sprinkled fairy dust over them, their friendship became more romantic. Deb lived nearby and Louis would sometimes walk to her house for an afterschool visit. Soon he began to ask if she could stop by our house on Saturday afternoons. Both mothers agreed, and Louis and Deb often sat at our dining room table, playing bingo or tic-tac-toe, or drawing pictures on large pieces of white paper with colored markers. They both enjoyed music, too, and Louis would sometimes play some of her favorite records on his stereo. I chaperoned these afternoons and frequently I noticed them sharing a starry-eyed gaze over a snack of cookies and milk or bowls of warm, homemade chocolate pudding.

Through the years their friendship continued to grow. At school and at afternoon recreation programs one could hardly be seen without the other. However, their bliss was soon to end. Louis announced that he had spotted a "For Sale" sign on Deb's front lawn as he approached her house one day. When Deb's mother dropped her off the next Saturday, my mother mentioned the sign and Deb's mother explained that she and her husband had put the house up for sale and were moving to a more pleasing southern climate. It had been arranged, she said, that Deb would remain in New York and live in a community residence for the developmentally-disabled run by a local organization.

"But she's so young," my shocked mother said. "You're placing her already?"

"She's twenty-one," Deb's no-nonsense mother explained. "It's time for her to move out."

Louis had also turned twenty-one and after graduation from school, he planned to attend a workshop program starting in the fall. That meant that Louis and Deb had only the remaining few days of school and eight weeks in summer camp together. My mother sat Louis down. "Deb is moving," she explained.

"Where?" Louis asked.

"She's going to a group home when camp is finished."

"No."

"Yes."

"Why?"

"Her family is moving and Deb needs a new place to live."

"Not me," Louis said as he pointed to the floor, "I'm staying right here."

"Yes, you can stay here, but do you understand that Deb is moving away?"

Louis looked down and nodded his head, "Yes."

That summer reports came from camp that Louis and Deb could not be separated. They held hands on the bus and during camp. They even held hands during lunch, maneuvering their respective sandwiches and juice boxes with their one free hand each. Deb's mother complained that despite the beautiful weather Deb was moody and though Louis made no mention of their looming separation my mother voiced her concerns about Louis' reaction on the last day of camp.

The final day arrived and friends and family were invited to a camp show given by counselors and campers. As always, it was a grand event and Deb danced a number with some other young ladies, after which Louis and his friends performed to a sassy tune from *A Chorus Line*. Then the camp director came to the stage and announced that this year there would be a very special final event. Louis' counselor entered from behind the curtain wearing a black plastic garbage bag and white clerical collar over his T-shirt and shorts. Louis followed him dressed in his green camp shirt and a makeshift cardboard top hat. Then strains of the wedding march began and Deb walked on adorned with a paper veil, carrying a bouquet of white paper flowers.

The counselor addressed the crowd, "Everyone here knows these two special people and everyone knows that they belong together. By the power vested in me I pronounce them Louis and Deb, friends forever." He lifted his right hand over their heads and gave his benediction, "Live long and prosper."

Louis faced the cheering group and took a bow as Deb looked on, smiling sweetly. Polaroid photos were taken and each member of the mock wedding party was presented with a picture as a memento.

That afternoon they rode the bus home together as they had for more than fifteen years. When it reached his stop, Louis exited, stood at the curb, waved, said "Goodbye Deb," and watched her tear-streaked face pressed to the bus window until it faded out of sight. For weeks after, he would take out that Polaroid photo of them, shake his head and simply say, "No more Deb."

Twenty-one years later, at the age of forty-two, Louis moved into a community residence also. Although our mother had died four years earlier, my father still maintained the family home and Louis preferred to spend weekends with his dad to remaining at the residence and participating in their recreational activities. One weekend, however, Louis was convinced by the staff to forego a home visit to attend the monthly dance held at a local church to which all other group home residents were invited.

That Saturday night at 11:00 P.M., I was startled from my sleep by my ringing phone. I ran to the kitchen, picked up the receiver and before I had the chance to say "Hello," I heard Louis cry out from the other end, "I danced with Deb tonight!" He went on with the details of his evening and after the call ended I returned to bed with my heart bursting.

A few days later, the staff member who had escorted Louis' group to the dance relayed to me the details of the two friends' reunion. When they spotted each other across the room, they ran to each other, clasped hands and could not be pried apart for the rest of the evening. "I swear," she said, "I never saw anything like it in almost twenty years in this business."

She may have never seen anything like it before, yet the pure, innocent love between two special friends can be witnessed every third Saturday of the month in the activities room of St. Mary's Church where the dances are held. Just ask for Louis and Deb.

~Monica A. Andermann

98

Letting Go

Across the years I will walk with you —
in deep, green forests; on shores of sand: and when our time on earth is
through in heaven too, you will have my hand.
~Robert Sexton

My parents lived by themselves until about six months ago, when my dad became sick with congestive heart failure. He had a stroke and a slight heart attack. It was then that we discovered Mom's Alzheimer's was much worse than we thought. Dad had been "covering" for her.

As my dad's health continued to decline, it became obvious that they could no longer remain in their home alone. We tried so hard to find people to stay with them and help. The final straw was when Dad had a short hospital stay and developed Mercer's. The help we had for them quit on the spot when he came home. Four months after Dad's stroke, we were forced to admit that they needed to be "placed" in a facility. We were fortunate to get them placed together, and they even got to share a room.

Mom and Dad adjusted fairly well to being there, and the nurses developed a special relationship with Dad, who was one of the few patients there who did not have Alzheimer's. He joked with them, teased, and just won their hearts. Soon my parents became the darlings of the facility. Mom did not understand that Dad was sick, and she became more and more confused. The nurses were wonderful about bringing her back to her room when she became lost, helping her with the daily tasks that she could no longer perform, and reassuring Dad that Mom was alright. Many times, although they had twin beds, Mom would be found in Dad's bed with him when morning came.

Unfortunately, Dad's condition worsened. There were many times that the family was called in, but Dad somehow rallied through whatever crisis he was facing. We would leave shaking our heads, with the nurses apologizing for the false alarm. I cannot tell you how many times this happened. His feet became so swollen because of the congestive heart failure that they considered amputation, but Dad's heart was not strong enough to withstand surgery. We decided that Dad just was not going to leave Mom until he was absolutely forced to. This was his biggest fear, and he talked to all six of his children many times about Mom and what would happen to her when he was gone. We tried to reassure him that we would always be there for her, but still he did not want to leave her. Theirs was a relationship that had survived many years, six children, financial problems, sickness, and many more hardships, and had only gotten stronger through the years.

Finally Dad began to get worse. We were called to the facility. Dad was very weak, had not eaten, and could barely talk. At least Mom didn't realize what was going on. She just followed her normal pattern, spending much time wandering the halls, rearranging clothes in her closet, etc. It was almost as if she just didn't realize Dad was there.

This continued for the next four days. Dad's condition steadily worsened. One of us tried to be there most of the time, and each of us held Dad's hand and told him to just let go. It hurt so badly to see him suffering, and suffering he was! Hospice kept him on pain medication, and even with that, he was not comfortable. On the fourth day, I went to work, planning to sit with Dad right afterward. About noon, I just had a feeling that I should go right away. I left work, went to the facility, and found my sister Jo already there. She said she had been on her way to work and just got a feeling that she wanted to see Dad, so she turned her car around and headed for the facility. Jo and

I spent the day listening to Dad's horrible breathing and talking to him. The nurses would come in every two hours, change him, turn him and try to make him comfortable. He had not opened his eyes or communicated for the past four days except to moan in pain.

About 5:00, Jo had to leave. Another sister was coming in around 6:30, so I settled down to wait. Soon the nurses brought Mom back to the room. I said, "Come sit down and talk to me, Mom." She came over, sat beside me and I got ready to hear the same things over and over. Instead, Mom looked at me and then looked over to Dad. She said, "Jack's dying, isn't he?" I told her he was dying, and that he was in a lot of pain. Mom said, "I don't want him to hurt." I suggested that she go over and tell him that, wondering what would happen.

All of a sudden, this Alzheimer's patient became my mom again! She walked over to Dad, took his hand, and started talking to him. "Jack, I love you so much and you have been such a good husband and father. I have so many memories of things we have done. I don't want you to leave me, and I will miss you so much, but I don't want you to hurt anymore." She continued to talk to him for about thirty minutes. During this time, my dad opened his eyes and just stared at his wife. He tried so hard to talk to her.

A couple of the nurses joined us around Dad's bed. All three of us were crying and watching this miracle! Mom steadily held Dad's hand, kissed him and talked to him. A lot of what she said was said only to him, and we couldn't hear. This was a precious, private talk between a husband and wife. Things I'm sure that my dad needed to hear from the only person who mattered at that time to him.

The nurse said that Dad's lungs were quickly filling up with fluid and perhaps everyone should be called in. I went outside and made the dreaded calls once again. Within an hour, everyone was there. Mom was back in her regular state, not paying any attention to Dad. We got her dressed in her pj's and she went to bed and straight to sleep. Finally, a couple of hours later, nothing had changed. We all left for the night, except my sister Tammy, who was spending the night.

About an hour after arriving home, the phone rang. Tammy, between her sobs, said, "Daddy's gone."

I know in my heart that God gave my father a special gift… the ability to have Mom give him permission to go.

~Teresa Keller

99

The Most Glorious Vacation

For death is no more than a turning of us over from time to eternity.
~William Penn

When Dad was diagnosed with terminal lung cancer, the journey that he took was not alone. His God, family, and friends were with him the entire way. Chemotherapy could possibly put the stage four cancer into remission but we all knew it was ultimately incurable and the prognosis of six months to live could very well be the reality.

Watching Dad lose his hair and suffer was heartbreaking. But along with the pain and tears there was such beauty, so many miraculous gifts that we, his family and friends, were blessed with. As the months passed into years, we all knew how precious each day we had with him was. The memories and lessons learned are forever in my heart.

During the last two and a half years of his life Dad taught me about hope, how to fight, and when to surrender. He taught me about trust. Not only that he trusted in God, but also the most amazing trust between a husband and a wife. During the last few weeks of his life, Mom would sit by his hospital bedside, sleeping most nights in a hospital recliner. She truly showed me the sacredness of the Sacrament of Marriage and what "in sickness and in health" meant. Dad trusted in her and the commitment they made to each other forty-eight years ago. It was evident to me that he was so grateful for her love and devotion just by the way he looked at her.

One hot, muggy August day, the world seemed to go on as usual. But for me it was anything but usual—it was an unforgettable moment in time. A day in which I was blessed with experiencing one of the most amazing examples of the devotion my parents had for each other. Seventy-two hours earlier, Dad had a near-death experience after he unexpectedly stopped breathing. Now, he sat surrounded by machines, in the intensive care unit after just coming off the ventilator. He had survived, but if it were to happen again we had to know what he wanted.

As Mom started talking to him about his wishes on being resuscitated, I wasn't sure if I could keep my composure. It was so difficult for her to ask him. She started and stopped several times but, finally, after several deep breaths and many tears, she asked what he wanted regarding resuscitation. Dad grew quiet. For the first time ever, he was at a loss for words. The minutes seemed like hours as I sat there trying to avoid sobbing, I began to focus intently on the small wooden cross hanging in the center of the wall. "Please God, help me be strong," I prayed silently, over and over again. The he broke the silence with his old, familiar voice.

Tears glistened in his eyes as he looked lovingly at Mom. He slowly said, "I don't want to be a burden to you, but I don't want to leave you."

My mom gently reached for his hand and stroked his hair back. "Jerry, let's think of it as if you are going on one of the most glorious vacations ever, and I will catch up to you later."

With a simple nod of the head, my dad accepted this, and as tears streamed down our faces, a sense of peace filled the room.

His charts were marked, and he wore a band around his wrist designating him as a "do not resuscitate" patient. Even with this, he worked diligently for weeks trying to regain strength to return home. He was anxious for Thursday, September 6th, to arrive. We all were. This was the date the doctors and nurses had set for him to go home. He proudly let his many visitors know that he was going home then.

After their nightly ritual of praying together, Mom left his hospital room to go home and make the final preparations for his homecoming the next day. Shortly after midnight, the phone startled Mom, abruptly waking her. A nurse from the hospital called to let her know that Dad was having difficulty breathing and was being taken to the emergency room. With urgency in the nurse's voice, she told Mom she needed to come to the hospital right away.

When Mom arrived at the emergency room, Dad's eyes were open. He had been asking for Mary—my mom—over and over again. The nurses advised he had minutes, maybe hours left.

God had planned their final goodbye so perfectly. Mom stroked his hair back one last time, and with love in her voice, she courageously said, "Jerry, it's okay. Go ahead. It's time to take that vacation."

A tear fell down his cheek, and he closed his eyes. It was time to surrender. His fight was over. He had so diligently prepared for his return home. To his eternal home, where he now waits for his loved ones to join him on the most glorious vacation ever, with our Lord Jesus.

~Susan Babcock

A Paradigm Shift

What do we live for, if it is not to make life less difficult for each other?
~George Eliot

Peg lay prostrate on the wooden floor, unable to lift her head or move her body. Five minutes passed… ten… fifteen. All because she'd reached for their wedding picture and fallen out of her wheelchair.

What a day for John to be late, Peg thought, as her immovable position grew more and more uncomfortable. It had been years since Peg could remember what it had been like to have control over her body. The multiple sclerosis had come on slowly, but in the last few years it had attacked viciously.

Out of the corner of her eye, she saw the photo that had fallen on the floor beside her, a picture of a bride and a groom, each with blue eyes and dark hair. Friends told her that raising three children hadn't aged either of them one bit, that in fact she was still as beautiful as ever and John as handsome.

John's car tires crunched in the snowy driveway. Her heart pounded as she heard her lover leap the eight stairs of their split-level home two at a time, eager to see his wife. Stunned to find her on the floor, John dropped to his knees, covered her body with his arms, pressed his cheek against hers—and wept with her.

Not out of sympathy. Peg's quips disarmed any of that maudlin stuff. Out of love—the deepest kind.

At that almost sacred moment, I intruded. "Oh I'm sorry," I

said, standing in the half-open doorway, peeking through the stair railing.

According to my custom as Peg's physical therapist, I had knocked and let myself in. I walked up and stood beside them not knowing what to say. Concern for Peg's welfare occupied my mind, but my heart, wounded from a recent divorce, felt rather uncomfortable around such tangible expressions of marital devotion.

John dried his tears, scooped up her thin, paralyzed body, and carried her to the bathroom. This was his habit every lunch hour.

"I'd do the same for you if things were reversed," Peg told him, her pluck restored, her smile broad as she winked at me over his shoulder.

"No, you wouldn't. I'm too big for you," he said with an equally broad smile. He fixed Peg lunch and returned to his work at the phone company. As she ate using a therapeutic spoon strapped to her wrist, I sat at the kitchen table, my mouth open in amazement at what had just transpired before my eyes.

How could I be divorced when I had had such an easy life compared to Peg and John? When they had married "for better or for worse," they had no idea what would befall them. Yet they seemed to truly love each other and their lives. What was wrong with me?

"Do you hurt today after the fall?" I asked Peg, wanting to change my thoughts.

"No, I'm just a little stiff. Go ahead and do the exercise routine," Peg said, adding, "I went to the counselor yesterday." Peg was a good conversationalist.

"How did that go?" I stretched her arm.

"Okay, until he asked, 'How's your intimate life?' I answered him, 'Fine, how's yours?' That quieted him right down." She had that familiar twinkle in her eye.

I chuckled within. No one tampered with this lady's love life, or for that matter, with her willingness to persevere. When therapy was over, she asked me to place a puzzle on her lap tray so she could arrange it. She knew her fingers were useless, but hey, why not give it a try?

I shook my head in wonder. My life in my former marriage had health, adequate wealth, two wonderful kids, and no big challenges—except finding happiness. I always thought it was a husband's responsibility to create his wife's happiness. When he hadn't met my expectations, I became increasingly irritable until finally things fell apart. The truth about happiness in marriage had eluded me until, around Peg and John, something warm and wonderful and puzzling stirred in my heart.

One lonely evening, I decided to call on them. I baked cookies, not because that was my custom, but because I wanted an excuse to be around those who understood love, to try to discover their secret. A friend and I drove to their house and I peeked through their family room window to see Peg seated in her wheelchair in front of the TV. John stood behind her like a tall, protective sentinel.

John opened the door, welcomed us, and retreated to the back of the room where Peg sat. They both smiled but said very little. All of a sudden, I saw a side of them I hadn't seen before—a certain shyness. They weren't used to outsiders intruding into their sanctuary. After some small talk, I moved towards the door, my friend following. They thanked us for the cookies and as we walked away, I glanced back through the picture window at Peg's forever smile. Like a framed photo, her husband had resumed his attentive stance—her guardian, lover, friend for life. Oh, sure, Peg and John were pleased we had thought of them. But their happiness came not from others but from another source.

Inspired to discover it, I searched through resources for insight and found one mundane quote after another. Finally a saying by Elbert Hubbard stood out. "The love we give away is the only love we keep."

That was it! Just then a paradigm shift took place in my divorce-weary soul. I realized happiness in love came from giving not from receiving, from sacrifice not ease, from putting another person's interests first not second. Old selfish habits had to go and I hoped a new me... in time... would come forth. Happiness was worth a try.

~Margaret Lang

Saying Goodbye

I may wear the glass slippers… but my hero wears combat boots.
~Source Unknown

I clutched the car's door handle as I watched him walk away. He was my soulmate, my lover, my best friend, and the father of the baby asleep in the infant seat within the car.

He had told me that he didn't want to part in the terminal, so we said our goodbyes in the parking lot next to the car. "I'll call you tonight from San Francisco," was all that he said before he turned away. I frantically tried to think what I could do to hold him there a few more minutes, but the pragmatist in me knew that I had to restrain myself from running after him, putting my arms around him, and kissing him one more time. Sobbing, I stood and watched as his image become smaller. Not once did he turn back to look at me. I closed my eyes and wiped away the tears. When I opened them again, he had completely disappeared.

He had told me to go home, but I couldn't tear myself away. If the plane had mechanical problems and the flight was canceled, he would have no way to call me back.

For more than an hour, I sat in the car, tormented by knowing he was in the terminal a few hundred feet away. I knew we had said our goodbyes, and there was nothing more to say. We had made the break; it would hurt even more to see each other again. I concentrated on the airplane sitting on the tarmac and waited for it to leave but, at the same time, I dreaded seeing it lift off. In my mind, being able to hold the image of the plane in front of me was paramount. As long as it sat there, we had a small chance for our fortunes to change. A miracle might happen to keep him from leaving. Once the plane pulled away from the gate, I would have to recognize that we might never be a couple ever again.

He and I had met nine years earlier at a resort where we were both summer employees. From the beginning, we were friends. One evening he asked me to go along when he found himself without a date after his plans had been finalized for an evening with another couple. From then on, we were drawn to each other. We had much in common and enjoyed our time together. An affectionate and caring courtship led to recognition of an enduring love for each other. During the ensuing years, we married, finished college, moved across the country, and taught school. Then the war years descended on us in a black, choking cloud. In a matter of weeks, his teaching deferment was canceled, and he was told to report for duty. We had to sell our home, and in the next two years, we moved five times. Then the orders came that he was to be sent to a war zone for a year. Completely understanding the full essence of the orders for deployment was realizing that he might not come back, that he might die in combat.

The night before he left, we stopped by his parents' home where we had dinner and then with strained voice he said goodbye to them. That night we couldn't sleep. We held each other and talked until there were no words left to say. Our thoughts were full of anguish.

In the morning, we went about doing ordinary things that took on new meaning. I watched him take out the trash and check the oil in the car. He gave me instructions about lighting the furnace and hot water heater. We were going into winter, and he worried that we might not be warm. He talked about care of the car. I didn't want to know about those things; I wanted him to be with us and to take care of us as he always had. My heart ached, and my brain was exhausted. The hours we could still be together were bleeding away.

The wait was over when the plane roared down the runway and lifted into the sky. As I watched it disappear into the clouds, I felt devastated. What was I going to do? I had no picture in my mind of how to live without him. I did realize I could not go on feeling as I did at that moment. It was too painful, and I had a baby to love and care for. I had to get busy. I had to be optimistic that he would come back to us. It was the only way not to be eaten by despair.

Many months later, I was at the airport and watched the plane land. With me was the little fellow who had learned to turn over, sit up, and walk—events in a child's development that his father had missed. We stood in the terminal at one of the gates. Somehow, it seemed all right to express our joy in public, when earlier our grief had been too personal to share. Passengers walked down the plane's steps and onto the tarmac. Finally, he emerged. We were no longer waiting. He was home. We could go on with our lives. It meant that we could be ordinary people doing ordinary things. I ran to meet him, to hold him, and to be with him for all of our years to come.

~Suzanne Waring

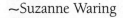

Meet Our Contributors
Meet Our Authors
Thank You
About Chicken Soup

Meet Our Contributors

Mary M. Alward lives in southern Ontario. Her work has been published in both print and online venues. When Mary isn't writing, she enjoys spending time with her family, reading and blogging. Mary can be reached via e-mail at malward2002@yahoo.ca.

Monica A. Andermann is an essayist and prize winning poet whose work has appeared or is forthcoming in various literary journals and anthologies. When she is not writing, she enjoys reading or spending time with friends and family.

Susan Babcock is a devoted wife and mother. Her three children and husband have been her greatest joys and the best job she could have ever hoped for. She has been a stay-at-home mom for the past fifteen years and has always found time to do volunteer work. Her hobbies include traveling, reading and spending many hours at her children's various sporting events.

Linda Baskin is a stay at home mom and loves spending every day with her son and daughter. She enjoys reading and journaling. She loves to golf with her husband and is working on getting her score under 100! Linda plans to continue writing as inspired. She thanks God for all the wonderful blessings in her life.

Martha Belknap is a teacher and the author of *Stress Relief for Kids: Taming Your Dragons,* and *Mind-Body Magic.* She has been married for twenty-six years and hopes that the Snitterfield story will inspire others to find creative, original, and humorous ways to handle challenges in their relationships.

Cynthia Bilyk joined the Army at nineteen and then became a Border Patrol Agent at twenty-four. She lives in Quemado, Texas with her husband, and two children. Cynthia enjoys leading a Girl Scout Troop and spending time with her family and friends.

Betty Bogart worked at Southwest Airlines for twenty-one years, often ghostwriting for Herb Kelleher and other company officers. Multiple writing associations have awarded her poetry and non-fiction. Her writing has appeared in *The Palm Beach Post, Living the Law of Attraction*, and other *Chicken Soup for the Soul* books. E-mail her at texasgirlb@gmail.com.

Sage de Beixedon Breslin is a licensed psychologist and intuitive consultant. She is an accomplished author, whose latest publications have been written to inspire and touch those who have struggled with life's challenges. For further information about Sage and what she offers, visit her website at www.HealingHeartCenter.org.

Sheryl Brownlee has published a local parenting magazine, penned a weekly humor column in a local newspaper and produced radio commercials. She also has twenty years experience selling radio and television advertising. She is currently working on a novel. Her favorite position is being a wife and mother.

Beth Cato resides in Buckeye, Arizona with her husband and son. Her work has appeared in publications such as *Niteblade Fantasy and Horror Magazine, Crossed Genres, Six Sentences*, and the book *The Ultimate Cat Lover.* Information regarding her current projects can always be found at www.bethcato.com.

Stefani Chambers lives in New York City where she is a writer of creative non-fiction and personal essays. She received her Masters of Journalism from the University of North Texas and has taken courses from Gotham Writers' Workshops. Her dream is to publish a collection of short essays. Contact her via e-mail at stefiwefi@yahoo.com.

A writer of humor and satire for more than twenty-five years, **Reid Champagne's** family still doesn't think he's very funny. His most recent contribution, "The Six Stages of Golf Grief" appeared in the 2009 edition of *Chicken Soup for the Soul: The Golf Book*. Contact him via e-mail at reid4bar@comcast.net.

Elynne Chaplik-Aleskow, Founding General Manager of WYCC-TV/PBS and Distinguished Professor Emeritus of Wright College in Chicago, is an author, public speaker and award-winning educator and broadcaster. Her non-fiction stories and essays have been anthologized. Elynne is married to her best friend Richard Noel Aleskow. Visit http://LookAroundMe.blogspot.com.

Jennifer Colvin is a marketing manager and freelance writer. Her stories about travel and misadventure have been published in numerous anthologies. These days, bike rides with her husband Bob take place much closer to their home in the San Francisco Bay Area, with their daughter in tow.

Harriet Cooper is a freelance writer, editor and language instructor. She specializes in writing creative non-fiction humor and articles, and often writes about health, exercise, diet, cats, family and the environment. A frequent contributor to Chicken Soup for the Soul, her work has also appeared in newspapers, magazines, newsletters and websites.

Debra A. Crawford lives in Florida with her husband, John. Diagnosed with SPS in 1994, Debra has a personal outreach with her website: www.livingwithsps.com. She enjoys family, church, outdoors, and reading. Future plans include writing short stories and autobiographical non-fiction.

Jean Davidson resides in Pocatello, Idaho. Her greatest writing interests are family stories and historical fiction stories about colorful individuals of the Old West. Her greatest joys are her family members, particularly her grandchildren and her cat Simba.

Dan DeVries received his Bachelor of Science degree in Electronic Engineering Technology from DeVry University in 1984 and is currently an Engineering Manager for The Boeing Company in Seattle, WA. Dan enjoys fishing, camping, spending time with his wife, and watching his five children grow up to become adults. Contact him at danandsheila@comcast.net.

Jamie Driggers writes about marriage and family issues whenever possible. The rest of the time she shares her thoughts about life at www.jamiedriggers.com. Her children and husband provide plenty of fodder and she counts herself fortunate that they give her something to laugh at and write about every single day.

Janet Perez Eckles is a speaker, writer and author of the inspirational book, *Trials of Today, Treasures for Tomorrow — Overcoming Adversities in Life*. Her stories, which appear in dozens of books including *Guidepost* books and numerous magazines, relate how adversity turned to triumph, to success and contagious joy. www.janetperezeckles.com, jeckles@cfl.rr.com.

Melissa Face and her husband, Craig, celebrated their fifth anniversary in July. They live in Wakefield, VA with their fur-child, Tyson. Melissa teaches Special Education and writes as often as possible. She has contributed several stories to the *Chicken Soup for the Soul* series. E-mail Melissa at writermsface@yahoo.com.

P. A. Flaherty earned degrees from Barnard College of Columbia

University and Smith College. She writes and edits fiction and creative non-fiction as well as grants. She recently planned her wedding. Follow her adventures in food writing at www.examiner.com/x-12601-Cheese-Examiner.

Jackie Fleming, a native Californian, grew up in the Bay Area and raised three boys on an Island in the California Delta. Her hobby is traveling the world by freighter, Yoga, reading and writing. For six years, she wrote columns for two weekly newspapers. She now lives in Paradise, California.

John Forrest is a retired educator. This is his third *Chicken Soup for the Soul* publication. His personal anthology of Christmas stories, *Angels Stars and Trees, Tales of Christmas Magic*, (Your Scrivener Press 2007) is in its second printing. He and his "true love" Carol still live in Orillia, Ontario, Canada. E-mail him at johnforrest@rogers.com.

Carole Fowkes is a registered nurse who also holds a BA in Communication. She currently works as a clinical trainer. She's originally from Cleveland, Ohio, but admits that her heart belongs to the Lone Star State, where she currently lives. Please e-mail her at cgfowkes@yahoo.com.

Jeannette Gardner works as a Medical Secretary at a private clinic. She taught herself to play guitar and began writing songs shortly thereafter. Her music can be heard at www.tenderangelmusic.com. Jeannette also enjoys fishing, playing guitar and tambourine, and loves Mother Nature. Please e-mail her at ji@tenderangelmusic.com.

Kimberlee B. Garrett spends most of her time caring for her wonderful husband and three children Emalee, Michael and Doug. When she does get a minute to herself, she enjoys reading, writing, and dreaming of being the first woman to win the Tour de France!

Nathan Danger Geist served a 2008-2009 combat tour as a Sergeant in Eastern Afghanistan under Operation Enduring Freedom. A graduate of Southern Illinois University Edwardsville, he now pursues his dream of being a film actor in the Chicago area. You can contact him or his wife Joanna at linkamo@comcast.net.

Sharon Graham received her Bachelor's degree in 2006, at the University of the Fraser Valley. She enjoys reading and writing, sometimes to the exclusion of all else. She and her husband hope to buy some property and create a home for under-privileged children.

Catherine Grow is a retired college teacher and writer happily co-existing with her husband and large, mixed-breed dog in a tiny, two-hundred-year-old house in rural northeastern Connecticut. Her work has appeared in a variety of journals, anthologies, and college-level composition texts.

Jean Hale graduated from the University of Tennessee with a Bachelor of Science degree in Business. She is a licensed Property and Casualty Insurance Agent. She is currently working part time as an Assistant Manager in retail. Her primary job is at home with her twin boys.

Cynthia Hamond has had over fifty stories in the *Chicken Soup for the Soul* series and other major publications, including *Woman's World* magazine and King Features Syndication. She received two awards and was feature writer in *Anthology Today*. Two stories have been made for TV. She enjoys school visits and group talks. www.CynthiaHamond.com.

Melissa Harding lives in Colorado Springs with her husband and three small children. She loves to travel and has lived in New Zealand and Costa Rica. When she's not changing diapers or breaking up fights, she enjoys hiking, boating, camping, and writing. She is currently working on an inspirational non-fiction book.

Laurel Hausman received her Master of Education from George

Mason University in Northern Virginia, where she now teaches high school mathematics. She plans to continue writing creative non-fiction. Laurel lives with her husband, Wayne, and their two Beagles, Newton and Summer. Please contact her via e-mail at Beegulls2Luv@aol.com.

Wes Henricksen is an author, attorney, and frequently-consulted expert on academic success. With his wife and young son, he travels to Argentina every chance he gets, and enjoys Malbec wine and engaging conversation. You can find out more about Wes at weshenricksen.com.

Jennifer Hofsommer currently resides with her husband in Chicago, Illinois where she is pursuing her Masters in Spanish Linguistics from the University of Illinois at Chicago. She has a passion for traveling, with her favorite destinations being in South America. Contact her via e-mail at jennifer.hofsommer@gmail.com.

Cara Holman worked for several years in the computer industry before making the easy decision to stay home full-time and raise her three children. She currently lives in Portland, Oregon with her husband and their youngest son. Her writings have appeared in various online journals and on her blog: http://caraholman.wordpress.com.

See **Judy Howard's** 200 Buckboard Antique Quilts at affordable prices on www.BuckboardQuilts.com. Exhibit her God Bless America Patriotic Quilts for $100. All profits go for quilts for wounded soldiers. See quilt photos, programs and read sample stories from her four award-winning books on www.HeavenlyPatchwork.com. BuckboardQuilts@cox.net.

Pamela Humphreys received her Bachelor of Science in Clinical Dietetics from the University of Oklahoma in 1978. She is a freelance writer, Bible teacher and registered dietitian. She enjoys traveling, cooking, reading and writing short stories and poetry. Please e-mail her at DelandPam1@sbcglobal.net.

Sheila Sattler Kale believes words have the power to change lives. She owns and manages The Closer Walk Christian Bookstore as well as writes and speaks encouragement to groups of all sizes. Her devotions can be viewed at www.thecloserwalk.com. Please e-mail her at closer@austin.rr.com. See her profile on Facebook.

Teresa Keller has been a social worker for the past twenty years for Department of Social Services. Teresa has written poetry for pleasure for years but this is only her second short story. She lives in Virginia with her husband and two Golden Retrievers. Please e-mail her at nugsmom@yahoo.com.

Elsie Schmied Knoke, a retired RN, earned her BGS from Roosevelt University and MM from the Kellogg School of Management. She sings in her church choir, volunteers at Recording for the Blind and Dyslexic and travels extensively with her husband. Her writings include essays, fiction and poetry. E-mail her at esknoke@bellsouth.net.

Marylane Wade Koch has over twenty-five years of experience in writing, editing, speaking, consulting, publishing, and coaching. She home schools her daughter and serves as adjunct faculty at the Loewenberg School of Nursing, University of Memphis. Contact her via e-mail at mwkoch@att.net.

Margaret Lang loves to draw from her life experience to write poignant true stories, having had about forty published. She is a speaker at women's and children's meetings, and a planter of afterschool Good News Clubs in the public schools. Her favorite role is that of grandma of three.

Dina A. Leacock lives in Southern New Jersey with her husband, her two sons and her cat. She is a founding member and past president of the Garden State Horror Writers, a multi-genre writing organization and past president of the Philadelphia Writers' Conference. Visit her at www.dinaleacock.com.

Linda Leary, mother, grandmother, and business owner for twenty years until she decided to transition at midlife to pursue her writing, which includes short stories, poetry, editing, ghost writing and magazine articles. She is involved in the international alternative justice movement called Restorative Justice and is a member of eWomen Network. siouxlu@comcast.net.

Delia Lloyd is an American writer/journalist/blogger based in London. Her essays have appeared in *The International Herald Tribune*, *The Christian Science Monitor*, and Mothering.com. She blogs about adulthood at www.realdelia.com.

Gary B. Luerding is a retired army NCO and high school administrator and lives in Southern Oregon with his wife of forty-seven years. He has contributed numerous stories to the *Chicken Soup for the Soul* and *Cup of Comfort* anthologies and several magazines and newspapers. He can be reached at garyluer@frontiernet.net.

Natalia K. Lusinski created her first newspaper, "Nat's Neat News Notes," at age ten, and has been writing ever since—from short stories to TV and film scripts. Most recently, she associate produced a documentary for The History Channel. E-mail her at writenataliainla@yahoo.com.

Melinda Richarz Lyons earned a Bachelor of Arts in Journalism from the University of North Texas. Her freelance work has appeared in numerous publications, and she is the co-author of *WOOF: Women Only Over Fifty* (Echelon Press). She enjoys genealogy and currently resides in Tyler, Texas.

David Martin's humor and political satire have appeared in many publications including *The New York Times*, the *Chicago Tribune* and the *Smithsonian Magazine*. His humor collection, *My Friend W*, was published in 2005 by Arriviste Press. David lives in Ottawa, Canada with his wife Cheryl and his daughter Sarah.

Timothy Martin is the author of four books and seven screenplays. He has two children's novels, *Scout's Oaf* (Cedar Grove Books) and *Fast Pitch* (Blitz Publishing), scheduled for publication in 2009. His web page can be viewed at www.timothymartin.org. Please e-mail Tim at tmartin@northcoast.com.

Margaret M. Marty is a retired wife, mother, grandmother, and professional secretary. Margaret enjoys flower gardening, yard work, and scrapbooking. She has pursued a memoir writing career in retirement, taking classes and establishing a personal historian business, Portraits in Prose. Please e-mail her at mmarty@northlc.com.

Dena May is an elementary Special Education teacher in Texas. She teaches Sunday School and plays the piano at her church, is on the local Child Welfare Board, and volunteers in the local Rainbow Room for CPS. Her first priority is being a wife and mother.

Caroline S. McKinney teaches in the School of Education at the University of Colorado at Boulder where she earned her PhD. She enjoys spending time with her children and grandchildren, hiking Colorado's mountains and traveling in Italy. She has written numerous articles for educational journals, and poetry for spiritual publications.

Lynn Maddalena Menna is happily married to her one true love, Prospero. They live in Hawthorne, NJ, with their cat, Toonsie. A retired educator, Lynn has been doing some freelance writing. She and Prospero enjoy sports cars, motorcycles, and traveling Europe and Hawaii. Friends can contact them at prolynn@aol.com.

Anthony J. Mohr's essays and short stories have appeared in the *Christian Science Monitor, The Sacramento Bee*, three anthologies, and several literary magazines including *Bibliophilos, The LBJ: Avian Life—Literary Arts, Literary House Review, Oracle*, and *Word Riot*. He lives in Los Angeles.

Alice E. Muschany lives in Flint Hill, Missouri and is looking forward to retirement after forty years of employment. Her hobbies are swimming, hiking, writing and photography—her eight grandchildren are wonderful subjects. She has been published in *Cup of Comfort* and is currently an opinion shaper for the Suburban Journal.

Toni-Michelle Nell lives with her husband Martin in Metro Atlanta. She enjoys being with those she loves and sharing in laughter, something the world needs more of. Toni-Michelle is currently enrolled at the University of Phoenix where she maintains a 4.0 GPA and is working on her AA in Psychology with the hopes of continuing on to get her Master's degree. Please e-mail her at tmnell@comcast.net.

Diane C. Nicholson is a freelance writer based in beautiful British Columbia. She is also a photo-artist, specializing in families of all species and memorial art (when it wasn't possible to get a professional portrait). She can be reached at mail@twinheartphotp.com and some of her work can be viewed at www.twinheartphoto.com.

Through **Karen O'Keeffe's** effort to glorify God, she strives to be the balanced, diverse woman that He created her to be—a wife, mother, sister, friend, writer, artist, homemaker, volunteer, teacher, and steward. She is a member of Words For The Journey Christian Writers' Guild. E-mail her at moneyhoney@q.com.

Elaine Herrin Onley and her late husband served as missionaries in the Caribbean for fourteen years. Following his death, she worked in public relations in Georgia. A published poet, author and visual artist, Elaine has three sons and six stepchildren. She and her second husband, Ed Onley, reside in Dothan, Alabama.

Laurie Ozbolt received her B.A. in Psychology from the University of Virginia and her M.B.A from the College of William and Mary. She works in HR and is training to be a Spiritual Director. She enjoys gardening, dancing and spending time with her family. Please e-mail her at laurie_ozbolt@hotmail.com.

Saralee Perel is an award-winning nationally syndicated columnist and novelist. She is honored to be a multiple contributor to *Chicken Soup for the Soul*. Saralee welcomes e-mails at sperel@saraleeperel.com or via her website: www.saraleeperel.com.

Jill Pertler writes a weekly syndicated column, "Slices of Life," which is printed in newspapers throughout her home state of Minnesota and beyond. She also dabbles in short fiction and photography. She lives in a cozy house with her husband, four children and assorted critters. Visit her website at: http://marketing-by-design.home.mchsi.com.

Marilyn Phillips, a teacher, has articles published in *A Chicken Soup for the Soul Christmas* and *Chicken Soup for the Surviving Soul*. Marilyn has three books that are sold by Christian Cheerleaders of America. Her webpage is www.mphillipsauthor.com. Marilyn lives in Bedford, TX, with her husband. They have two grown children.

Stephanie Piro lives in New Hampshire with her husband and three cats. She is one of King Features' "Six Chix" (she is the Saturday chick!). Her single panel, "Fair Game," appears in newspapers and on her website: www.stephaniepiro.com. She is also an illustrator, a designer of gift items for her company Strip T's, and a part-time librarian. Contact her at stephaniepiro@gmail.com.

Kay Conner Pliszka and her "unromantic hubby" were both teachers in the Milwaukee public school system. They met in 1972, were married a year later, and have enjoyed life together for thirty-six years. They are now retired and living in a fantastic retirement village in Florida. For speaking engagements e-mail kmpliszka@comcast.net.

Jennifer Quasha is a published author of more than forty books. Her book, *The Dog Lover's Book of Crafts*, won the DWAA Best General Interest Book in 2002. Currently, she is a freelance writer and editor. Check out her website at www.jenniferquasha.com.

Sheri Radford lives in Vancouver, BC, Canada with her husband and three cats. She is the author of three very silly picture books for children: *Penelope and the Preposterous Birthday Party*, *Penelope and the Monsters*, and *Penelope and the Humongous Burp*. You can visit her on the web at www.sheriradford.com.

Gayle Danis Rinot is an experienced journalist, copywriter, columnist and editor. She is a 1987 graduate of Emerson College in Boston, where she majored in Broadcast Journalism. Gayle lives in central Israel with her charming husband and three beautiful and talented daughters. You may contact her at gaylerinot@gmail.com.

Sallie A. Rodman is an award-winning author whose stories have appeared in numerous *Chicken Soup for the Soul* anthologies, magazines and newspapers. She lives with Paul in Los Alamitos, CA. They still visit General Lee's and wonder what the next fortune cookie will bring. Reach her at sa.rodman@verizon.net.

Laurel Rosenberg, a Los Angeles native, is a prize winning artist and writer. Her work is collected throughout the United States and seen in film and television. She founded Survivors Against Violent Encounters, has written screenplays, a children's book, and "Laurel Creations" features her butterfly products. Please contact her via: www.Laurelrosenberg.com.

Jay Rylant graduated from Mountain View College in Dallas, TX, after which he went on to spend fourteen years as a freelance musician. He now pursues a career as a writer and novelist. He has served the last year as editor for *Different Strokes*—a weekly newsletter for golfhelp.com, and he was published in *Chicken Soup for the Soul: The Golf Book*.

Arthur Sanchez hails from the sunny state of Florida. Primarily a Fantasy writer he loves telling the story of how he met his wife. For more information on Arthur's work, links to free stories on the web, or to find out about his books, visit his website: www.ArthurSanchez. com.

Jeffrey Nathan Schirripa studied Communications and graduated from Marist College in 2000. Jeffrey is currently finishing his first motivational psychology book, *Carpe Diem*, which will inspire readers to cultivate their inner strength and create the life of their dreams. Jeffrey can be reached at JeffreySchirripa@gmail.com.

Elizabeth Schmeidler is happily married and a mother to three wonderful sons. She is an author of poetry, children's stories, novels, short stories, and is an inspirational speaker. Elizabeth has composed/recorded three CDs of original music. She is working on her newest CD, "Believe." Contact her at www.elizabethshop.org.

Michael Jordan Segal, who defied all odds after being shot in the head, is a husband, father, social worker, author (including a CD/Download of twelve stories entitled *Possible*) and inspirational speaker. He's had many stories published in *Chicken Soup for the Soul* books. To contact Mike or to order his CD, please visit www.InspirationByMike. com.

Ann M. Sheridan founded Bimbos Buddies (www.bimbosbuddies. org) and published a picture book for children with cancer called *Dogs Get Cancer Too*. Ann has contributed stories to *Chicken Soup for the Woman Golfer's Soul* and *Chicken Soup for the Soul: What I Learned* *from the Dog.* She resides in Long Branch, NJ. Please contact her at ASheridan529@aol.com

Toni Somers is a retired photographer and drawing teacher. She has a Bachelor of Arts in Studio Art from Columbia College. She enjoys drawing and playing classical guitar and hammered dulcimer. Toni lives on the Texas Gulf Coast with her husband of fifty-four years. Please e-mail her at txlaughinggull@yahoo.com.

Deb Stanley lives in Michigan with her husband and three daughters. She teaches 6th grade Special Education. Deb's hobbies include spending time with family, inspirational writing, singing, and working with children with special needs, especially those with autism. E-mail her at dstanley64@gmail.com.

Susan Staunton received her BA in Elementary Education and her Master's in Guidance Counseling. She taught for nine years in Maryland and now home schools in Minnesota. Susan hopes to continue writing stories that teach and inspire in addition to writing home school curriculums. Please e-mail her at s.staunton@comcast.net.

Jean H. Stewart writes and edits from her home, where she lives with her husband of forty-nine years and stays involved with their twin daughters and families. An award-winning writer, her stories can be found in numerous *Chicken Soup for the Soul* books as well as other anthologies, magazines and newspapers. You can reach her at jeanstewart@cox.net.

A city girl, **Evelyn L. Stringham** found being a farmer's wife so interesting, she wrote a weekly column, "Farm Wife," for several Michigan newspapers for fifty years. Night Visit happened to her shortly after her husband's death. Moving to Arizona, she wrote about snowbirds for the *Arizona Republic*. Contact her at estringham@juno.com.

Sylvia Suriano-Diodati is a pianist and songwriter; her short stories have been featured in *Angels on Earth* and *Woman's World* magazine, as well as previous volumes of *Chicken Soup for the Soul*. Her greatest joy—along with her husband, Ludovico—is their new baby, Isabella! Sylvia can be contacted via e-mail at sylviadiodati@rogers.com.

Anji Limón Taylor is a writer and poet. She is currently working towards a BS degree in Digital Communications and Media at New York University. She enjoys reading, running and laughing. Her future writing projects include a very unique children's book series. Feel free to e-mail her at anji@anjiwrites.com.

B.J. Taylor and her husband vacation on the islands as often as they can, with Maui holding a special spot in their hearts. B.J. is an author whose work has appeared in *Guideposts*, many *Chicken Soup for the Soul* books, and numerous magazines and newspapers. She and Roger have four children and two adorable grandsons. Visit her website at www.bjtayloronline.com.

Tena Beth Thompson writes about life and shares her experiences with a touch of humor. She's published in *Chicken Soup for the Shopper's Soul*, *Chicken Soup for the Soul in Menopause*, and *Chicken Soup for the Soul: Divorce and Recovery*. Miss Thompson co-founded the *Patchwork Path* anthology series. She can be reached at editor@patchworkpath.com.

Lisa Tiffin is a freelance writer from Upstate New York, where she lives with her husband and twin sons. Her essays and articles have appeared in a variety of magazines. She is the author of *The Eagle Ridge Prep Technological Adventure* series for children. Find out more at www.lisatiffin.com.

Christine Trollinger took up writing as a hobby after retiring from the insurance business in 1991. She has been published in several magazines and books of inspiration. She enjoys painting, gardening and has two great granddaughters, who are the love of her life. Please e-mail her at gabby_trolly@yahoo.com.

Samantha Ducloux Waltz is an award-winning freelance writer in Portland, Oregon. She currently has numerous essays in the *Chicken Soup for the Soul*, *The Ultimate*, *A Cup of Comfort* series, and other anthologies. She has also written fiction and non-fiction under the name Samellyn Wood. Learn more at www.pathsofthought.com.

A retired college teacher and administrator at Montana State University in Great Falls, **Suzanne Waring, Ed.D.**, is now a freelance writer. Recently celebrating their forty-fifth wedding anniversary, Suzanne and her husband, Leonard, have two adult sons. Please e-mail her at swaring7@yahoo.com.

Stefanie Wass lives in Hudson, OH with her husband and two daughters. Her essays have appeared in the *Los Angeles Times*, *Seattle Times*, *Christian Science Monitor*, *Cleveland Magazine*, *Akron Beacon Journal*, *Akron Life and Leisure*, and four *Chicken Soup for the Soul* anthologies. She may be reached at www.stefaniewass.com or swass@roadrunner. com.

Laura Wisniewski is a registered nurse, motivational speaker, and freelance writer. She is a training specialist for a large healthcare system on the West coast of Florida. Her hobbies include biking, kayaking, sailing and grandparenting. Please e-mail her at laura@ nursingvoice.com.

Ferida Wolff is author of seventeen books for children and three essay books for adults. Her essays appear in anthologies, newspapers and magazines. She also writes online at www.grandparents.com and is a columnist for www.seniorwomen.com. A former elementary school teacher and Yoga instructor, she now teaches stretching and meditation. Her website is www.feridawolff.com.

Sheryl Young is an award-winning freelance writer specializing in family values topics for magazines, newspapers and the Internet. She's written the book, *What Every Christian Should Know About the Jewish People: Improving the Church's Relationship with God's Original Chosen Nation*, and has been happily married to her husband Jerry for twenty-five years.

Meet Our Authors

Jack Canfield is the co-creator of the *Chicken Soup for the Soul* series, which *Time* magazine has called "the publishing phenomenon of the decade." Jack is also the co-author of many other bestselling books.

Jack is the CEO of the Canfield Training Group in Santa Barbara, California, and founder of the Foundation for Self-Esteem in Culver City, California. He has conducted intensive personal and professional development seminars on the principles of success for more than a million people in twenty-three countries, has spoken to hundreds of thousands of people at more than 1,000 corporations, universities, professional conferences and conventions, and has been seen by millions more on national television shows.

Jack has received many awards and honors, including three honorary doctorates and a Guinness World Records Certificate for having seven books from the *Chicken Soup for the Soul* series appearing on the New York Times bestseller list on May 24, 1998.

You can reach Jack at www.jackcanfield.com.

Mark Victor Hansen is the co-founder of Chicken Soup for the Soul, along with Jack Canfield. He is a sought-after keynote speaker, bestselling author, and marketing maven. Mark's powerful messages of possibility, opportunity, and action have created powerful change in thousands of organizations and millions of individuals worldwide.

Mark is a prolific writer with many bestselling books in addition to the *Chicken Soup for the Soul* series. Mark has had a profound influence in the field of human potential through his library of audios, videos, and articles in the areas of big thinking, sales achievement, wealth building, publishing success, and personal and professional development. He is also the founder of the MEGA Seminar Series.

Mark has received numerous awards that honor his entrepreneurial spirit, philanthropic heart, and business acumen. He is a lifetime member of the Horatio Alger Association of Distinguished Americans.

You can reach Mark at www.markvictorhansen.com.

Amy Newmark is the publisher of *Chicken Soup for the Soul*, after a thirty-year career as a writer, speaker, financial analyst, and business executive in the worlds of finance and telecommunications. Amy is a *magna cum laude* graduate of Harvard College, where she majored in Portuguese, minored in French, and traveled extensively. She is also the mother of two children in college and two grown stepchildren who are recent college graduates.

After a long career writing books on telecommunications, voluminous financial reports, business plans, and corporate press releases, Chicken Soup for the Soul is a breath of fresh air for Amy. She has fallen in love with Chicken Soup for the Soul and its life-changing books, and really enjoys putting these books together for Chicken Soup's wonderful readers. She has co-authored more than two dozen *Chicken Soup for the Soul* books.

You can reach Amy through the webmaster@chickensoupforthesoul. com.

Thank You!

*W*e owe huge thanks to all of our contributors. We know that you pour your hearts and souls into the thousands of stories and poems that you share with us, and ultimately with each other. We appreciate your willingness to open up your lives to other Chicken Soup for the Soul readers.

We can only publish a small percentage of the stories that are submitted, but we read every single one and even the ones that do not appear in the book have an influence on us and on the final manuscript.

We want to thank Chicken Soup for the Soul Assistant Publisher D'ette Corona for reading the thousands of stories and poems that were submitted for this book. She shaped the initial manuscript and this book is as much hers as it is ours. We also want to thank our editor and webmaster Barbara LoMonaco and editor Kristiana Glavin for their expert editorial and proofreading assistance.

We owe a very special thanks to our creative director and book producer, Brian Taylor at Pneuma Books, for his brilliant vision for our covers and interiors. Finally, none of this would be possible without the business and creative leadership of our CEO, Bill Rouhana, and our president, Bob Jacobs.

Chicken Soup for the Soul®
Improving Your Life Every Day

eal people sharing real stories—for fifteen years. Now, Chicken Soup for the Soul has gone beyond the bookstore to become a world leader in life improvement. Through books, movies, DVDs, online resources and other partnerships, we bring hope, courage, inspiration and love to hundreds of millions of people around the world. Chicken Soup for the Soul's writers and readers belong to a one-of-a-kind global community, sharing advice, support, guidance, comfort, and knowledge.

Chicken Soup for the Soul stories have been translated into more than forty languages and can be found in more than one hundred countries. Every day, millions of people experience a Chicken Soup for the Soul story in a book, magazine, newspaper or online. As we share our life experiences through these stories, we offer hope, comfort and inspiration to one another. The stories travel from person to person, and from country to country, helping to improve lives everywhere.

Chicken Soup
for the Soul.

Share with Us

We all have had Chicken Soup for the Soul moments in our lives. If you would like to share your story or poem with millions of people around the world, go to chickensoup.com and click on "Submit Your Story." You may be able to help another reader, and become a published author at the same time. Some of our past contributors have launched writing and speaking careers from the publication of their stories in our books!

Our submission volume has been increasing steadily—the quality and quantity of your submissions has been fabulous. Starting in 2010, we will only accept story submissions via our website. They will no longer be accepted via mail or fax.

To contact us regarding other matters, please send us an e-mail through webmaster@chickensoupforthesoul.com, or fax or write us at:

Chicken Soup for the Soul
P.O. Box 700
Cos Cob, CT 06807-0700
Fax: 203-861-7194

One more note from your friends at Chicken Soup for the Soul: Occasionally, we receive an unsolicited book manuscript from one of our readers, and we would like to respectfully inform you that we do not accept unsolicited manuscripts and we must discard the ones that appear.

Dating and courtship, romance, love, and marriage are favorite Chicken Soup for the Soul topics. Everyone loves to read true stories about how it happened for other people. This book includes the 101 best stories on love and marriage that appeared in a wide variety of past Chicken Soup for the Soul books. These heartwarming stories will inspire and amuse readers, whether they are just starting to date, are newly wed, or are veterans of a long marriage.

978-1-935096-10-8

More Love Stories

Almost everyone thinks their own family is "dysfunctional" or at least has a dysfunctional member or two. These stories of wacky yet lovable relatives, holiday meltdowns, and funny foibles, along with more serious stories about abuse, controlling family members, and flare-ups, show readers that they aren't alone. All in the Family is a quirky and fun holiday book, and a great bridal shower or wedding gift! Norman Rockwell's famous "Freedom from Want" Thanksgiving family painting appears on the back cover and is lovingly parodied on the front, driving home the point that all our families, no matter how much we love them, are just a little dysfunctional!

978-1-935096-39-9

A Great Wedding
or Anniversary Gift